SWEET

SWEET

YOTAM OTTOLENGHI

HELEN GOH

WITH TARA WIGLEY

EBURY
PRESS

For my mother, Cheng, who never
fails to cook with her heart and soul;
and for my sister, Lily, who ignited
my passion for baking and has been
with me every step of the way.

——

HELEN

For my three sweet treats, Karl, Max
and Flynn, who always refuse to share
their chocolate chip cookies with me.

——

YOTAM

SWEET

There's so much sugar in this book that we thought about calling it, well, *Sugar*. There's nothing like a perfectly light sponge flavoured with spices and citrus, for example, or a mega-crumbly icing-sugar-dusted cookie, straight out of the oven, to raise the spirits and create a moment of pure joy. These are the moments we're rejoicing in here, celebrating the sweet things in life.

We say this not to be irreverent or flippant – we are completely aware of current concerns about the adverse effects of sugar – but we want to make it clear that this is a recipe book full of over 110 wonderful sweet things.

In the fickle world of food fads and fashions, 'public enemy number one' is constantly changing: eggs, fats, carbs – we are told to restrict our intake of them one year, and then to make them a major part of our diet the next. To those who do as they're told, it's all very confusing.

In the midst of this confusion, we try to stick to the simple rule of 'what you see is what you get'. People will make responsible choices about what to eat and how much as long as they are not consuming things without realizing it – hidden sugars, hidden salts, hidden elements with names we can't even pronounce, let alone understand what they are. There is nothing wrong with treats, as long as we know what they are and enjoy them as such.

Just as we don't hide anything, we're also never 'free-from' anything, just for the sake of it. We're lucky to not have any food allergies and pleased that those who can't eat gluten have lots of 'free-from' choice, but 'free-from' cooking, for the sake of it, is just not something that excites us. If a recipe is 'free-from' gluten or nuts or dairy, it is the result of accident rather than design. A happy accident, certainly – we had no idea we were creating over 20 gluten-free recipes here, and are delighted that we have! – but it's not something we specifically set out to do. (To make things easier, we have added gluten-free (GF) and nut-free (NF) symbols to the recipes where this happy accident occurs.)

The Ottolenghi way has always been about abundance, inclusion and celebration. It's the way we've always cooked and it's the way we've always baked. It's the way we've always eaten and the way we've always lived.

My first job in a professional kitchen was whisking egg whites. Yes, just that. It was the 1990s and I was doing my training as a chef during the day, and assisting the pastry chef in a fancy central London restaurant at night. On the dessert section most of the work is done before service starts. Since I was so junior and tended to do the late shift, there was one job I spent a lot of time doing: beating egg whites to order for our very popular vanilla soufflés. By the end of three months, I was a bona fide expert in the right consistency of egg whites needed for the perfect soufflé.

It must be fate then, or some kind of direction from above, that I ended up making my name on egg whites, sugar and lots and lots of air. The famously giant Ottolenghi meringues, which have adorned our windows for many years, have become our trademark. I am crediting this to divine intervention, rather than all of my whisking, because it would not have been my plan-A for Ottolenghi to be referred to, by some, as 'the meringue shop'. There are worse names to be called, I know, but my ambivalence towards them is no secret. I do actually love meringue, just not so much of it! The Louise Cake on page 173, for example, wearing a white crown of meringue on its head and gilded with flaky almonds and bits of delicious coconut, is, in fact, one of my favourite cakes in the book.

Looking beyond the Ottolenghi window, or, rather, through it, it wouldn't have been hard to spot my love for all things sweet and the fact that I eventually honed my skills as a pastry chef beyond the holy trinity of egg white, sugar and air. Sitting alongside our grilled vegetables, grain salads and the rest of the savoury dishes inspired by Sami Tamimi's and my childhoods in Jerusalem, were a bunch of sweet treats that were not at all fluffy or airy. Fruit galettes, little cheesecakes, Amaretti cookies, danishes and muffins, tarts filled with citrusy curds and all manner of chocolate delights: these were rapidly rallying a crowd of lively devotees keen to augment their salad box with a little (or big) sweet finale.

In fact, it was precisely this juxtaposition of good, yet different, things – strikingly appetizing salads alongside wonderful, hand-crafted sweet treats – that has come to define the Ottolenghi experience. And by 'good things' I mean anything that is freshly made, with love, a bit of flair, real ingredients and lots of attention to detail.

Helen's arrival

I assume that it is this tacit philosophy – plus the window, no doubt – that attracted Helen to Ottolenghi and brought her to us as soon as she had come off the proverbial boat from Australia in 2006.

I can actually remember getting a phone call from her and then meeting for the first time outside one of our shops, hearing her story and not quite understanding what drives such a star to leave behind a very successful career – Helen's professional history both as a pastry chef and as a psychotherapist is remarkable – in a very sunny Melbourne in favour of a rather elusive future in a rather grey London.

It took seeing Helen at work – first cooking savoury food with Sami in Notting Hill and running our Kensington kitchen, later spending much of her time dreaming up pastries, cakes and all manner of sweet things for the company – for the penny to drop. I finally realized that it was Helen's restlessness and her insatiable drive for perfection that had brought her to us. What we shared, which Helen had identified right from the start and I took a bit longer to realize, was the notion that there is no upper limit to the number of times you can bake a cake or the amount of thought that can go into the components of a tart in order to get it just right; that you can discuss the minutiae of a chocolate ice cream or a nut brittle as if the fate of the entire universe rests on the conversation, without worrying for a second that this may be, just may be, a tiny bit over the top.

This kind of intensity and commitment has been a constant throughout Helen's different roles in Ottolenghi. Over the years she has been involved in creating canapés, testing breakfast dishes, trying out salads and offering her insights into anything, really, that appeared on our menus or was placed on our shelves and required the kind of depth and breadth of knowledge of food that she has. More than anything else, though, it is with her cakes – a term I use very loosely here, to mean anything from a dreamy chocolate chip cookie, to a light-as-a-feather meringue roulade, to a rum and raisin bundt with caramel dripping down its sides – that Helen carved her inspired mark on our food.

Our tasting sessions

Forming friendships and collaborations around a spread of food is the Ottolenghi way. I bonded with Sami in this way all those years ago, then with Ramael Scully, co-author of *NOPI: The cookbook*, who taught me to love miso and appreciate a few new cooking techniques. My friendship with Helen was mostly formed around a piece of cake.

Here is an image that I can't shake: it's a Sunday afternoon, around 4pm probably; my husband Karl looks out the window of our first-floor West London flat, an expression of clear foreboding appears on his face and then, very quietly, he says: 'Helen's here ... with her cakes.' Helen then walks through our front door like a gust of wind or, rather, an over-zealous dusting of icing sugar, carrying more brown carton boxes than humanly possible and, before even setting them down, begins apologizing for all the things that went wrong with her cakes. This one hasn't risen properly, the other bowed around the centre, an icing has split halfway through its application, a sabayon lost its air, a sorbet failed to churn, a sugar syrup crystallized, a cookie crumbled and so on and on and on.

Helen would then open up her boxes and take out what seemed like at least three solid days' worth of standing in the kitchen and baking. In one Sunday session we could, very easily, sample three versions apiece of two cakes-in-progress, each with its own minuscule variation (one flavoured with vanilla, for example, the other with pandan, the third with Chinese five-spice), a biscuit Helen had in America, tried at home and wanted to Ottolenghify, a couple of confectionery items (say, a chocolate-nut brittle and an Italian nougat), three flavours of summer cordials, and, to round it all up nicely, she would quickly cook up a batter she'd brought with her for a new pancake or waffle to add to Islington's breakfast menus.

You'd think there's a touch of embellishment here but there really isn't, I promise. The sinking of Karl's heart was entirely justified. It had nothing to do, though, with the cakes that failed – according to Helen – or the cookies that crumbled, and everything to do with how hard it was to stop yourself indulging in all those incredible sugary pleasures. Helen's 'failures', you see, are the stuff the sweetest of dreams are made of for mere mortals. Our Sunday afternoons tended to end up with all participants nearing a perfect state of sugar-induced delirium.

This book

Many of the cakes in this book are a result of those elated Sunday sessions. Items that eventually received our seal of approval, after endless tests and infinite discussions, were, if I may say so myself, pretty magnificent. Other recipes are older, going back to the early days of Ottolenghi. Those evolved organically in our stores, based on feedback from our customers and staff. Many were brought to us by a great number of talented pastry chefs who have worked with us over the years; we acknowledge them with gratitude in the introductions to the recipes. Some recipes have been developed especially for the book, when we felt we were missing a particular angle, a specific style of cake, or just something that we love to eat and that happened to be sweet.

What all of the recipes share is having been through the full Ottolenghi treatment, which is exactly the way I described a 'good thing' earlier: they were all conceived with love and a bit of flair and made with real ingredients and lots of attention to detail. I feel confident that you'll be able to find all of these components in each of our 'cakes' here.

One final note

These days, my tastings with Helen are not quite the same as they used to be. I suspect it's to do with the fact that we both became parents in recent years.

In our first meeting after Helen's Sam was born, the three-week-old was resting in his Moses basket next to us while Helen and I were debating the merits of different consistencies of marshmallow for making s'mores. To my regret, I sent an offhand tweet reporting that an infant is the third wheel in our regular tastings, only to receive a bunch of grave warnings from concerned followers about the fatal risks of feeding cakes to newborns.

Setting aside this particular mishap, Sam and his brother Jude's arrival and, later on, the birth of my boys, Max and Flynn, did slightly alter the nature of our meetings. Our attention now has to be harnessed and somewhat focused, deliberations are shorter and, unconsciously, we find our cakes a bit more child-friendly (you wouldn't know that, though, looking at the number of cakes in the book with serious quantities of booze in them). Children's birthday parties are now natural testing grounds for sponges and the boys themselves are some of our fiercest critics. Just the other day I offered Max a slice of cake, to which he quickly replied: 'Did Helen make it?' 'I am afraid not,' I said. 'No, then,' was his resolute and final answer. What a few years back may have been a very lengthy discussion was over before it had even started. Having been put so clearly in my place, all I could do was go back to the kitchen and whip up some egg whites.

———

YOTAM OTTOLENGHI

Cookies and biscuits

—

Making cookies and biscuits is fun, quick and easy. We'd say this about all forms of baking, of course, but cookies and biscuits are particularly happy-making. This is for all sorts of reasons. Here are just a few.

KIT-FREE › Making a batch of cookies or biscuits doesn't require much kit. Assuming that anyone with an interest in baking has baking trays, baking parchment, measuring spoons, wooden spoons and mixing bowls, then you're pretty much ready to go. If you want to develop your interest in baking and don't already own a free-standing electric food mixer, we'd highly recommend investing in one. It is a thing of great beauty! We use our electric mixer so often throughout the book that we've taken the liberty of assuming you have one. Beyond this, though, you won't need much more to open the (oven) door on to a whole world of cookies and biscuits. There are occasions when a little something extra is needed – a piping bag and a non-stick silicone mat for the Cats' Tongues (see page 27) for example, or stamps and cookie cutters for the Soft Gingerbread Tiles with Rum Butter Glaze (see page 42) – but we'll suggest a shortcut or alternative where we can, so that you don't have to buy a specific piece of kit if you don't want to.

HASSLE-FREE › The lack of kit and general fuss makes baking cookies and biscuits an ideal activity to do with kids. Baking with little people is often, secretly, more fun in theory than in practice – the chaos! the flour! the sheer disregard for detail! With cookies, though, you really can get your mini-helpers involved in rolling, shaping and mixing without being too precious about whether the dough is slightly over-mixed, or the size and shape of a particular biscuit is somewhat idiosyncratic. There are enough recipes in the book for which precision and timing is everything – making the Frozen Espresso Parfait (see page 298), for example, requires an empty kitchen and full focus – but here you really can embrace the chaos and relax in the knowledge that your dough is going to be robust enough to handle a spot of four-year-old improvisation.

RULE-FREE(ISH) › Many cookie and biscuit recipes are also able to handle a spot of grown-up improvisation. Recipe writers ask something completely contradictory of their readers: at the same time as saying that baking is a science – if you don't own measuring spoons, put the book down and buy some now, please! – and that instructions need to be followed closely, we also ask you to use your initiative as to whether a little bit more or less of something is needed (time in the oven, water in the dough, whisking in the mixer). So too with ingredients: alongside the instruction to put precisely ⅛ teaspoon of something in a batter, we then blithely say, 'but if you don't have it, you can use this or this as an alternative, variation or substitute'. It's not meant to be a paradox: we have tested and re-tested these recipes until we think we have created a perfect version. Our strong advice to you – rolling pin in hand, waving it in the air for emphasis – is to do the same. Don't bake a batch of cookies once and then move on to the next recipe. Bake and re-bake (or test and re-test, if you like) the same recipe so that you can make all the tweaks, changes and alterations you need to create the exact amount of 'crisp' or spice you want in your biscuit. If you don't like aniseed or brandy, don't add it; if you don't have any date syrup, use golden syrup; if you like your biscuits particularly crisp, give them an extra minute in the oven; if you want to jazz up a simple biscuit, sandwich two together with something delicious. Bake something enough times for it to become yours. Then you can move on to the next one of ours.

FREEZER-FRIENDLY › Cookie and biscuit doughs are really happy to be hidden away in the freezer for a while, ready to be popped into the oven as and when the moment arrives. It's one of life's great pleasures, we think, to know that, whatever else is going on in your day, you're only ever about 14 minutes away from a perfectly baked chocolate chip cookie. We generally prefer to bake from frozen (we roll the dough into balls, then freeze them), rather than baking the biscuits first and freezing them after they've cooled. There are exceptions to this rule, however, which will appear alongside all the standard 'getting ahead' and 'storage' notes.

FESTIVE-FRIENDLY › There is a perfect cookie or biscuit for every occasion: some of our recipes are so festive, for example, that they actually look like snowballs. Whether they resemble snow – the Pecan Snowballs (see page 63) or Amaretti with Honey and Orange Blossom (see page 38) – or simply taste of the spices we associate with festive times – the Orange and Star Anise Shortbread (see page 46) – there's always something to link in with a special occasion. The cranberries in the Cranberry, Oat and White Chocolate Biscuits (see page 24) for Thanksgiving, for example, or the Chocolate 'O' Cookies (see page 55) for the classic kids' party.

We've been making and selling some of the biscuits and cookies featured here in our shops for years. And as with all old friends, we're feeling excited (but also a little bit protective) to be sharing these. Look after them, please! Some are twists on household or childhood classics: our Garibaldis (see page 57) and Chocolate and Peanut Butter S'mores (see page 48); some were made for the shops but didn't quite work –– the Chocolate, Banana and Pecan Cookies (see page 29), which went too soft too quickly because of the banana in the mix, but which are heaven to make at home; others were developed specifically for *Sweet*: the Soft Date and Oat Bars (see page 45) and the Speculaas Biscuits (see page 37).

And the difference between a cookie and a biscuit for those pondering this, of all of life's great questions? The straightforward answer is that cookies bend and biscuits snap. Cookies are often softer and thicker than biscuits. Delve a bit deeper, though, and you could say that cookies are sweet and often chunky, while biscuits can be savoury and are often crisp. We can think of crisp cookies, however – and then we have our 'Anzac' Biscuits (see page 52), which also go by the name of Honey, Oat and Raisin Cookies. Is it just a case of American vs British terminology? It's a can of worms we are very happy to keep closed, in return for a jar of cookies (or biscuits), which we are more than happy to keep open.

Whatever you call them and whichever recipes you choose to make your own, we hope they make you happy. A house with a full cookie jar becomes a home.

Custard Yo-Yos with roasted rhubarb icing

Yo-Yos were a staple of Helen's Antipodean childhood, ubiquitous in all of the cafés where she sweetened her tooth. Their popularity with our customers shows that the old-fashioned combination of roasted rhubarb and custard takes a lot of people back to the sweet treats of their youth.

As an alternative to custard powder, you could use cornflour. It won't have the wonderful old-school yellow of custard powder but the Yo-Yos will still taste great: you might just want to up the amount of vanilla extract you use from ¼ to ½ teaspoon. And if you're not opposed to food colouring, a drop or two of yellow will also help to simulate the colour of the custard.

MAKES 15

The icing can be made up to 2 days in advance and kept in the fridge. If your icing is a bit loose – this can happen if you overwork it – it will benefit from time in the fridge anyway, to firm up. The dough tends to go very hard if left in the fridge, so it is best to roll them on the day the dough is made.

Once assembled, the Yo-Yos can be kept for up to 5 days in an airtight container, so long as they are not anywhere too warm (in which case the icing will soften).

175g plain flour, plus 1 tbsp extra for dusting
65g custard powder
65g icing sugar
⅛ tsp salt
170g unsalted butter, at room temperature, cubed
¼ tsp vanilla extract (or ½ tsp, if using cornflour)

RHUBARB ICING
1 small stick of rhubarb, trimmed, washed and cut into roughly 3cm lengths (70g)
65g unsalted butter, at room temperature, cubed
130g icing sugar
½ tsp lemon juice

1   Preheat the oven to 180°C/160°C Fan/Gas Mark 4. Line a small baking tray with baking parchment.

2   **To make the rhubarb icing,** spread the rhubarb out on the lined baking tray and roast for 30 minutes, or until softened. Remove from the oven and allow to cool before transferring to the small bowl of a food processor. Blitz to a purée, then add the butter. Sift in the icing sugar, add the lemon juice and continue to process for a couple of minutes: it seems like a long time, but you want it to thicken, which it will do as it's whipped. Transfer to a small bowl and chill in the fridge for a couple of hours to firm up. You don't want the icing to be at all runny, so add a little more icing sugar if necessary: it needs to hold when sandwiched between the biscuits.

3   **To make the dough,** sift the flour, custard powder, icing sugar and salt into the bowl of an electric mixer with the paddle attachment in place. Mix on a low speed to combine. Add the butter and continue to mix on a low speed until the mixture resembles breadcrumbs. Add the vanilla extract, increase the speed to medium and beat for about 30 seconds, until the dough comes together.

4   Reduce the oven temperature to 170°C/150°C Fan/Gas Mark 3. Line two baking trays with parchment paper. ››

5   Pinch off small bits of dough and use your hands to roll them into 3cm round balls: you should have enough dough for 30 balls, about 15g each. Place them on the lined baking trays, spaced about 4cm apart. Dip the back prongs of a small fork in the remaining flour before gently but firmly pressing down into the middle of each biscuit: the balls will increase to about 3.5cm wide, but don't press all the way to the bottom; you just want to create firm lines in the dough rather than force them to spread out.

6   Bake for 25 minutes, rotating the trays halfway through, until the biscuits are dry on the bottom but have not taken on too much colour. They will be relatively fragile when warm but still firm to the touch. Set aside on the trays to cool for 5 minutes before transferring to a wire rack to cool completely.

7   **To assemble,** sandwich pairs of biscuits together with the icing, with the 'forked' sides facing outwards. You should use about 15g of icing in each biscuit. It will seem like a lot, but trust us – the biscuits can take it.

Peanut sandies

These are lovely as they are – simple, nutty, moreish – but can also be used as a base for other things, if you want to build them up. A layer of melted chocolate, or Nutella straight from the jar, sandwiched together and served with a spoon of ice cream, they make for a sort of scaled down and deconstructed Snickers bar. The marshmallow filling from the Chocolate and Peanut Butter S'mores (see page 48) also works well, with a thin layer of melted chocolate or raspberry jam.

MAKES ABOUT 18 (IF USING A 7CM CUTTER)

90g raw peanuts (skinless, unroasted and unsalted), or roasted peanuts

150g plain flour

125g unsalted butter, at room temperature

50g icing sugar

1 tsp vanilla extract

¼ tsp salt

¼ tsp baking powder

2 tbsp demerara sugar

1   Preheat the oven to 190°C/170°C Fan/Gas Mark 5.

2   Spread the peanuts out on a baking tray and roast for 8–10 minutes (or 3–4 minutes if using roasted) until golden brown. Set aside until completely cool, then transfer to a food processor with 50g flour. Blitz until the nuts are finely chopped, then set aside. The oven is not used for over an hour so can be turned off at this point.

3   Place the butter and icing sugar in an electric mixer with the paddle attachment in place. Beat on a medium-high speed for about 2 minutes until light and fluffy. Add the vanilla extract, mix to combine, scrape down the sides of the bowl with a rubber spatula, then reduce the speed to medium-low. Sift the remaining flour, salt and baking powder into the bowl and continue to mix. Add the nuts and beat again, just to combine.

4   Tip the dough on to a clean work surface and knead gently to bring it together, then form it into a ball. Wrap loosely in cling film, press to form a disc, and chill in the fridge for at least 1 hour to firm up.

5   Preheat the oven to 190°C/170°C Fan/Gas Mark 5. Line two baking trays with baking parchment.

6   Roll the dough between two sheets of baking parchment to just under 0.5cm thick. Using a 7cm round cutter, cut out 18 circles, re-rolling the offcuts so that you have enough dough. Place these on the lined trays, spaced about 1cm apart. Sprinkle with the sugar and bake for 15 minutes, or until golden brown all over. Remove from the oven and set aside on their trays to cool before serving.

This recipe can easily be doubled if you want to make more, or if you want to freeze half the batch, ready rolled and all set up to be baked as and when you want.

Once baked, these will keep for up to a week in an airtight container.

Almond, pistachio and sour cherry wafers

These are lovely to snack on with tea or coffee, of course, but they also work well after a meal with a spoonful of ice cream. Don't be put off by how many slices one loaf makes: the slices are wafer thin so you can easily eat four or five at a time! Play around with the dried fruit: raisins, roughly chopped figs or apricots can be used instead of (or in combination with) the sour cherries.

Thanks to Carol Brough, previously head pastry chef at Ottolenghi, for introducing us to these.

MAKES 1 LARGE LOAF, ABOUT 55–60 WAFER-THIN SLICES

400g plain flour	240g soft dark brown sugar
1 tsp bicarbonate of soda	70ml water
½ tsp ground cinnamon	150g whole almonds, skin on
½ tsp salt	90g shelled pistachio kernels
100g unsalted butter, cubed	100g dried sour cherries

1   Line the base and sides of a regular 900g loaf tin with baking parchment and set aside.

2   Sift the flour, bicarbonate of soda, cinnamon and salt into a large bowl and set aside.

3   Place the butter, sugar and water in a small saucepan over a medium-low heat. Cook for about 5 minutes, until the sugar has dissolved, then pour into the dry ingredients, along with the almonds, pistachios and cherries. Mix to form a smooth, glossy dough, then tip the mixture into the prepared tin, pressing down firmly. Cover the top with a piece of baking parchment and transfer to the fridge or freezer for several hours to firm up: it should be cold but pliable when pressed for ease of slicing (see notes).

4   Once the dough is firm, preheat the oven to 190°C/170°C Fan/Gas Mark 5. Line a baking tray with baking parchment.

5   Slice the loaf as thinly as you can without the slices breaking – 2–3mm thickness is ideal – and lay them out on the parchment-lined tray; they won't spread during baking, so don't worry about spacing them apart.

6   Bake in batches in the oven for 10–14 minutes (timing will vary, depending on how thick the slices are) until golden brown. Remove from the oven and set aside until completely cool: they will be slightly soft when warm but will harden and crisp up as they cool.

At the bakery we use a meat slicer to produce very fine, uniform slices. Using a large kitchen knife also works well, though. Freeze the dough once it's shaped into a loaf (but before it's sliced and baked), then transfer it to the fridge the night before you want to bake it, or just remove it from the freezer for a couple of hours before slicing; it is much easier to slice when not completely frozen: it should be cold but pliable when pressed.

The unbaked dough can be kept in the freezer for up to 3 months.

Once baked, the crisp wafers keep for up to 1 week in an airtight container.

Cranberry, oat and white chocolate biscuits

We first made these to sell around Thanksgiving, but our customers soon demanded them all year round. They have enough going for them to appeal to all senses, as well as seasons: tartness from the cranberries, chewiness from the oats, nuttiness from the wholemeal flour and almonds, and a bit of sweet luxury from the white chocolate coating. Sour cherries or plump Californian cherries can be used instead of the cranberries, if preferred.

MAKES ABOUT 30 (IF USING A 7CM CUTTER)

———

150g whole almonds, skin on
150g plain flour, plus extra for dusting
75g wholemeal flour
150g jumbo rolled oats
¼ tsp salt
225g unsalted butter, at room
   temperature, roughly cut into
   3–4cm pieces
100g caster sugar

finely grated zest of 1 large orange
   (1 tbsp)
125g dried cranberries, chopped in half
   (if they are not already chopped),
   soaked in 25ml orange juice
250g white chocolate

These will keep for up to a week in an airtight container.

———

1   Preheat the oven to 180°C/160°C Fan/Gas Mark 4.

2   Spread the almonds out on a baking tray and roast for 10 minutes. Remove from the oven and, once cool enough to handle, roughly chop into 0.5–1cm pieces. Transfer the nuts to a large bowl and add the flours, oats and salt. Mix together and set aside.

3   Increase the oven temperature to 190°C/170°C Fan/Gas Mark 5. Line two or three baking trays with baking parchment and set aside.

4   Place the butter, sugar and orange zest in the bowl of an electric mixer with the paddle attachment in place. Beat on a medium speed for about 2 minutes, until combined and light. Add the almond and flour mix to the butter and sugar and continue to mix on a low speed until the dough just comes together. Add the cranberries and orange juice and mix for another few seconds to combine, then tip the dough on to a lightly floured work surface. Knead into a ball, sprinkling over more flour if needed to prevent it getting too sticky.

5   Cut the dough in half and roll out one half so that it's just over 0.5cm thick. Use a 7cm cookie cutter to cut the dough into rounds. Transfer these to a lined tray while you continue with the remaining dough. Bake for 18 minutes, until lightly coloured all over. Remove from the oven and set aside until completely cool.

6   Meanwhile, place the white chocolate in a small bowl over a pan of gently simmering water, stirring occasionally, until melted. Do not let the base of the bowl touch the water. To coat the cookies, use the back of a dessertspoon to spread a tablespoon of melted chocolate over each. Set aside on a cooling rack for the chocolate to set, which can take up to an hour, before serving.

Chocolate chip and pecan cookies

Our version of this classic American cookie is a huge seller in the Ottolenghi delis. In fact some of our customers have become such cookie connoisseurs that each store tailors its bake to their particular preference. It's true! Our Ledbury Road regulars, for example, like them crisp on the edges and soft in the centre. This is achieved by cooking the rolled dough when it is fridge-cold (rather than room temperature). Our customers on Upper Street, on the other hand, prefer them crisp all the way through. To achieve this you just flatten the balls slightly before they are baked and give them an extra minute in the oven.

The pecans can be substituted with either walnuts or hazelnuts, if you prefer. Whichever nut you choose, they'll need to be roasted. The cookies also work without any nuts at all: if you go for this option, you'll need to increase the amount of chocolate to 370g. It's important to start with chips or callets here, rather than chopping from a block of chocolate – see page 352.

MAKES ABOUT 36 (THE BATCH IS QUITE LARGE, BUT THE BALLS ARE SO EASY TO ROLL, FREEZE AND BAKE FROM FROZEN THAT WE HAVE NOT TRIED TO REDUCE IT)

120g pecan halves (or walnut halves or hazelnuts)
250g unsalted butter, at room temperature, cut into 2cm cubes
200g light brown sugar
200g caster sugar
1½ tsp vanilla extract
2 large eggs
560g self-raising flour
1 tsp salt
250g dark chocolate chips or callets (60-70% cocoa solids)

1   Preheat the oven to 170°C/150°C Fan/Gas Mark 3.

2   Spread the pecans out on a baking tray and roast for 10 minutes. Remove from the oven and, when cool enough to handle, roughly chop into 1.5cm pieces and set aside. You can turn the oven off at this point, as the dough will need to chill in the fridge before baking.

3   Place the butter and sugars in the bowl of an electric mixer with the paddle attachment in place. Beat on a high speed for about 2 minutes, until light and fluffy. With the machine still running, add the vanilla extract and eggs, one at a time, beating well after each addition. Reduce the speed to low, sift in the flour and salt and continue to beat until combined. Finally, add the chocolate chips and roasted nuts, mixing until just combined. Turn off the machine and gently bring the dough together by hand: the consistency should be firm and come together easily.

4   Use your hands to form the dough into large golf-ball-sized balls, about 45g each, and set aside in the fridge for an hour to firm up.

5   When ready to bake, preheat the oven to 200°C/180°C Fan/Gas Mark 6. Line two large baking trays with baking parchment.

6   Spread the balls of dough out on the lined baking trays – you'll need to bake them in two batches – spaced at least 6cm apart. Bake for 12 minutes, rotating the trays halfway through, until golden brown and slightly cracked on top. Remove from the oven and set aside to cool on the trays for 10 minutes until firm, then transfer to a wire rack to cool completely.

Once the unbaked dough has been rolled into balls, they can be frozen for up to 3 months. You can also bake them from frozen: you'll just need to add an extra minute of cooking time (unless, like our Ledbury Road customers, you like a soft centre).

The cookies keep well for 5 days in an airtight container.

Cats' tongues

Langues de Chat, Lenguas de Gato, Katte Tong, Cats' Tongues: whatever the name you use, these long and delicate biscuits are so light that you can nibble a load. We've kept the flavour deliberately simple so they can be served alongside all sorts of flavoured ice creams, sorbets and set puddings: the Campari and Grapefruit Sorbet (see page 304), for example, or the Yoghurt Panna Cotta with Basil and Crushed Strawberries (see page 282). You can also sandwich two together with chocolate ganache, if you like, for something more substantial.

The lemon zest can be substituted with orange or lime zest, perhaps, or a pinch of spice can be added – ground cloves, ginger, cardamom or mahleb all work well.

MAKES AROUND 36

___

120g unsalted butter, at room temperature, cubed
120g caster sugar
scraped seeds of ¼ vanilla pod
finely grated zest of ½ lemon (½ tsp)

⅛ tsp salt
60g egg whites (from 1½ large eggs)
90g plain flour
a drop or two of lemon oil

___

1   Preheat the oven to 210°C/190°C Fan/Gas Mark 6.

2   Place the butter, sugar, vanilla seeds, lemon zest and salt in the bowl of an electric mixer with the paddle attachment in place. Beat on a medium speed for about 3 minutes, until light. Reduce the speed to low and gradually dribble in the egg whites, beating all the time and scraping down the bowl to ensure even mixing. Sift the flour into a separate bowl, then, with the mixer still on a low speed, add the flour in three batches. When completely combined, add the lemon oil – just a drop or two – mix through and then scrape the mixture into a piping bag fitted with a 1cm wide nozzle.

3   Pipe 9cm long fingers on to a non-stick silicone mat, or a parchment-lined baking tray, spaced about 4cm apart, as they will spread during baking. Bake for 8 minutes, rotating the tray halfway through, until the biscuits are light brown around the edges. Remove from the oven and wait for a minute or two before transferring to a cooling rack. Set aside until completely cool, then store in a kitchen paper-lined airtight container (the paper will prevent the delicate biscuits breaking when being moved about).

Use a non-stick silicone baking mat here, if you have one, instead of regular baking parchment. It will help the delicate biscuits cook more evenly. If you only have baking parchment, that's fine: just switch the oven to conventional heat (rather than fan-assisted) to prevent the paper and light biscuits fluttering around inside and becoming misshapen; the biscuits might need an extra minute in the oven on this setting.

You will need a piping bag with a 1cm wide nozzle here. You can either invest in a piping bag which comes with a range of nozzles, or you can buy a disposable piping bag and just cut a 1cm hole in the end.

These will keep well in an airtight container for up to 5 days, or in the freezer for up to 10 days. Once baked, they're actually very good eaten straight from frozen!

Chocolate, banana and pecan cookies

These were introduced by Jim Webb, an original member of the Ottolenghi team along with Sami, Noam and Yotam. Jim mostly worked on pastry, bringing with him some brilliant ideas, along with a serious knowledge of bread and viennoiserie. It was Jim's suggestion to add banana to the dough here, both for the moisture and the distinct flavour it brings to the cookies. The pecans are a classic match, but walnuts can be used instead, if you prefer.

The secret here is to slightly under-bake the cookies, which keeps them soft and fudgy. It's for this reason that they've never become a feature in the shops, particularly in the summer, where they'd bend and break after an hour or two piled up in a bowl. There are worse things to happen, though, than to be told you need to eat a whole batch of cookies within a day or so of them being baked.

MAKES ABOUT 24

110g unsalted butter, at room temperature, cubed
110g caster sugar
1 large egg, lightly beaten
125g plain flour
½ tsp baking powder
20g Dutch-processed cocoa powder
½ tsp ground cinnamon
¼ tsp salt
100g chocolate chips (70% cocoa solids), or 100g dark cooking chocolate, cut into 0.5cm pieces
50g mashed banana (about ½ small banana)
170g pecan halves, finely chopped
100g icing sugar, for dusting

1   Place the butter and sugar in the bowl of an electric mixer with the paddle attachment in place. Beat on a medium-high speed until light and fluffy, then gradually add the egg and continue to beat until incorporated. Sift the flour, baking powder, cocoa powder, cinnamon and salt into a bowl, then add to the butter and sugar. Mix on a low speed for about 15 seconds, then add the chocolate and banana. Beat until combined, then transfer to the fridge for 2 hours to firm up.

2   When firm, use your hands to form the dough into 3cm round balls, about 20g each: you might need to wash your hands once or twice when making them, if they get too sticky. Place the pecans in a medium bowl and drop the balls into the nuts as you form them, rolling them around so that they are completely coated and pressing the nuts in so that they stick.

3   Line a baking tray with baking parchment, place the cookies on the tray – there is no need to space them apart at this stage – and transfer to the fridge for at least an hour.

4   When ready to bake, preheat the oven to 190°C/170°C Fan/Gas Mark 5. Line two baking trays with baking parchment.

5   Place the icing sugar in a bowl and roll the cookies in the icing sugar, pressing it in as you go so that it sticks well. Place on the lined baking trays, spaced 2–3cm apart, and flatten the cookies to 1cm thick.

6   Bake for 10 minutes. They will be soft to the touch when they come out of the oven, so allow them to cool on the tray for 10 minutes before gently transferring to a wire rack. These can be served warm, when they will be a little gooey in the centre, or set aside until completely cool.

Once the unbaked dough has been rolled into balls, they can be kept in the fridge for up to 2 days, or frozen for up to 3 months. You can also bake them from frozen: you'll just need to add an extra minute of cooking time.

These cookies are best eaten within a day of being made.

Brown butter almond tuiles

These tuiles (or 'tiles') are, like the Cats' Tongues (see page 27), deliciously simple biscuits to eat with ice cream, sorbet (they work well with the Campari and Grapefruit Sorbet, see page 304) or just with a cup of coffee. It's 'browning' the butter that gives them their nutty caramel note. And if you've made the ice cream yourself, you'll already have the egg whites ready and waiting to be put to good use.

Traditionally, tuiles are cooled over a rolling pin to produce their characteristically curved shape. We tend to cool ours flat, however, as they store more easily this way and are less prone to snapping, but feel free to stick with tradition, if you prefer.

MAKES ABOUT 20

45g unsalted butter, cubed
120g flaked almonds
120g caster sugar

35g plain flour
70g egg whites (from 2 large eggs)
¼ tsp vanilla extract

Provided they are cooked through (completely crisp), they will keep for up to 10 days in an airtight container. If they do soften, you can crisp them up in the oven for 5 minutes at 180°C/ 160°C Fan/Gas Mark 4 before setting aside to cool completely.

1   To brown the butter, place it in a small saucepan over a medium heat. Once melted, continue to cook until the butter is foaming. Swirl the pan gently from time to time, to allow the solids to brown more evenly, until you see dark brown sediments begin to form on the sides and bottom of the pan. Continue to bubble away until it turns a rich golden brown. It will also smell heavenly, like toasted nuts and caramel. Remove the pan from the heat and let it stand for 5 minutes, to allow the burnt solids to collect at the bottom of the pan. Strain through a fine-mesh (or muslin-lined) sieve, discarding the solids. You need 25g browned butter, so pour away any excess (this can be reserved for cooking), then set aside to cool to room temperature.

2   Place the flaked almonds, sugar and flour in a medium bowl and pour over the cooled butter. Add the egg whites and vanilla and mix with a wooden spoon until combined.

3   Preheat the oven to 180°C/160°C Fan/Gas Mark 4. Line a baking tray with baking parchment.

4   Drop tablespoons of the almond mixture – about 15g each – on to the baking tray, spaced about 5cm apart. Flatten the mixture by patting them down with moistened fingers – keep a small bowl of warm water nearby to dip into – until the almonds are just about in a single layer and each tuile is about 6cm wide.

5   Bake for 18 minutes, rotating the tray halfway through, until the tuiles are golden brown all over. Remove the tray from the oven and allow them to cool for 5 minutes before gently transferring them with a small metal spatula to a wire rack (or drape them over a rolling pin, if you prefer the traditional shape) until completely cool.

Gevulde Speculaas

Speculaas are spiced shortcrust biscuits, hugely popular in the Netherlands. 'Gevulde' means stuffed, which – with their almond paste filling – these certainly are. Both are eaten by the Dutch around Sinterklaas – the 5th and 6th December – when the legendary figure rides into town on his white horse, bearing presents for those who've been good. You'll worry that the dough is not going to come together when rolling it, but trust in the recipe – it works!

You'll have twice as much spice mixture as you need for this recipe, but it keeps well in a sealed container, so can be used in your next batch of Gevulde Speculaas or in the Speculaas Biscuits (see page 37) – one batch needs exactly the amount of spice mixture you'll have left over.

Thanks to Hennie Franssen for this recipe (as well as for translating all of Yotam's books into Dutch).

SERVES 12

Once baked, these will keep for up to 5 days in a sealed container.

SPICE MIX

1 tbsp ground cinnamon
1 tsp ground aniseed
¾ tsp ground white pepper
¾ tsp ground ginger
½ tsp ground coriander
1 tsp ground cardamom
¼ tsp ground nutmeg
¼ tsp ground cloves

DOUGH

100g unsalted butter, softened, plus
    an extra 15g, melted, for brushing
100g dark brown sugar
1 tbsp full-fat milk, plus up to 1 tbsp
    extra, if the dough needs it
½ tsp bicarbonate of soda
180g plain flour, plus extra for dusting
⅓ tsp salt

ALMOND PASTE

200g whole blanched almonds
150g caster sugar
1 large egg
finely grated zest of 1 small lemon
    (¾ tsp), plus 2 tsp lemon juice
60g mixed candied peel

TO DECORATE

1 large egg, lightly beaten, to glaze
30g whole blanched almonds

1   **For the spice mix,** combine all the ingredients in a bowl and set aside until ready to use.

2   **To make the dough,** place the butter in the bowl of an electric mixer with the paddle attachment in place. Add the sugar and milk and beat on a medium speed until smooth. Sift the bicarbonate of soda, 4 teaspoons of spice mix, the flour and salt into a bowl, then add this to the dough. Continue to mix until the dough is soft and pliable, adding a little more milk if needed. Transfer the dough to your work surface and lightly knead. Wrap in cling film and keep in the fridge until ready to use. ››

3 **For the almond paste,** place the almonds in a food processor and blitz for 30 seconds – you don't want the texture to be completely smooth. Add the sugar, egg and lemon juice and blitz again, until it is slightly smoother but still grainy. Finally, add the lemon zest and candied peel and blitz once or twice, just to mix through. The paste should be sticky and softer than the dough, but still hold its shape. Transfer to a small bowl until ready to use.

4 Preheat the oven to 190°C/170°C Fan/Gas Mark 5.

5 Roll the dough out on a lightly floured 40 x 30cm sheet of baking parchment to form a 35 x 20cm rectangle, just over 0.5cm thick. Dust with more flour if you need to, to prevent it sticking.

6 Transfer the dough and parchment sheet to a large baking tray and brush two-thirds of the melted butter evenly over the dough. Spoon the almond paste lengthways down the centre of the dough to form a long sausage, about 6cm wide. Brush the almond paste with the remainder of the butter and then, using the parchment paper to help you, draw in the left side of the dough on top of the paste. Bring in the right side on top of this (again, using the paper to help you) so that the two sides are slightly overlapping. Press gently to secure and carefully turn the whole thing over so that the seal is at the bottom and the paste is secured – a bit like a giant sausage roll. Brush evenly and lightly with the beaten egg, arrange the whole almonds on top – decorating as you like – and then brush again with the egg.

7 Place in the oven and bake for 30 minutes, until the dough begins to colour and the almonds are golden. Don't be alarmed that the roll flattens out – this is meant to happen! Set aside until completely cool on the baking tray, then cut into 12 slices, each about 2.5cm thick, and serve.

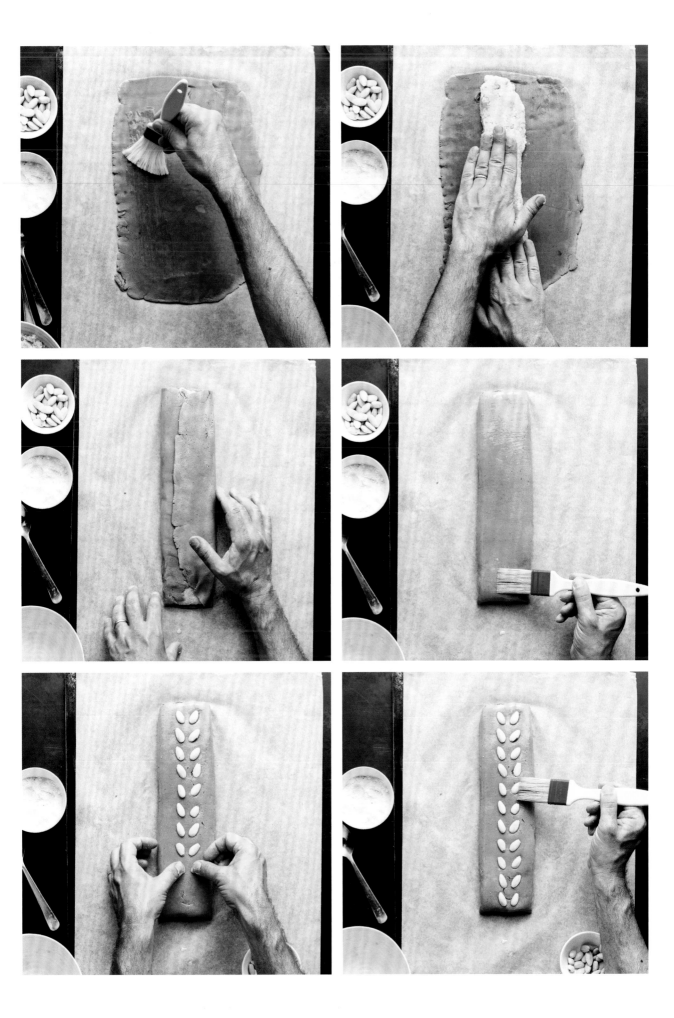

Speculaas biscuits

We originally made these crisp biscuits to use up the spice mix left over from making the Gevulde Speculaas (see page 33). Yet they swiftly became the very reason to make the spice mix in the first place! Either way, you're on to a festive winner. Both the Gevulde Speculaas and these biscuits are traditionally eaten in the Netherlands around Sinterklaas, during the first week of December. They're delicious all year round, though, perfect for snacking on or for serving with ice cream.

Use any size or shape of cookie cutter you like, depending on the occasion and season. The more frilly the edge of your cutter, the quicker your biscuit edges will cook, so keep an eye on timings as you might need to reduce them by a minute or two. Be sure not to under-bake them, though: you want them to be super crisp and they are meant to take on a lot of colour.

MAKES ABOUT 60 BISCUITS (IF USING A 7CM ROUND CUTTER)

The dough can be frozen before or after it is rolled and shaped; if the latter, bake from frozen and increase the cooking time by 1 minute.

Once baked, these will keep for up to a week in an airtight container.

450g plain flour
1 tbsp baking powder
3½ tsp spice mix (approximately; see Gevulde Speculaas, page 33)
½ tsp salt
250g unsalted butter, at room temperature

330g soft dark brown sugar
50ml dark rum or brandy
1 large egg white, lightly beaten until frothy, for brushing
100g flaked almonds, to decorate

1   Sift the flour, baking powder, spice mix and salt into a medium bowl and set aside.

2   Place the butter and sugar in the bowl of an electric mixer with the paddle attachment in place. Beat on a medium-high speed for about 3 minutes, until the mixture is light and fluffy. Add the rum or brandy and beat until incorporated. Finally, add the sifted dry ingredients and continue to mix on a low speed; the dough can initially feel dry and difficult, but trust us, it will come together. Tip on to a clean work surface and knead lightly to bring together. Divide the dough into two pieces, wrap each loosely in cling film, then press down to form flattish discs and transfer to the fridge for 30 minutes (or freeze one of the discs if you just want to make 30 biscuits).

3   When ready to bake, preheat the oven to 210°C/190°C Fan/Gas Mark 6. Line two large baking trays with baking parchment and set aside.

4   Roll out the dough on a lightly floured work surface until it is just under 0.5cm thick. Using a 7cm round cutter (or whatever size or shape you like), cut out the biscuits and place them on the lined baking trays, spaced 2cm apart. Re-roll the scraps to cut out more biscuits. Use a pastry brush to lightly paint a thin layer of egg white over each biscuit, then sprinkle lightly with the flaked almonds (use 50g if you have frozen half the dough).

5   Bake for 12 minutes, rotating the trays halfway through, until golden brown and the almonds are toasted. Remove from the oven and set aside for 10 minutes on the trays for the biscuits to cool slightly, before transferring to a wire rack to cool completely.

Amaretti with honey and orange blossom

With no flour at all, the ground almonds are allowed to be the star here, so use the freshest, best-quality almonds you can find.

MAKES 20

200g ground almonds
110g caster sugar
finely grated zest of 1 lemon (1 tsp)
finely grated zest of 1 small orange
    (1 tsp)
⅛ tsp salt

60g egg whites (from 1½ large eggs)
25g runny honey
⅛ tsp best-quality almond extract
¼ tsp orange blossom water
100g flaked almonds, for rolling
25g icing sugar, for dusting

1   Combine the almonds, sugar, lemon zest, orange zest and salt in a large bowl and set aside.

2   Place the egg whites in the bowl of an electric mixer with the whisk attachment in place and whisk on a medium speed. Heat the honey in a small saucepan over a medium heat, and just before it comes to the boil, increase the speed of the whisk to medium-high while the honey continues to boil for 30 seconds and the egg whites form soft peaks. Remove the honey from the heat and carefully pour into the egg whites, in a continuous stream, whisking all the time. When all the honey has been added, keep whisking for a minute until the meringue is fully whipped and cooled. Stop the mixer, remove the whisk attachment and change to the paddle attachment.

3   Add the almond and sugar mixture, along with the almond extract and orange blossom water. Mix until it all comes together to form a soft, pliable paste. Alternatively, use a wooden spoon or your hands to bring everything together. Transfer to a bowl, cover with cling film and transfer to the fridge for 1 hour to firm up. The mixture will still be very soft but the chilling will help when rolling out.

4   Once chilled, divide the mixture into four portions of about 90g each. Sprinkle a quarter of the flaked almonds on a clean work surface and roll out one piece to form a log 30cm long and 1.5cm wide, covered with almonds.

5   Line a baking tray (that will fit inside your fridge) with baking parchment, and either lift the log on to the tray by hand or roll it on to a clean ruler and use that to transfer it to the tray. Continue until you have rolled all four pieces into logs, sprinkling more flaked almonds on the work surface with each batch. Place them all on the tray, cover with cling film, and place in the fridge for at least 2 hours, or up to 2 days.

6   When ready to bake, preheat the oven to 190°C/170°C Fan/Gas Mark 5. Line a baking tray with baking parchment.

7   Remove the tray from the fridge and cut each log into five smaller logs, 6cm long. Sift the icing sugar into a bowl and roll each piece in the icing sugar so that they are covered all over. Spread out on the parchment-lined baking tray, spaced 2cm apart, and bake for 13–15 minutes, rotating the tray halfway through, until the Amaretti are golden brown but still soft. Remove from the oven and set aside on the tray for 10 minutes. These can be served warm or transferred on to a wire rack to cool and firm up before serving.

The key to making these is in the timing. As with any recipe with an Italian meringue component (see page 347 for more on Italian, French and Swiss meringues), the sugar syrup – in this case, honey syrup – needs to be at exactly the right temperature just as the egg whites have formed soft peaks. The trick is to have the egg whites whipping slowly, and then be ready to increase the speed as the honey comes to the boil.

The unbaked, rolled dough can be kept in the fridge, covered in cling film, for up to 2 days.

Once baked, these will keep well for up to 10 days in an airtight container.

SOFT GINGERBREAD TILES
WITH RUM BUTTER GLAZE

Soft gingerbread tiles with rum butter glaze

Helen has been slightly obsessed with these ever since she saw them on the front cover of the *Tartine* baking book by Elisabeth M. Prueitt and Chad Robertson. They used an antique embossed rolling pin to create the imprint before cutting them into rectangles; here, we use round biscuit stamps for the imprint before cutting them out with a round biscuit cutter. Once the glaze is applied, they really do look like antique tiles. Try to get hold of some stamps if you can – they're very popular in Scandinavian countries and can easily be bought online. If you can't get hold of any, the gingerbreads can also be made as regular biscuits, using round cutters, or cut into squares or rectangles with a knife.

If you want to keep the glaze booze-free, the rum in the icing can be replaced with lemon juice.

MAKES 12–14 (DEPENDING ON THE SIZE OF STAMP AND CUTTER)
—

85g unsalted butter, at room
    temperature
90g soft dark brown sugar
100g black treacle (or blackstrap
    molasses)
1 large egg yolk
235g plain flour, plus extra for dusting
    and printing
½ tsp bicarbonate of soda
1 tsp ground ginger
½ tsp ground cinnamon
⅛ tsp ground cloves
1 tbsp Dutch-processed cocoa powder
¼ tsp salt
¼ tsp freshly ground black pepper

RUM BUTTER GLAZE
80g icing sugar
⅛ tsp ground cinnamon
15g unsalted butter, melted and warm
1 tbsp dark rum (or lemon juice)
1 tsp warm water

Once the dough is made, it can be wrapped in cling film and kept in the fridge for up to 2 days before baking.

These will keep for up to 5 days in an airtight container. The glaze will discolour and crack a little, but this will not affect how they taste.

1   Place the butter, sugar and treacle in the bowl of an electric mixer with the paddle attachment in place. Beat on a medium speed until smooth and incorporated. Add the egg yolk and continue to beat until fully combined.

2   Sift all the dry ingredients into a bowl, reduce the speed of the mixer, and add the dry ingredients to the butter and treacle. Once the mix comes together, tip the dough on to a lightly floured work surface and knead gently. Roll out the dough so that it is about 6mm thick. If the dough is very soft, you will need to chill it.

3   Preheat the oven to 190°C/170°C Fan/Gas Mark 5. Line two baking trays with baking parchment and set aside.

4   Dip the biscuit stamps in a small bowl of flour, shake off any excess and then press them firmly into the dough, one at a time, to create a deep imprint. How far you need to press to get an imprint will depend on your stamp: the patterns on some are more deeply cut than others. Bear in mind that the biscuits rise a little when cooked, so any soft imprints will disappear. Then, using a round biscuit cutter which is slightly larger than the pattern, cut out the pieces of imprinted gingerbread. Transfer the biscuits to the lined baking trays, spaced about 2cm apart. Re-roll the dough and continue to stamp and cut biscuits until all the dough is used up.

5   Bake for 9–10 minutes, rotating the trays halfway through, until firm to the touch. They will continue to firm up as they cool, so don't be tempted to bake them for any longer.

6   **Prepare the glaze** while the gingerbreads are in the oven, as the glaze needs to be brushed on to the biscuits while they are still warm. Sift the icing sugar and cinnamon into a small bowl. Add the melted butter, rum (or lemon juice) and water and mix with a spoon until smooth. The glaze will thicken slightly if it sits around, so stir through a little more warm water if you need to – it should be the consistency of runny honey.

7   Remove the biscuits from the oven, leave them to rest for 5 minutes, then brush or dab the glaze all over with a pastry brush. Transfer to a wire rack to cool completely.

Soft date and oat bars

We have decided to call these 'bars', as flapjacks conjure up American-style pancakes to many, which these are very much not. Whatever you want to call them, these nut-and-seed-filled slices have a crunchy edge and a slightly chewy middle. It's the way we like them, but they might be a bit softer than you're used to. If you want to firm them up – so they're robust enough to cart about in Tupperware, for example – store them in the fridge, where they'll soon harden up.

MAKES ABOUT 14

These will keep for up to 5 days in an airtight container.

50g almonds, skin on
50g cashew nuts
200g jumbo rolled oats
35g pumpkin seeds
35g sunflower seeds
15g sesame seeds
7–8 large Medjool dates, pitted (120g), halved lengthways and each half cut into 3 pieces

200g unsalted butter, cut into 3–4cm cubes
180g demerara sugar
75g date syrup (or golden syrup)
finely grated zest of 1 small orange (1 tsp)
2 tsp orange blossom water
1 tsp ground cinnamon
¼ tsp salt

1   Preheat the oven to 180°C/160°C Fan/Gas Mark 4. Grease and line a 30 x 20cm baking tray and set aside.

2   Spread the almonds and cashew nuts out on a separate tray and roast for 10 minutes, or until the nuts are lightly browned. Remove from the oven and allow to cool for a few minutes before chopping into roughly 1.5cm pieces. Transfer to a large mixing bowl and set aside.

3   While the nuts are in the oven, place 80g of the oats in a food processor and roughly blitz: you want them to be broken into small pieces rather than turned to powder. Add the blitzed oats (which will help keep the bars together when baked) to the unblitzed oats in a bowl and set aside.

4   Place the seeds in a dry frying pan and toast over a medium-low heat, shaking the pan frequently, so that they toast evenly. Add the seeds to the chopped nuts along with the dates and all of the oats. Mix to combine and set aside.

5   Place the butter, sugar, date syrup and orange zest in a medium saucepan and place over a medium-low heat. Stir gently until the butter has melted (don't worry if the demerara sugar has not melted, it will add to the crunch) and the mix comes together. Remove from the heat, stir through the orange blossom water, cinnamon and salt, then pour over the oat mixture. Mix well and tip out into the lined baking tray. Use a small spatula or the back of a spoon to spread and press the mixture evenly on to the tray.

6   Bake for about 35 minutes, or until bubbling and a dark golden colour. Remove from the oven and allow to cool for about 30 minutes before cutting into squares or 8 x 3cm rectangles; however you slice them you want to do so before they set hard. Don't remove them from the tray until they are completely cool, however, as they will crumble and fall apart.

Orange and star anise shortbread

Using two types of flour here – the finely milled Italian '00' flour and the white rice flour – creates a shortbread with a crisp and buttery texture. For the rice flour, you need the grainy type – a brand such as Bob's Red Mill, for example – rather than the finely milled Asian variety used to make dumpling wrappers.

If you are looking for ideas for biscuits to give as gifts, these should go on the list: they're sturdy enough to be wrapped in cellophane bags, with a shelf life that allows them to be enjoyed at leisure.

The recipe calls for a round pastry cutter but feel free to use any shape that you like, particularly festive shapes if you are gifting them as a holiday treat.

MAKES ABOUT 40 BISCUITS (IF USING A 7–8CM CUTTER)

360g Italian '00' flour
70g white grainy rice flour
165g caster sugar
⅛ tsp baking powder
1½ tsp ground star anise
    (about 3 whole star anise)
1 tsp flaky sea salt

finely grated zest of 1 large orange
    (1 tbsp)
scraped seeds of ½ vanilla pod
250g unsalted butter, fridge-cold,
    cut into 2cm cubes
1 large egg, lightly beaten

1   Sift the flours, sugar, baking powder and ground star anise into a large mixing bowl. Add the salt, orange zest and vanilla seeds and mix to combine. Add the butter and use the tips of your fingers to rub it into the dry mix until there are no large bits of butter and the consistency is that of breadcrumbs. Add the egg and mix gradually, using your hands or a wooden spoon, until the dough comes together. Shape into a rectangle and wrap tightly in cling film. Set aside in the fridge for at least 1 hour to firm up.

2   Preheat the oven to 180°C/160°C Fan/Gas Mark 4. Line two baking trays with baking parchment and set aside.

3   Cut the dough in half and roll out one half on a lightly floured work surface until it is just under 0.5cm thick. Using a 7–8cm round cutter, cut out the biscuits and place them on the lined baking trays, spaced 1cm apart. Re-roll the scraps to cut out more biscuits.

4   Bake for 16–17 minutes, in batches if necessary, rotating the trays halfway through to get an even colour. They should be golden brown on the edges, lightly golden in the centre and have a golden brown underside. Transfer to a cooling rack until completely cool.

The dough can be made a day ahead and kept in the fridge overnight; make sure you remove it from the fridge and allow it to sit at room temperature for 30 minutes before rolling, so it becomes malleable. The dough can also be frozen before or after it is rolled and shaped; if the latter, bake from frozen and increase the cooking time by 1 minute.

Once baked, these will keep well for up to 10 days in an airtight container.

Chocolate and peanut butter s'mores

This is our take on s'mores, the campfire classic of melted marshmallows squished between two biscuits and dipped in melted chocolate. These are a little more elaborate, but there's got to be a scout's badge for making your own marshmallow, surely?

Helen's childhood memories of Wagon Wheels – chocolate-coated biscuits with a marshmallow centre – predispose her to keeping these simple, leaving out the crunchy peanut butter in the filling. Yotam, whose own childhood memories are rich in nutty tahini, prefers them with. They work both ways.

MAKES 22 (IF USING A 6CM CUTTER)
___

BISCUITS

150g unsalted butter, at room
    temperature, cut into 2cm cubes

75g caster sugar

1 large egg yolk (save the egg white
    for the marshmallow)

40g maple syrup

50g roasted (unsalted) peanuts,
    finely ground in the small bowl
    of a food processor

260g plain flour

⅛ tsp salt

MARSHMALLOW

1½ sheets (about 11 x 7cm)
    platinum gelatine, or 1½ tsp
    powdered gelatine

85ml cold water

90g caster sugar

1½ tsp liquid glucose

scraped seeds of ¼ vanilla pod

30g egg whites (from 1 medium egg)

TO FINISH

140g crunchy peanut butter,
    for spreading

15g roasted (unsalted) peanuts,
    roughly chopped into 0.5cm pieces

¼ tsp flaky sea salt

130g dark cooking chocolate
    (70% cocoa solids), roughly chopped
    into 0.5cm pieces

You will need a piping bag with a 1cm wide nozzle here. You can either invest in a piping bag which comes with a range of nozzles, or you can buy a disposable piping bag and just cut a 1cm hole in the end. You will also need a sugar thermometer to make the marshmallow.

The dough for the biscuits can be made a day ahead and kept in the fridge.

Once baked and filled, these will keep for 3 days in an airtight container.

1   **To make the biscuits,** place the butter and sugar in the bowl of an electric mixer with the paddle attachment in place. Beat on a medium-high speed for about 2 minutes, until light and fluffy. Add the egg yolk and, when combined, add the maple syrup and ground peanuts. Once combined, sift in the flour and salt and mix together until a dough forms. Tip on to a clean work surface and knead gently for a few seconds to bring it together. Wrap the dough loosely in cling film, press to form a disc, and keep in the fridge for at least 1 hour or overnight.

2   Preheat the oven to 190°C/170°C Fan/Gas Mark 5. Line two baking trays with baking parchment and set aside.

3   Remove the dough from the fridge about 5 minutes before rolling, so that it has some malleability. On a lightly floured work surface, roll out the dough so that it is just under 0.5cm thick: you can divide it in half before rolling, if that's easier. Using a 6cm round cutter, cut out 44 circles and place them on the parchment-lined baking trays. Bake for about 15 minutes, rotating the trays halfway through, until the biscuits are firm and turning a light golden colour around the edges. Remove from the oven and set aside, still on their tray, to cool.

4   Once cool, turn the biscuits over so that the underside sits up. Spread half of the biscuits with peanut butter and set aside.

5   **Next, make the marshmallow.** Place the gelatine sheets or powder in a small bowl. Cover with 40ml of the water and set aside.

6   Place the sugar, glucose, vanilla seeds and remaining water in a small saucepan and place over a medium heat. Stir until the sugar has melted, then increase the heat to medium-high. Bring to the boil and simmer for about 8–10 minutes, until the mixture turns a very light amber colour and starts to thicken (you are looking for it to eventually reach 128°C on a thermometer).

7   Keep a close eye on the sugar as it's simmering, and when the temperature reaches about 120°C, place the egg whites in the bowl of an electric mixer. Starting off with a hand-held whisk (there is not enough egg in the bowl for the machine whisk to take effect at this stage), beat the egg whites until stiff peaks form. Continue beating with the machine from this stage.

8   When the sugar reaches 128°C, remove from the heat, slide the softened gelatine and soaking water into the sugar mix and stir to combine. With the electric mixer still running, slowly and carefully pour the sugar syrup over the egg whites, and continue to whisk until the mixture is glossy and thick and the bowl of the mixer is completely cool: about 15 minutes. Immediately spoon the marshmallow into a piping bag and pipe the mix in a circular pattern over the remaining upturned biscuits, covering the whole of the base with a generous amount of the marshmallow. Sandwich a peanut-butter-covered biscuit on top of a marshmallow-covered biscuit and press gently together. Continue with the remaining biscuits in the same way, then leave for about half an hour to set.

9   Combine the chopped peanuts and sea salt in a small bowl, rubbing the salt between your fingers to break it up. Set aside.

10   **Next, melt the chocolate.** Place the chocolate in a small bowl over a pan of simmering water, stirring occasionally, until melted. Do not let the base of the bowl touch the water.

11   Gently hold the peanut side of the 'sandwich' and dip the marshmallow half lightly into the melted chocolate, so that the biscuit is covered. Sprinkle a pinch of the peanut and salt mix into the centre of the biscuit (on the side with the melted chocolate) and allow to set before serving.

SWEET

CHOCOLATE AND PEANUT BUTTER S'MORES

'Anzac' biscuits (aka Honey, oat and raisin cookies)

Anzac biscuits – a mix of rolled oats, desiccated coconut and sugar, held together by flour, golden syrup and butter – are very popular in Australia and New Zealand. Traditionally, they are sweet, flat and crispy. Very untraditionally (as Yotam was informed in no uncertain terms by his Antipodean Instagram followers, after posting a picture of our Anzacs), ours are plump, chewy and slightly malty. With outcries of 'travesty!' we both applauded the loyalty of the Southern Hemisphere to their bakes at the same time as defending our version as a twist on (rather than a cruel departure from) the original. They get their 'chew' from the addition of the raisins and the honey, while the bran flakes give them a slight but distinctive malty flavour. They're lovely to have sitting on the kitchen counter for snacking on throughout the day.

MAKES 22

100g rolled oats (not the quick-cook breakfast type)
50g bran flakes, lightly crushed by hand
90g desiccated coconut
185g plain flour
100g caster sugar
40g soft light brown sugar

100g raisins
finely grated zest of 1 lemon (1 tsp)
185g unsalted butter
60g runny honey
30ml water
1 tsp bicarbonate of soda

Once baked, don't keep these in an airtight container as they will soften very quickly. Place them in an open container, separating the layers of biscuits with baking parchment, and wrap the whole thing in kitchen foil. This way, they will keep for 3–4 days.

1   Preheat the oven to 170°C/150°C Fan/Gas Mark 3. Line two large baking trays with baking parchment and set aside.

2   Combine the oats, bran flakes, coconut, flour, sugars, raisins and lemon zest in a large bowl and set aside.

3   Heat the butter, honey and water in a small saucepan over a low heat until the butter melts. Remove from the heat and quickly stir in the bicarbonate of soda, for about 15 seconds, until the mixture becomes light and frothy. Pour the mixture into the dry ingredients, mix thoroughly, then roll into golf-ball-sized balls, about 40g each. Spread the balls out on the two baking trays, spaced about 5cm apart.

4   Bake for 18–20 minutes, until the cookies are golden brown but still slightly soft. Remove from the oven and set aside for 5 minutes on the tray before transferring them to a wire rack to cool completely. The cookies should be crispy on the outside but still retain a chew on the inside.

Chocolate 'O' cookies

Helen set herself the challenge of making a cookie to rival the popularity of our chocolate chip cookie. These were the result and they've become something of a signature cookie in the shops. We find their combination of salty, sweet and spicy both delicious and intriguing.

    The 'O' in the name nods three ways: first to Thomas Keller, whose own version of the Oreo biscuit inspired the base for our cookie; second to their small pound-coin shape; and third, of course, to the big round 'O' in the name on the door.

MAKES 22 (IF USING A 6CM CUTTER)

The dough can be made in advance and kept in the fridge for up to 2 days, or frozen for future use.

Once baked and filled, these will keep for 5 days in an airtight container.

COOKIES

190g unsalted butter, at room
    temperature, cubed
130g caster sugar
½ tsp flaky sea salt
220g plain flour
75g Dutch-processed cocoa powder
¼ tsp bicarbonate of soda

WATER GANACHE

½ cinnamon stick
shaved peel of ½ orange
½ tsp chilli flakes
90ml boiling water
125g dark cooking chocolate
    (70% cocoa solids), roughly
    chopped into 1cm pieces
scraped seeds of ½ vanilla pod
¼ tsp flaky sea salt
50g caster sugar
50g liquid glucose
50g unsalted butter, cut into
    2 cm cubes

1   **To make the cookies,** place the butter, sugar and salt in the bowl of an electric mixer with the paddle attachment in place. Beat on a medium-high speed for about 3 minutes, until light and fluffy. Sift the flour, cocoa powder and bicarbonate of soda into a bowl, reduce the speed of the mixer to low, then add the dry ingredients in two batches until a dough forms. Tip on to a clean work surface and knead gently until smooth and uniform. Wrap the dough loosely in cling film, press to form a disc, and keep in the fridge for at least 1 hour to firm up.

2   Preheat the oven to 180°C/160°C Fan/Gas Mark 4. Line two baking trays with baking parchment and set aside.

3   Remove the dough from the fridge about 5 minutes before rolling, so that it has some malleability. On a lightly floured work surface, roll out the dough so that it is about 3mm thick: you can divide it in half before rolling, if that's easier. Using a 6cm round cutter, cut out 44 circles and place them on the parchment-lined baking trays. Bake for 13–15 minutes, rotating the trays halfway through, until firm, then remove from the oven and set aside on the trays until completely cool.

4   **To make the ganache,** place the cinnamon, orange peel and chilli flakes in a small bowl and cover with the boiling water. Set aside to infuse for 30 minutes. After the water has been infusing for about 20 minutes, prepare the sugar syrup.

5   Place the chocolate, vanilla seeds and salt in a medium bowl and set aside. ››

6 Place the sugar and glucose in a small pan and warm through over a medium heat, stirring from time to time, until the sugar has melted. Increase the heat to medium-high and boil until the caramel turns a light amber colour, about 5 minutes. Remove from the heat and add the infused water and aromatics. Don't worry if the sugar seizes in the pan: just return it to the heat and stir until the sugar has dissolved. Return the caramel to the boil, then strain the liquid over the chocolate and vanilla; the aromatics can be discarded. Leave for 2–3 minutes until the chocolate has melted, then mix together.

7 Add the butter, one piece at a time, stirring continuously until all the butter is incorporated and the chocolate is smooth. Place in the fridge for 30 minutes until the ganache is firm.

8 Spoon a heaped teaspoon of the ganache on to the underside of a biscuit, then, using a knife or the back of a dessertspoon, spread it evenly all over the biscuit. Place another biscuit, underside down, on top of the ganache and sandwich together. Set aside while you repeat with the remaining biscuits and ganache.

Garibaldis

These are an altogether more decadent version of the so-called 'squashed fly' biscuit. Where the original is dry and not too sweet, our butter-rich pastry is flaky and positively oozing with caramel. Commercial garibaldis come in strips of stuck-together biscuit, which are then snapped off one at a time. Ours can also become stuck together as the caramel oozes out when the biscuits are baked. Don't worry, though: once they are cool enough to handle, just cut through the caramel and neaten the biscuits up with scissors. The result is quite rustic, but this is as it should be!

MAKES 20

The caramel can be made a day ahead; if it becomes too firm, warm it gently to soften: you want it to be spreadable rather than runny. The dough can also be made ahead and will keep in the fridge for 3–4 days. Once assembled, the biscuits can be frozen before baking; when ready to eat, they can be baked from frozen: you'll just need to add an extra minute of cooking time.

Once baked, these will keep for a week in an airtight container.

FILLING
120g raisins
20ml sweet Marsala wine
finely grated zest of 1 small orange
    (1 tsp)
20ml orange juice

PASTRY
250g plain flour
75g icing sugar
finely grated zest of ½ a lemon (½ tsp)
⅛ tsp salt

160g unsalted butter, fridge-cold,
    cut into 2cm cubes
1 large egg yolk
1 tbsp cold water
1 large egg, lightly beaten, to glaze

CARAMEL
60ml water
120g caster sugar
90ml double cream
¼ tsp flaky sea salt

1   **Prepare the filling** by placing the raisins in a small jar or container with the Marsala, orange zest and juice. Cover and leave at room temperature for 6 hours (or up to 24 hours), shaking it occasionally, until all the liquid has been absorbed and the raisins are soft and plump.

2   **To make the pastry,** place the flour, icing sugar, lemon zest and salt in the bowl of a food processor and blitz to combine. Add the butter and blitz until the consistency of breadcrumbs, making sure there are no large lumps of butter left. Add the egg yolk and water and continue to mix until the dough just comes together. Take care not to mix any longer than necessary: the dough doesn't so much come together as hold when pressed into a ball, so don't worry if it appears slightly crumbly. At the same time, you might need to add an extra tablespoon or two of water, if the dough needs it.

3   Transfer the dough to a clean work surface and knead very lightly, just to shape it into a smooth ball. Cut the dough in half, wrap one half in cling film and place in the fridge while you roll out the other. Place a large piece of baking parchment on your work surface and lightly flour. Roll out the first piece of dough on the parchment to about 30 x 25cm and 3mm thick. Transfer the dough and parchment paper together to a baking tray and set aside while you roll out the second piece of dough in the same way. Place this, along with the parchment paper, on top of the first sheet of dough. Cover with cling film and place the tray in the freezer for at least 30 minutes. This allows the pastry to firm up so that it can be sandwiched together. ››

4   **To make the caramel,** place the water and sugar in a small saucepan and place over a medium heat. Stir to combine and when the sugar has dissolved, increase the heat to medium-high. Cook until the caramel is the colour of golden syrup, approximately 6 minutes. Remove the pan from the heat and slowly pour in the double cream. Return to a low heat, stir until completely smooth, add the sea salt and set aside to cool to room temperature.

5   Preheat the oven to 190°C/170°C Fan/Gas Mark 5. Line two baking trays with baking parchment.

6   Remove the pastry sheets from the freezer and, moving quickly, spread a thin layer of the caramel sauce over both sheets. The caramel will start to set as soon as it touches the cold pastry, so spread a little at a time to get a thin, even layer. Sprinkle the raisins over the top of one of the sheets, in one even layer, then place the other sheet of pastry, caramel side down, on top of the raisins.

7   Place a sheet of parchment paper on top of the pastry and gently roll a rolling pin over it, applying a light pressure to 'seal' the two layers. Egg wash the top of the pastry and trim a tiny bit of the edge away – just 0.5cm – to neaten. Slice the rectangle into even strips (5 strips lengthways and 4 strips across to get 20 rectangles), then place the rectangles on the lined baking trays, spaced well apart.

8   Bake for 22–25 minutes, or until a nice golden brown colour. Remove from the oven and allow to cool for 10 minutes. If some of the caramel and raisins ooze out, you can easily pop the raisins back into the edges of the biscuits while they are still hot. Then use a fish slice or offset spatula to gently transfer the biscuits from the baking sheet to a wire rack and cool completely before eating.

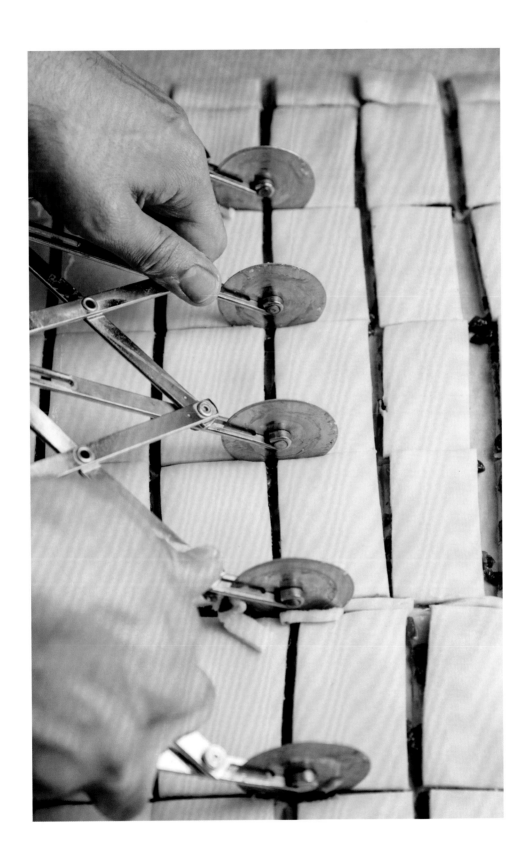

GARIBALDIS

Pecan snowballs

Various versions of these cookies are popular throughout the world. They are sometimes called Mexican wedding cakes (even though they're a short, nutty cookie rather than a cake) and given out at festivals and celebrations, and in Greece they're known as kourabiedes and made with walnuts or almonds and flavoured with ouzo. We've used brandy in ours, but go with whatever bottle is open: ouzo, Pernod and rum all work well. Or you can leave out the alcohol altogether, if you prefer. For those cooking with kids (or for anyone who enjoys the bowl-and-spoon-licking stage of baking), the raw dough for these cookies is hard to resist.

Packed in cellophane bags and tied with ribbon, these make great gifts, particularly in the festive season, as they look all snowy and wintry with their thick icing sugar coating.

MAKES ABOUT 21

These will keep well for up to 7 days in an airtight container. They also freeze well for up to a month (after baking), and are uncommonly good eaten straight from the freezer!

90g pecan halves
120g unsalted butter, at room
    temperature, cubed
65g icing sugar, plus an extra
    50g for coating

scraped seeds of ¼ vanilla pod
¼ tsp vanilla extract
½ tsp brandy (optional)
⅛ tsp salt
165g plain flour, plus extra for dusting

1   Preheat the oven to 180°C/160°C Fan/Gas Mark 4.

2   Spread the pecans out on a baking tray and roast for 8–10 minutes, until they have taken on some colour and smell nutty, then leave to cool. Transfer to a food processor, blitz until fine – stop the machine before the nuts turn into an oily paste – and set aside.

3   Place the butter and icing sugar in the bowl of an electric mixer with the paddle attachment in place. Beat on a medium-high speed, scraping down the sides of the bowl a few times to ensure even mixing, until the mixture is light. With the machine still running, add the vanilla seeds, extract, brandy (if using), salt and the ground pecans. Finally, add the flour and mix on a low speed until everything comes together and there are no longer any bits of flour visible. Tip the mixture on to a clean work surface and knead gently for 30 seconds, then form into a ball. Wrap loosely in cling film, press to flatten into a disc and chill in the fridge for 30 minutes to firm up.

4   Increase the oven temperature to 190°C/170°C Fan/Gas Mark 5. Line a baking tray with baking parchment.

5   Roll the dough into balls, about 20g each. Spread out on the lined baking tray and bake for 16–18 minutes: the underside of the cookies should be firm and a light golden brown. Remove from the oven and allow to rest for 3 minutes on the baking tray.

6   Sift the extra icing sugar into a bowl, then, one at a time, gently roll the warm cookies in the icing sugar. Return them to the still-hot baking tray to allow the icing sugar to set into a thin coating. Leave for 5 minutes before coating the cookies for a second time; you may need another tablespoon or two of icing sugar.

Not-quite-Bonnie's rugelach

Bonnie Stern, aka Yotam and Sami's Canadian mother, has been looking after 'her boys' since they started doing book signing tours in Canada. As well as being told which restaurants they need to try, Sami and Yotam have come to expect a bag of Bonnie's exceptional rugelach. Filled with apricot jam, pecans and demerara sugar, they're simple, brittle and perfectly buttery.

It's the substitution of apricot jam with membrillo (quince paste) in our version that makes these 'Not-quite-Bonnies', as well as the addition of the baking powder in the dough, which makes the pastry flakier. Apricot jam still works well, though (and is more widely available than membrillo), so feel free to use the jam, if you like. We've fallen for a number of rugelach over the years, from the yeasted varieties so popular in Israel, to this flakier version, preferred in North America. The yeasted variety behaves more like bread and doesn't keep as well as the flaky kind.

MAKES 24

The addition of the baking powder here, and the fact that the dough is made using the 'cutting-in' method (in a food processor with a metal blade, rather than whisked in an electric mixer), makes the pastry so light and flaky. The presence of the cream cheese also makes it a dream to roll. For more on this cream cheese pastry, see page 230.

The pastry can be made a day ahead and kept in the fridge, or frozen for up to 3 months: remember to thaw it overnight in the fridge before using. The rolled rugelach can also be frozen (before glazing) for up to 3 months. When you are ready to bake them, brush with the glaze and bake from frozen, adding an extra minute or two to the cooking time.

These will keep for up to 4 days in an open container, separated by pieces of baking parchment, and the whole thing wrapped loosely in aluminium foil. Don't keep them in an airtight container: the sugar will 'weep' if you do and turn the rugelach soft and sticky.

PASTRY
160g plain flour
⅛ tsp salt
¼ tsp baking powder
finely grated zest of 1 small lemon (¾ tsp)
scraped seeds of ¼ vanilla pod
125g unsalted butter, fridge-cold, cut roughly into 3cm cubes
125g cream cheese, fridge-cold

FILLING
40g walnut halves
100g soft light brown sugar
½ tsp ground cinnamon
150g shop-bought quince paste (membrillo)
1 tsp lemon juice

TO GLAZE
1 large egg, lightly beaten
25g demerara sugar

1   **To make the pastry,** place the flour, salt, baking powder, lemon zest and vanilla seeds in a food processor and blitz for about 15 seconds to combine. Add the butter cubes and blitz for a few more seconds, until the mixture has the texture of fresh breadcrumbs. Add the cream cheese and process just until the dough comes together in a ball around the blade: be careful not to over-process or the pastry will be tough. Tip the dough on to a lightly floured work surface and knead for a few seconds, just to bring it together.

2   Divide the pastry in two, wrap each half loosely in cling film, then press to flatten into discs. Transfer to the fridge for at least 1 hour.

3   Preheat the oven to 180°C/160°C Fan/Gas Mark 4. Line two baking trays with baking parchment and set aside.

4   **To prepare the filling,** spread the walnuts out on a baking tray and roast for 5 minutes. Remove from the oven, set aside to cool, then chop finely and place in a small bowl with the brown sugar and cinnamon. Mix together and set aside.

5   In a separate bowl, combine the quince paste and lemon juice to form a smooth paste. If your quince paste is very firm, warm it gently over a low heat to soften (or heat for 10 seconds in a microwave), until the texture is thick like jam but spreadable, then set aside to cool before using. ››

6 Take one of the pieces of dough from the fridge and roll out on a lightly floured work surface to form a 24cm circle, about 2mm thick. Use a small spatula or the back of a spoon to spread half of the quince paste evenly over the surface and then sprinkle with half of the sugar and nut mixture. Using a sharp knife or a pizza wheel, if you have one, cut the dough as though you are slicing a cake into 12 equal triangles: the best way to get even-sized triangles is to cut it first into quarters, then each quarter into thirds. One at a time, roll each wedge quite tightly, starting from the wide outside edge and working towards the point of the triangle, so that the filling is enclosed. Place them on the lined baking trays, seam side down, spaced about 3cm apart. Repeat the rolling process with the remaining disc of dough and filling ingredients, then chill the rugelachs in the fridge for at least 30 minutes before baking.

7 Increase the oven to 200°C/180°C Fan/Gas Mark 6.

8 **When ready to bake,** lightly brush the tops of the rugelachs with the egg wash and sprinkle with the demerara sugar. Bake for 20–25 minutes, rotating the trays halfway through, until golden brown all over. Don't worry if some of the filling oozes out: this will add a lovely toffee taste to the edges of the biscuits. Remove from the oven and allow to rest on the trays for 5 minutes before transferring to a wire rack to cool completely.

Mini-cakes

—

We love mini-cakes for lots of reasons. Being able to eat rather a lot of them is one. They also look so very lovely, all mini-me sized and often iced in bright colours, which can't help but make you smile. And they come in all shapes and sizes, which makes them fun to make as well as to eat.

This chapter is home (sweet home) to so many of our signature cakes. Arranged in rows as neat and orderly as little soldiers, just the sight of our mini-cakes pulls hungry customers through the door. And it's not hard to see why, frankly. There's something about 'mini' things that encourages especially big care to be taken of them, in the way they're made and displayed. There is also something about them that encourages people to make space for them, whether it's morning, noon or night.

We have syrup-soaked mini-cakes, reminiscent of Yotam's childhood, gluten-free cakes, cakes drenched in boozy caramel and cakes that have been on our shop counters since day one – the Flourless Chocolate 'Teacakes', for example (see page 108). If you want to bring out your inner cake shop, this is the chapter to start covering with specks of chocolate and flour.

THE SMALLER SOMETHING IS, THE MORE YOU CAN EAT › Some mini-cakes are so mini and light that you find yourself eating a few more than one at a time! The Baby Black and Orange Cakes (see page 94), for example, or either of our Powder Puffs (see page 82), which come as close to biting through air as we can imagine; super-light sponge cakes, held together with whipped cream and fresh strawberries; citrus-spiked cupcakes; little and light fresh madeleines – they are all bite-sized delights.

CAKES TO RELAX WITH, CAKES TO REBEL WITH › Other mini-cakes are more for the 'us against the world' days, when something decadent is needed to sustain and strengthen. It's not every day that you're going to be making and eating a doughnut piped with saffron custard cream, or a brownie filled with chunks of halva and swirls of tahini. But on the days you do, you'll be guaranteed to conquer all that comes your way!

MAKE THE MINI MIGHTY › Although we tend to think of mini-cakes as something to be enjoyed throughout the day, many of them also work well served with the sort of fanfare usually reserved for desserts. No one is ever going to feel short-changed when presented with their very own Tahini and Halva Brownie (see page 87), for example, served with a generous scoop of vanilla ice cream, or a Banana Cake with Rum Caramel (see page 100) served with some rum and raisin ice cream. With literally a spoonful of help, mini-cakes can be made mighty.

HAVE YOUR CAKE AND EAT IT (OR NOT) › Mini-cakes love to be eaten on the day they're iced. There are always things you can do to get ahead – 'teacakes' (and even a sponge, if you really need to) can be made a day in advance and kept in an airtight container – but always hold back on icing until the day you are planning to serve them. You don't want to keep anything iced out of the fridge for too long, and the icing will often lose its shiny gloss after a day. Don't be too precious with any leftovers, however: they'll be fine in the fridge for a day or two for you to snack on.

Even when un-iced, some cakes like to be eaten on the day they are baked: the Saffron, Orange and Honey Madeleines (see page 76), or the Hazelnut Crumble Cake (see page 90), for example. Other cakes, on the other hand, taste better the day after they're made: the flavours and texture of the Persian Love Cakes (see page 74), for example, deepen with a little bit of time.

Kit

The fact that they come in all shapes and sizes means, inevitably, that making mini-cakes requires a wider variety of tins and trays than other chapters. We've tried not to go too far with specialist moulds and tins, and we always suggest alternatives where we can so that you may be able to improvise with what you already have. That being said, the cost of a tray or mould is often the same price as two or three shop-bought cakes, so there's always that justification, if you need one, for purchasing more kit. Home-baked bundt cakes for ever!

Below is a list of all the kit you'd need were you to make every recipe in this chapter. Alternatives are suggested, where relevant, and instructions given in individual recipes for amending cooking times to suit the alternative tin size.

REGULAR MUFFIN TINS › These have 12 moulds: 7cm wide at the top, 5cm wide at the bottom, and 3.5cm deep.

LARGE ('JUMBO') MUFFIN TINS › These have 6 moulds: 8.5cm wide at the top, 6cm wide at the bottom, and 4cm deep. You could use a regular muffin tin instead – you'll just make more muffins, smaller in size, and the baking time will need to be reduced.

MINI-MUFFIN TINS › These have 24 moulds: about 4cm wide at the top, 3cm wide at the bottom, and 2–2.5cm deep. Again, you could use a regular muffin tin instead – you'll make fewer but larger cakes.

BOTTOMLESS CAKE RINGS › We like to make our mini Victoria Sponges (see page 96) in 8cm wide cake rings. Alternatively, you can make one large cake instead – you'll need a 20cm round springform tin and will need to increase the cooking time accordingly. We also use these small cake rings for our individual cheesecakes, so if you think you're going to be making these too, the rings are a bit of kit worth having.

INDIVIDUAL BUNDT TINS › We love making our 'teacakes' in individual bundt tins, which are 10cm wide at the top and 5cm deep. They're big enough to be a real treat, but light enough to not be intimidating, and exciting enough to share. And that's before the icing has been drizzled over, falling down the sides unevenly as well as through the well in the centre of the cake. Alternatively, you can use one large bundt tin: 20cm wide at the top, 14cm wide at the bottom, and 10cm deep. The method will be the same, but the baking time will need to be increased. You could also use a large muffin tray – the moulds are not quite as big as the bundt tins, so you'll generally make one more muffin than bundt.

SILICONE HALF-SPHERE MOULDS › We make our Baby Black and Orange Cakes (see page 94) in these silicone trays with hole-shaped moulds, 5cm wide at the top and 2.5cm deep. They make for very cute orb-shaped mini-cakes. Alternatively, if you have the traditional mince pie tin that we use for the Pineapple Tartlets with Pandan and Star Anise (see page 255), you can use this instead.

SMALL RECTANGULAR SILICONE FINANCIER MOULDS › We make our Persian Love Cakes (see page 74) in small 8 x 3 x 3cm rectangular moulds. You could also make these in a regular muffin tin, but make sure you use paper liners: the cakes won't come out if they are only greased and floured.

MADELEINE TRAYS › Our Saffron, Orange and Honey Madeleines (see page 76) are made in standard madeleine trays, the shell-shaped moulds of which are about 7.5 x 5cm. Available in silicone or metal, we far prefer the metal – you don't get the nice crust in the silicone tray – but either is fine; you'll just need to grease and flour the metal tray before the batter is added. The trays usually have 12 moulds, but because it is so very easy for one person to eat about a third of these, we would encourage you to buy two trays rather than one and make 24! Madeleines are so much about their shape, but if you do need an alternative, a mini-muffin tin would work, or a domed traditional mince pie tin. In either case you will just make more cakes, smaller in size.

POPOVER TINS › Similar to large muffin tins, with 6 large moulds, but with straight sides: 6.5cm wide and 5cm deep. We like to make our Strawberry and Vanilla Mini-cakes (see page 95) in popover tins, but a regular or large muffin tin would also work.

MINI-LOAF TINS › We make our Chocolate Guinness Cakes with Baileys Irish Cream (see page 117) in mini-loaf tins which are 9.5 x 6.5cm at the top and 7 x 4cm at the bottom. You can convert the recipe into one larger cake, if you like, using an 18cm round springform tin. The changes you'll need to make to the recipe are all written in the kit note on page 117.

NO SPECIAL TINS OR TRAYS › If you don't want to stock your cupboards with any more kit, that's fine – we understand! Doughnuts, brownies and powder puffs are your friends.

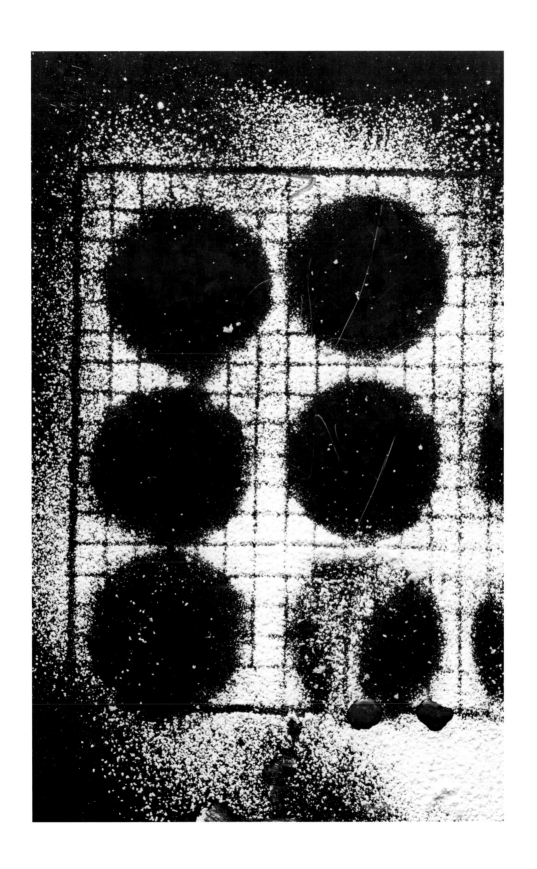

Persian love cakes

These little Persian cakes came to us by way of our Glaswegian colleague John Meechan, who adapted them from a Gerard Yaxley recipe in *Gourmet Traveller*. John's stroke of genius was to add buckwheat flour, distinctive for its nutty and slightly sour taste, and the mahleb, a spice made from grinding the seed kernel of the St Lucie cherry. The spice is not often used outside of Greece, Turkey and the Middle East, so don't worry if you can't get hold of any: a few drops of almond extract work well as an alternative.

The cakes can be served warm, without the mascarpone, pistachio and pomegranate seed topping, or at room temperature with all the toppings. Presentation-wise, it's a nice little trick to lay a piece of baking parchment on top of each cake, on the diagonal, held down flat, and sprinkle the icing sugar over the exposed side of the cake.

MAKES 12
—

240g ground almonds
135g demerara sugar
135g soft light brown sugar
50g buckwheat flour
80g unsalted butter, fridge-cold, cubed
¾ tsp salt
160g Greek-style natural yoghurt
90g eggs (roughly 1½ large eggs)
1 tbsp mahleb (or ¼ tsp almond extract)
¾ tsp ground nutmeg

TO SERVE (AT ROOM TEMPERATURE)
60g mascarpone
1½ tsp pistachio kernels, slivered
  or finely crushed
12 pomegranate seeds (optional)
icing sugar, for dusting

—

1   Preheat the oven to 180°C/160°C Fan/Gas Mark 4.

2   Place the ground almonds, both sugars, flour, butter and salt in a food processor and blitz a few times, until the mixture has the consistency of breadcrumbs. Transfer two-thirds of the mix – about 430g – to a large bowl along with the yoghurt, eggs, mahleb and nutmeg. Mix to combine and set aside.

3   Line the base of 12 financier (or muffin tin) moulds with the remaining third of the crumb mix: it should come about a third of the way up the sides of the moulds. Use your fingers or a teaspoon to press the mix into the base of the moulds, as you would a cheesecake, so that it is compact.

4   Using two teaspoons, fill each mould to the top with the yoghurt mix, and level off with a palette knife for an even finish. Place the moulds on a baking tray and cook for 30–35 minutes, rotating the tray halfway through, until the cakes are dark golden brown on top and a skewer inserted into the centre comes out clean. The cakes will look slightly uncooked and damp inside, but this is the way they should be and is part of their charm. Allow the cakes to cool in their tins for 15–30 minutes before unmoulding them. Serve as they are, slightly warm, or leave to cool before spooning a little mascarpone on top of each cake and topping with the crushed pistachios and 1 pomegranate seed, if using. Sprinkle a little icing sugar on one half of each cake, at a diagonal (see introduction), and serve.

We make our cakes in small rectangular silicone financier moulds, which look so elegant. Alternatively, use a regular muffin tin.

These cakes are at their best the day after they are made. They can be eaten on the day, however, and kept for up to 2 days in a sealed container (without the mascarpone topping). They don't keep for much longer than this – which is surprising, given how moist they are – because the texture becomes a bit gummy. Once the cakes have been topped with the mascarpone, they can be stored in the fridge and brought back to room temperature before serving.

Saffron, orange and honey madeleines

Traditionally, madeleines are best eaten as close to coming out of the oven as possible. The beating together of the eggs and sugar makes them super light and fluffy, but it's all the air incorporated into them that also makes them dry out so quickly if left to sit around for too long.

Here, untraditionally, we forgo all the beating and just place the ingredients in a food processor. Mixing them this way means that the resulting madeleines won't be quite as light as those made by hand-whisking, but they're every bit as delicate and buttery as you'd hope. We do it this way to build in a little bit of robustness, which allows them to still be eaten hours (rather than minutes) after they come out of the oven.

We love the saffron here, but the spice is not to everyone's liking (particularly in a sweet context), so you can leave it out, if you prefer, and focus on the orange and honey instead.

MAKES ABOUT 22

90g unsalted butter, plus an extra 20g, melted, for brushing
2 tsp honey, plus an extra 3 tbsp, for glazing
¼ tsp saffron threads (optional – see above)
2 large eggs
75g caster sugar

scraped seeds of ¼ vanilla pod
finely grated zest of 1 small orange (1 tsp)
90g plain flour, plus extra for dusting
1 tsp baking powder
⅛ tsp salt
20g shelled pistachio kernels, finely blitzed

Ideally, use a standard madeleine tray here – metal or silicone.

These are best eaten on the day they are made, as fresh from the oven as possible. We know it's not madeleine protocol, but leftovers can be kept in an airtight container and eaten as they are (without needing to be warmed through) the following day.

1   Place the butter, honey and saffron threads (if using) in a small saucepan over a low heat until the butter has melted. Remove from the heat and set aside to come to room temperature.

2   Place the eggs, sugar, vanilla seeds and orange zest in a food processor and mix until smooth and combined. Sift the flour, baking powder and salt into a bowl, then add to the egg mixture. Pulse a few times, just to mix in, and add the cooled butter, honey and saffron mixture. Process once more, to combine, then pour the batter into a small bowl. Cover with cling film and allow to rest in the fridge for about an hour.

3   Preheat the oven to 200°C/180°C Fan/Gas Mark 6. If you are using metal madeleine trays, brush the moulds with melted butter and sprinkle liberally with flour. Silicone trays should not need any greasing or flouring, but you can lightly brush with a little melted butter here, if you like. Tap to ensure that all the moulds are dusted and then shake off the excess flour.

4   Spoon a heaped teaspoon of batter into each mould: it should rise two-thirds of the way up the sides of the moulds. If you only have one madeleine tray, place the remaining batter in the fridge until you have baked the first batch. You will need to wash and dry the mould completely before greasing and flouring again and repeating with the second batch. ››

5   Bake for 9–10 minutes, until the madeleines are beginning to brown around the edges and they spring back once tapped lightly in the middle. Remove the tray(s) from the oven and set aside for a minute before releasing the cakes. The best way to do this, with a metal tray, is to go around the edges of each madeleine with a small knife or spatula (to make sure they are not stuck) and then tap the edge of the tray on the bench until they fall out. With a silicone tray they should just fall out of their moulds. Transfer the cakes to a wire rack to cool.

6   Pile the blitzed pistachios on to a plate in a straight line and set aside. Melt the 3 tablespoons of honey in a small saucepan (a microwave is also good here) until very runny, then brush lightly over the shell-patterned side of one madeleine. With the shell side facing down towards the nuts, roll the narrower end of the madeleine along the pile of pistachios so that you have a straight 1cm strip of pistachios at the base of the madeleine. Repeat with the remaining madeleines, and place on a serving platter, nut side up.

Lemon and raspberry cupcakes

The difference between a cupcake that stands the test of time and one that vanishes into obscurity is, we think, all to do with the icing. The actual cake has to be light, tender and moist, of course, but the icing has to be sensational. Is it not the reason, secretly, why some people choose cupcakes in the first place? Here, the simple trick of whipping the lemon curd into the mascarpone works an absolute treat.

Making your own lemon curd is satisfying and delicious, but feel free to shortcut and buy some ready-made, if you like. Since discovering a 'seriously zesty' own-brand supermarket version, Helen admits that her rate of production on the homemade lemon curd front has rather reduced.

MAKES 12

The lemon curd can be made up to 3 days before icing the cakes and stored in the fridge. To prevent lemon zest from drying out, pop it in a zip-lock bag or plastic container and freeze it, where it will keep for a couple of months.

Once baked, the cakes are best eaten on the same day. If un-iced, they will keep in an airtight container for an extra day.

LEMON CURD
1 large egg, plus 2 extra egg yolks
90ml lemon juice (from 2 lemons; the zest of these lemons needs to be used for the cake batter, so grate the zest before juicing)
90g caster sugar
75g unsalted butter, at room temperature, cut into 2cm cubes

CUPCAKES
125g unsalted butter, at room temperature
finely grated zest of 2 lemons (2 tsp)
225g caster sugar
3 large eggs
120g soured cream
160g plain flour
1½ tsp baking powder
¼ tsp salt
150g fresh raspberries, plus 12 extra for garnish (about 60g)

ICING
prepared lemon curd (270g)
300g mascarpone

1   **Make the lemon curd.** Whisk together the whole egg and egg yolks in a bowl and set aside. Put the lemon juice and sugar into a small saucepan and place over a medium-high heat. Stir until the sugar dissolves, then, as soon as it comes to the boil, pour the syrup over the eggs, whisking the whole time. Return the mixture to the saucepan and cook over a low heat for 4–5 minutes, stirring constantly with a wooden spoon until the mixture has thickened and one or two bubbles appear on the surface.

2   Remove from the heat and stir in the butter, one cube at a time, waiting until each piece melts before adding the next. When all the butter has melted and the mixture is smooth, transfer the curd to a clean container and cover the surface with cling film: you want the cling film to actually touch the surface to prevent it forming a skin. Set aside to cool completely before placing in the fridge until needed.

3   Preheat the oven to 190°C/170°C Fan/Gas Mark 5 and line the 12 moulds of a regular muffin tin with paper liners; if you don't have liners, brush the moulds and the top of the muffin tray with barely melted butter and dust all over with flour, tapping away the excess. ››

4   **To make the cupcakes,** place the butter, lemon zest and sugar in the bowl of an electric mixer with the paddle attachment in place. Beat on a medium-high speed for about 3 minutes, until the mix is light and fluffy. Add the eggs, one at a time, scraping down the paddle and sides of the bowl after each addition. Add the soured cream and beat until incorporated. Sift the flour, baking powder and salt into a bowl and add this to the mixer. Continue to mix until combined, again scraping down the paddle and sides of the bowl. Increase the speed to high and beat for another 20 seconds. Reduce the speed, add the raspberries and mix for just a few seconds so that the fruit breaks up and the mixture is roughly rippled with the raspberries.

5   Spoon the batter into the paper liners – they will be nearly full – and bake for about 22 minutes, or until a skewer inserted into the centre of a cake comes out clean. Set aside in the tray to cool for 5 minutes before transferring the cakes to a wire rack to cool completely.

6   **Make the icing** when the cupcakes are cool. Place the lemon curd and mascarpone in the bowl of an electric mixer with the whisk attachment in place. Whisk on a medium speed until thick, about 1 minute, then use a small spatula or butter knife to ice the cakes. Finish with a whole raspberry in the centre of each cake, a dusting of icing sugar and serve.

Powder puffs

Helen had her first taste of powder puffs at a funeral in Victoria, Australia, over 20 years ago. Too embarrassed to ask what they were – a funeral is no time to be sourcing recipes! – Helen wondered about the recipe for years before she came across it again thanks to Stephanie Alexander, whose insights into the magic of sifting (three times), as well as not over-mixing allowed the penny to drop for Helen.

Looking at the biscuits alone, you'd be forgiven for wondering what all the fuss is about. They're nothing more than baked sponges – a little like the Italian Savoiardi biscuits used to make tiramisu. It's when they're sandwiched together and left to soften for several hours, however, that they become so very light that you feel as though you're biting into thin air.

We've included two versions here: raspberry and rose for the height of summer, and chocolate and chestnut for a more autumnal feel. Strawberry jam and the vanilla whipped cream from the chocolate and chestnut version are good alternatives to the raspberry jam and rose water, if you don't have (or like) rose water.

MAKES ABOUT 24

Raspberry and rose

3 large eggs, whites and yolks
    separated
½ tsp cream of tartar
180g caster sugar
1 tsp vanilla extract
75g plain flour
70g cornflour
½ tsp bicarbonate of soda
⅛ tsp salt
about 130g raspberry jam
15g icing sugar, for dusting

ROSE WHIPPED CREAM
300ml double cream
25g icing sugar, sifted
1¼ tsp rose water

Chocolate and chestnut

3 large eggs, whites and yolks
    separated
½ tsp cream of tartar
180g caster sugar
1 tsp vanilla extract
75g plain flour
50g cornflour
½ tsp bicarbonate of soda
⅛ tsp salt
3 tbsp Dutch-processed cocoa
    powder, plus an extra 1 tbsp
    for dusting
250g sweetened chestnut spread
1½ tsp icing sugar, for dusting
100g marron glacés in syrup,
    thinly sliced (optional)

VANILLA WHIPPED CREAM
300ml double cream
25g icing sugar, sifted
½ tsp vanilla extract
⅛ tsp salt

Sift three times – One of the secrets to the incredible pillow-y lightness here is in the sifting of the flour three times. Though always passionate about the benefits of sifting, Helen is positively evangelical about the need to sift not once or twice but three times. This will create the aeration you need to produce the fluffy results.

Don't over-work the mix – Key to success, also, is not to over-work the mix: there shouldn't be any more stirring after the flour has been folded in, otherwise air pockets will be created and the mixture will deflate.

Give them the time they need to sit around and soften – It's also important to give the biscuits the time they need, once sandwiched together with cream, to really soften. They are nice and soft after 5 hours, but can happily be left for up to 24 hours in the fridge.

After baking, the un-sandwiched biscuits can be stored for up to 5 days in an airtight container. They can also be frozen for up to 3 months.

Once sandwiched together, they can happily be left for up to 24 hours in the fridge: just hold back on dusting with the icing sugar (if using); this needs to be sprinkled over just before serving. Remove from the fridge about an hour before serving: you want them to be room temperature, not fridge-cold.

 (RASPBERRY AND ROSE ONLY)

1   Preheat the oven to 210°C/190°C Fan/Gas Mark 6. Line four baking trays with baking parchment (or line two trays, and cook them in batches).

2   Place the egg whites in the bowl of an electric mixer with the whisk attachment in place and beat on a medium-high speed for about 1 minute, until frothy. Add the cream of tartar and continue to beat for another minute until soft peaks form. Gradually add the sugar and keep whisking for about 5 minutes, until the mixture forms a stiff and glossy meringue. Add the vanilla extract and the egg yolks, one at a time, and continue to beat until just combined.

3   Place the flour, cornflour, bicarbonate of soda, salt and cocoa powder, if making the Chocolate Puffs, in a bowl. Sift twice before sifting for a third time into the bowl with the meringue mixture: it's vital to sift three times here to aerate the mixture as much as possible. Fold the dry ingredients into the batter gently but thoroughly, stopping as soon as it's combined. Do not stir the mixture again after this point.

4   Use 2 teaspoons to drop heaped spoonfuls of the mix on to the lined trays. They should be about 4cm wide and spaced 5cm apart. Don't be tempted to use a piping bag here, as all the air will be knocked out. Place in the oven and bake for 11–12 minutes, rotating the trays halfway through, until golden brown around the edges and starting to go crisp. Remove from the oven and set aside for about 10 minutes, until completely cool. If you need to cook them in two batches, remove the first batch with a palette knife once cooked, then wipe down the baking parchment with a slightly damp cloth before continuing with the next batch.

5   Gently ease the biscuits away from the parchment paper and separate them into similar-sized pairs.

6   **To make the rose cream,** place the cream, icing sugar and rose water in the bowl of an electric mixer with the whisk attachment in place. Whisk together on a high speed for about a minute, until soft peaks form, taking care not to over-whisk or it will become thick and grainy. **To make the vanilla cream,** place the cream in the bowl of an electric mixer with the whisk attachment in place. Add the sugar, vanilla and salt and whisk on a high speed for about a minute, until soft peaks form, taking care not to over-whisk or it will become thick and grainy.

7   At least 5 hours (or anything up to 24 hours) before serving, spread a tablespoon of the whipped cream on to the base of half of the biscuits, followed by about ½ teaspoon of jam if making the Raspberry Puffs, or a heaped teaspoon of the chestnut spread if making the Chocolate Puffs. Sandwich together with the top biscuits and place the puffs in the fridge for around 4 hours – layered with baking parchment in an airtight container – until the biscuits are completely softened. Remove the puffs from the fridge an hour before serving – they need to be room temperature rather than fridge-cold. If making the Raspberry Puffs, just dust with icing sugar. If making the Chocolate Puffs, sift the icing sugar into a bowl with 1 tablespoon of cocoa powder and sprinkle through a fine-mesh sieve over each puff. Place a piece of marron glacé on top, if using, along with a small drizzle of the syrup, and serve.

RASPBERRY AND ROSE
POWDER PUFFS

CHOCOLATE AND CHESTNUT
POWDER PUFFS

Tahini and halva brownies

The combination of tahini, halva and chocolate is so good that some members of staff (Tara, we see you!) had to put a temporary ban on their eating of these particular brownies during the making of this book. It is very hard to eat just the one.

In order to achieve the perfect balance of cakey and gooey – that sweet spot that all brownies should hit – the cooking time is crucial. It will vary by a minute or so between different ovens, and depending on where the tray is sitting in the oven, so keep a close eye on them.

MAKES 16

We made these in a 23cm square baking tin, but a 30 x 20cm rectangular tin also works well.

These will keep well for up to 5 days in an airtight container. They also freeze well, wrapped in cling film, for up to a month. When you take them out of the freezer, they are uncommonly good eaten at the half-frozen, half-thawed stage.

250g unsalted butter, cut into 2cm cubes, plus extra for greasing
250g dark chocolate (70% cocoa solids), broken into 3–4cm pieces
4 large eggs
280g caster sugar
120g plain flour
30g Dutch-processed cocoa powder
½ tsp salt
200g halva, broken into 2cm pieces
80g tahini paste

1   Preheat the oven to 200°C/180°C Fan/Gas Mark 6. Grease and line a 23cm square or 30 x 20cm rectangular baking tin with baking parchment and set aside.

2   Place the butter and chocolate in a heatproof bowl over a pan of simmering water, making sure that the base of the bowl is not touching the water. Leave for about 2 minutes, to melt, then remove the bowl from the heat. Stir through, until you have a thick shiny sauce, and set aside to come to room temperature. Place the eggs and sugar in a large bowl and whisk until pale and creamy and a trail is left behind when you move the whisk: this will take about 3 minutes with an electric mixer, longer by hand. Add the chocolate and fold through gently using a spatula – don't over-work the mix here.

3   Sift the flour, cocoa and salt into a bowl, then gently fold into the chocolate mixture. Finally, add the pieces of halva, gently fold through the mix, then pour or scrape the mixture into the lined baking tin, using a small spatula to even it out. Dollop small spoonfuls of the tahini paste into the mix in about 12 different places, then use a skewer to swirl them through to create a marbled effect, taking the marbling right to the edges of the tin.

4   Bake for about 23 minutes, until the middle has a slight wobble and it is gooey inside – they may be ready anywhere between 22 and 25 minutes. If using the 30 x 20cm tin, they will need a couple of minutes less. They may seem a little under-cooked at first, but they firm up once they start to cool down. If you want to serve them warm-ish (and gooey), set aside for just 30 minutes before cutting into 16 pieces. Otherwise, set aside for longer to cool to room temperature.

Lemon, blueberry and almond 'teacakes'

We've always called these 'teacakes' at Ottolenghi. There's no link to the traditional raisin-filled bready cake that's toasted and slathered with butter – it's more to do with how good they taste with a cup of tea. We make these in a muffin tin – without a paper liner, in order to keep the edges neat and straight – inverting them on to a wire rack before drizzling with icing. 'Upside-down-muffins' sounds a lot less elegant than 'teacakes', however, so we've taken the liberty of keeping the misnomer both here and elsewhere.

MAKES 12

190g unsalted butter, at room temperature, cubed, plus extra for greasing
190g caster sugar
finely grated zest of 1 lemon (1 tsp)
4 large eggs, lightly beaten
190g ground almonds
45g plain flour, plus extra for dusting

¼ tsp baking powder
⅛ tsp salt
60ml lemon juice
100g blueberries, plus an extra 70g to garnish

ICING
160g icing sugar
35ml lemon juice

Un-iced, these keep well for 3 days in an airtight container. They also freeze well. Once iced, they're best stored in an airtight container in the fridge and eaten within a couple of days.

1   Preheat the oven to 180°C/160°C/Gas Mark 4. Grease all 12 moulds of a regular muffin tin with butter and dust lightly but thoroughly with flour. Tap away any excess flour and set aside.

2   Place the butter, sugar and lemon zest in the bowl of an electric mixer with the paddle attachment in place. Beat on a medium-high speed until light, then add the eggs and ground almonds in three or four alternate batches. Sift the flour, baking powder and salt into a bowl, then add this to the mixer and reduce the speed to low. Finally, add the lemon juice. Spoon the mixture into the moulds and divide the 100g of blueberries between the cakes: push them down slightly so that they sink into the cake mix. The reason we do this (rather than stirring them through the batter) is to ensure that each cake gets an equal number of blueberries.

3   Bake for 30–35 minutes, until the edges are lightly golden and a skewer inserted into the middle of a cake comes out clean. Remove from the oven to cool for 10 minutes before gently tapping the cakes out on to a cooling rack so that they are sitting upside down. Set aside until completely cool.

4   **To make the icing,** combine the icing sugar and lemon juice in a bowl and stir until it has a thick pouring consistency. Spoon the icing over the cakes: you want it to dribble down the sides a little without covering the cakes entirely. Dot the remaining blueberries in the centre of each cake – you should have enough for 3 on top of each cake – and serve.

Hazelnut crumble cake with Gianduja (or Nutella) icing

In the shops we use Gianduja chocolate for our icing, which we're crazy about: with its addition of hazelnut paste, it's the most wonderful match for the hazelnut crumble. You can find it in chocolate shops or online; however, we've also offered a version with Nutella instead (admit it – we know you've got a jar of it somewhere).

With thanks to Belinda Jeffery, the wonderful Australian cook whose walnut cake recipe this is adapted from.

SERVES 11 (USING INDIVIDUAL BUNDT TINS) OR 12–14 (USING ONE LARGE BUNDT TIN)

—

250g soured cream
130g full-fat Greek yoghurt
1½ tsp bicarbonate of soda
3 large eggs
280g caster sugar
250g unsalted butter, at room temperature, cut into 3cm cubes, plus extra for greasing
1 tbsp rum or brandy
2 tsp vanilla extract
460g plain flour, plus extra for dusting
2 tsp baking powder
1 tsp salt
10g hazelnuts, blanched or skin on, thinly sliced (use a mandoline, if you have one, but don't worry if they seem to crumble more than slice)

HAZELNUT CRUMBLE
80g hazelnuts, blanched or skin on
80g caster sugar
1¼ tsp ground cinnamon
¼ tsp salt

GIANDUJA GANACHE
150g Gianduja chocolate, chopped into 1cm pieces
100ml double cream

NUTELLA GANACHE
80g milk chocolate (60% cocoa solids), chopped into 1cm pieces
80g Nutella
100ml double cream

We've used individual bundt tins here, but you can make it in one large bundt tin, if you prefer. You will also need a piping bag to layer the batter in the individual tins (you can just pour it into the large tin and use a spatula to spread it out).

The crumble mixture can be prepared up to 2 days ahead and stored in an airtight container until ready to use.

Hazelnuts behave like no other nuts and the cakes always dry out really quickly, so are best eaten on the day they are made. They'll be fine the following day, just not at their best.

1   Preheat the oven to 180°C/160°C Fan/Gas Mark 4. **For the crumble,** spread the hazelnuts out on a baking tray and roast for 12 minutes, until they begin to colour and smell nutty. Remove from the oven and, if starting with skin-on hazelnuts, place them in the middle of a clean tea towel, draw in the sides and rub together so that the brown papery skin falls off. If starting with blanched nuts, just set them aside to cool. Once cooled, place the nuts in a food processor, add the sugar, cinnamon and salt and process until the nuts are finely chopped. Set aside.

2   Increase the oven heat to 200°C/180°C Fan/Gas Mark 6. Grease and flour the bundt tins and set aside.

3   **To make the cake,** place the soured cream and yoghurt in a medium bowl and whisk in the bicarbonate of soda. Leave to stand for 15 minutes for the mixture to puff up and become light and airy.

4   Meanwhile, place the eggs and sugar in a food processor and process for a minute to combine. Add the butter and process for another minute. Don't worry if the mixture looks a little curdled at this point: it will come together in the end. Stir the rum or brandy and vanilla into the soured cream mixture and add this to the food processor. Use the pulse button to combine a few times, scraping down the sides of the bowl to ensure that the batter is evenly distributed. Tip the mixture into a large bowl. Sift the flour, baking powder and salt into a separate bowl, then stir this into the egg and butter mixture until the batter is just combined.

5   Transfer the batter to a piping bag and pipe a thin layer into the bottom of the prepared tins. Sprinkle a generous amount of the nut crumble all over: about a third (between all the tins). Continue to layer the batter and nut mix so that you have 3 layers of batter, finishing with a layer of nuts. Press this last layer of nuts gently into the cake batter with a spatula (so that they don't fall out when the cakes are baked and inverted).

6   Place the cakes in the oven and bake for 25 minutes (or 55–60 minutes, if making one large cake), or until a skewer inserted into the centre of a cake comes out clean. Set aside in the tins for 10 minutes to cool, before gently loosening the sides and inverting on to a wire rack to cool completely.

7   **To make the Gianduja ganache,** place the chocolate in a bowl and set aside. Put the cream into a small saucepan and place over a medium heat. Heat for 1–2 minutes, until bubbles begin to form at the edges and the cream starts to come to the boil. Remove immediately from the heat, then pour over the chocolate. (**If making the Nutella version,** combine the chocolate and Nutella in a bowl and pour over the hot cream.) Leave for a couple of minutes before stirring the chocolate until smooth: the ganache should not be so thin that it just dribbles off the cakes, but not so thick that it doesn't dribble at all. Spoon it over the cooled cakes so that it drips evenly down the sides. If you are making one large cake, you can either spoon all of the ganache over, or spoon over about two-thirds and serve the remainder alongside each portion. Finally, sprinkle with the sliced hazelnuts and serve.

HAZELNUT CRUMBLE CAKE WITH GIANDUJA (OR NUTELLA) ICING

Baby black and orange cakes

We like to make these simple 'teacakes' bite-sized, then bag up a mix of black and orange to give as gifts. They're especially fun to make around Halloween, ready for sweet-toothed trick-or-treaters. We've given both versions of the cakes in one recipe, so either choose to make one or the other, or both, if you want the mix. In this case you'll need to double the quantity of egg white, caster sugar and melted butter needed. Make both batches separately, though, from beginning to end (rather than whisking up double the egg mix all together and then dividing it in two).

MAKES ABOUT 22
——

60g egg whites (from 1½ large eggs)
80g caster sugar
70g unsalted butter, melted, plus extra
   for greasing

FOR BABY ORANGE TEACAKES	OR FOR BABY BLACK TEACAKES
30g plain flour	20g plain flour
20g ground almonds	20g ground almonds
10g cornflour	25g Dutch-processed cocoa powder
finely grated zest of 1 orange (1½ tsp)	

——

We make these cakes in silicone half-sphere moulds which are 5cm across and 2cm deep. Alternatively, you can use a mini-muffin tin: they won't have their cute orb shape but they'll still be perfectly bite-sized.

These will keep for up to 3 days in an airtight container.

1   Preheat the oven to 190°C/170°C Fan/Gas Mark 5. Lightly grease 22 holes of your silicone mould or mini-muffin tin and set aside. It's fine to cook the mix in two batches if you need to: the batter is happy to wait.

2   Place the egg whites and sugar in the bowl of an electric mixer with the whisk attachment in place. Whisk on a medium-high speed for about 2 minutes, until the sugar is dissolved and the mix is thick, glossy and heavy. You can check that it is whisked enough by feeling a little of the mix between your thumb and forefinger: you should barely be able to feel the sugar granules. Keep the mixer on a medium-high speed and slowly pour the melted butter down the side of the bowl. Beat until combined, scrape down the sides of the bowl and reduce the speed to low.
If making the Baby Orange Teacakes, sift the flour, almonds and cornflour into a bowl, then add to the mixer along with the orange zest. **For the Baby Black Teacakes,** sift the flour, almonds and cocoa into a bowl, then add to the mixer. Mix to combine, turn off the machine and scrape down the sides of the bowl.

3   Use a piping bag (or two teaspoons) to fill the moulds about three-quarters full. Bake for 12 minutes, until the centre of the cakes springs back when touched. Allow to rest in the moulds for 10 minutes before turning them out on to a wire rack to cool completely.

Strawberry and vanilla mini-cakes

The combination of strawberry and vanilla is another one that takes Yotam straight back to his childhood. It's a food memory so loved that he converted this mini-cake recipe to create one large 'number 1'-shaped cake for the first birthday of his second son, Flynn. If you'd also like to do this, the method remains the same, but the baking time will need to be increased. As a guide, Yotam's great big '1' took just over 60 minutes to bake.

MAKES 12 (USING LARGE MUFFIN TINS OR POPOVER TINS) OR 18 (USING REGULAR MUFFIN TINS)

We use popover tins for these cakes, which are fairly large. A large or regular muffin tin could be used as an alternative.

Whether iced or un-iced, these will keep for up to 3 days in an airtight container. They don't look their best after the first day, but the taste will not be affected.

250g unsalted butter, at room temperature, plus extra for greasing
250g caster sugar
1 tsp vanilla extract
scraped seeds from ½ vanilla pod
4 large eggs, lightly beaten
120g self-raising flour, plus extra for dusting
¼ tsp salt
140g ground almonds
200g strawberries, hulled and cut into 1cm dice

6 whole strawberries (or 9 if using a regular muffin tin), cut in half lengthways, or 2 tbsp freeze-dried chopped strawberries, to garnish (optional)

STRAWBERRY ICING
60g strawberries, hulled and roughly chopped
300g icing sugar
20g liquid glucose (or light corn syrup)
scraped seeds of ¼ vanilla pod

1   Preheat the oven to 200°C/180°C Fan/Gas Mark 6. Grease and flour the moulds of your chosen tins.

2   Place the butter, sugar, vanilla extract and seeds in the bowl of an electric mixer with the paddle attachment in place. Beat on a medium speed until light, then add the eggs, a little at a time, scraping down the sides of the bowl a few times as you go. Adding the eggs gradually should prevent the mix splitting, but don't worry too much if it does: it might look a bit curdled, but this will not affect the final result. Continue to beat until fully combined. Sift the flour and salt into a bowl, then stir in the ground almonds. Reduce the speed of the mixer to medium-low, then add the dry ingredients in three batches, and finally fold in the diced strawberries.

3   Spoon the mixture into the prepared moulds – it should come about three-quarters of the way up the sides (about two-thirds in a regular muffin tin) – and bake for about 22 minutes (about 20 minutes in a regular muffin tin), rotating the tray halfway through, until a skewer inserted into the middle of one of the cakes comes out clean. Remove from the oven and allow to sit for 15–20 minutes before easing the cakes out of the moulds. Transfer to a wire rack to cool completely before icing.

4   **To make the icing,** place all the icing ingredients in a food processor and blitz together until smooth. Drizzle the tops of the upturned cakes with the icing, allowing it to drip down the sides. If using, garnish with half a fresh strawberry on each cake, cut side facing up, or a sprinkle of dried strawberries.

Victoria sponge with strawberries and white chocolate cream

Nothing says 'summer garden party' more than this: the light-as-air sponge, the seasonally sweet strawberries, the white chocolate cream . . . Add a freshly mown lawn and a cup of tea and you're there. At least that was our vision before these were shot for the book by Peden + Munk. Taylor (the Peden side of the team) delighted in bringing a little bit of anarchy (or 'pile up', as he preferred to call it) to some of our more composed presentations. Perfectly organized, neat mini-cakes received the requisite Taylor treatment here, and we could not be more delighted with the results.

The secret to the sponge – which is light as air, but also rich and buttery – is the reliance on air being whipped into the eggs as the raising agent, rather than chemical leaveners. Melted butter is then trickled into the cake batter and folded in for extra richness. All this requires a deft and light hand (and a bit of elbow grease to begin with), but the result is a deliciously versatile sponge for your repertoire. There's something a little bit magic about making a perfect genoise sponge. Behind the magic, though, there's quite a lot of method. None of it is complicated; all of it is important. For more on making the perfect genoise, see page 346.

SERVES 8 (8 INDIVIDUAL CAKES OR ONE LARGE CAKE)

___

WHITE CHOCOLATE CREAM
70g white chocolate, finely chopped
70ml double cream, plus an extra
    120ml to finish

STRAWBERRIES
250g hulled strawberries,
    roughly chopped
70g caster sugar
1½ tsp lemon juice

SPONGE
4 large eggs
100g caster sugar
scraped seeds of ½ vanilla pod (keep
    the pod for the strawberry jam)
finely grated zest of 1 lemon (1 tsp)
60g unsalted butter
100g plain flour
⅛ tsp salt
150g hulled strawberries, sliced
    0.5cm thick
1 tsp icing sugar, for dusting

We have used 8cm wide cake rings here. But if you don't have eight of these, make one large cake in a 20cm round springform cake tin instead.

___

The sponge is best made on the day it's served, but can be made a day ahead, if necessary, and kept in an airtight container. It can also be frozen, wrapped in cling film, for up to a month.

___

Once assembled, the cakes should be eaten on the same day, and the closer to assembly the better, as cream does not like to sit around for too long.

___

___

1   **To make the white chocolate cream,** place the chocolate in a medium bowl and set aside. Put the cream in a small, heavy-based saucepan and place over a medium-low heat. Cook until it is just starting to simmer, then pour the hot cream over the chocolate. Leave to sit for 3 minutes, for the chocolate to soften, then stir gently until the chocolate is melted and fully combined. Cover with cling film and refrigerate for 1 hour until completely cold.

2   **To cook the strawberries,** place the strawberries, sugar and lemon juice in a small saucepan (along with the empty vanilla pod) and mix well. Bring to the boil over a medium heat and cook for 4–5 minutes, stirring regularly, until the sugar has melted and the mixture has thickened. Remove from the heat and set aside to cool. ››

3   Preheat the oven to 170°C/150°C Fan/Gas Mark 3. Line a large baking tray with baking parchment and place eight 8cm cake rings, ungreased and unlined, on top and set aside. If making this in a 20cm round springform tin, you don't need the baking tray, but you will need to line the bottom of the tin with baking parchment.

4   Put enough water into a medium saucepan so that it rises about 5cm up the sides: you want the bowl from your electric mixer to be able to fit in the saucepan and sit over the water without actually touching it. Bring the water to a boil, then reduce to a simmer.

5   **To make the sponge,** place the eggs, sugar, vanilla and lemon zest in the bowl of an electric mixer and place the bowl on top of the saucepan of simmering water, making sure (again) that the bottom of the bowl is not touching the water. Whisk continuously by hand for about 5 minutes, until the mixture is frothy, creamy and warm. Remove the bowl and place it on the electric mixer with the whisk attachment in place. Whisk on a high speed until the mixture has tripled in volume and is no longer warm.

6   While the mix is beating in the mixer, melt the butter and set aside to cool. Combine the flour and salt in a bowl and sift it twice. When the egg mixture has tripled in volume and is no longer warm, sift half the flour (yes, a third sift!) directly over the mixture and gently fold it in with a large rubber spatula. Sift the remaining flour over the mixture and fold in again. Now drizzle the cooled, melted butter down the sides of the bowl. Fold in gently and swiftly to incorporate.

7   Spoon the mixture into the cake rings – it should be filled two-thirds of the way up the sides – and bake for 15–18 minutes (or 25 minutes if baking one large cake), or until the cakes are a light golden brown and the sponge springs back when lightly pressed in the middle. Remove from the oven and set aside to cool for 20 minutes, in the rings, before using a small knife to remove them: take a bit of care here, to prevent the cakes tearing or sticking to the sides. Transfer to a wire rack to cool completely.

8   **When ready to assemble,** place the white chocolate cream in the bowl of an electric mixer with the whisk attachment in place. Add the extra 120ml cream and whip on a medium-high speed for about 30 seconds until combined and thick. It should just hold on the whisk – it can over-whip very quickly, so be careful.

9   Cut the cakes horizontally across the centre and spread the cooked strawberries on the cut side of the bottom piece (discard the vanilla pod). Spoon half of the white chocolate cream on top, followed by the sliced strawberries, followed by the remaining white chocolate cream. Finish with the top half of the sponge. If you have made one large cake, take care when slicing it in half; you'll need to support it underneath when lifting it back on top of the cream and strawberries. If you have a cake lifter or jumbo cookie spatula, now is the time to use it! Dust with icing sugar and serve.

Banana cakes with rum caramel

Banana bread can sometimes feel like the place over-ripe bananas go to when no one else wants them. These decadent cakes, on the other hand, feel like the place they go to party, a bottle of rum in hand.

MAKES 6 (USING INDIVIDUAL BUNDT TINS) OR 7 (USING LARGE MUFFIN TINS)

100g unsalted butter, at room temperature, cut into 2cm cubes, plus extra for greasing
70g caster sugar
70g soft light brown sugar
2 large eggs
1 tsp vanilla extract
110g self-raising flour, plus extra for dusting
100g ground almonds
2 tbsp malted milk powder (e.g. Horlicks)

⅛ tsp salt
½ tsp ground cinnamon
¾ tsp bicarbonate of soda
2–3 ripe medium bananas, peeled and mashed (225g)
100g soured cream
2 tbsp dark rum

RUM CARAMEL
200g caster sugar
125ml water
130ml double cream
1½ tbsp dark rum

We make these in individual bundt tins, but you can also use a large muffin tin.

Un-iced, these will keep for 5 days in an airtight container. Once iced, they should be eaten within 24 hours.

1   Preheat the oven to 180°C/160°C Fan/Gas Mark 4. Lightly grease the bundt or muffin tins, dust with flour and set aside.

2   Place the butter and sugars in the bowl of an electric mixer with the paddle attachment in place. Beat on a medium-high speed for about 3 minutes, until light but not too fluffy. Add the eggs, one at a time, beating well after each addition, then add the vanilla extract. Beat for another minute to combine.

3   Sift the flour, almonds, malted milk powder, salt, ground cinnamon and bicarbonate of soda into a large bowl: not all the almonds will make it through the sieve, but it's okay to tip in any that don't make it. Whisk to combine and set aside.

4   Place the mashed bananas in a separate bowl with the soured cream and rum. Mix well, then add a quarter of this to the butter-sugar mixture, beating on a low speed to incorporate. Add a quarter of the dry mix, continuing to beat, and continue in batches with the remaining wet and dry ingredients until everything is combined.

5   Spoon the mixture into the prepared tins, filling them about three-quarters of the way up the sides. Bake for 25–28 minutes, or until a skewer inserted into the centre of a cake comes out clean. Remove from the oven and set aside in their tins until completely cool. Once cool, place the cakes on a wire rack with a tray or sheet of baking parchment underneath.

6   **Make the caramel** while the cakes are in the oven. Place the sugar and water in a medium saucepan and stir to combine. Bring to the boil, then simmer over a medium-high heat for 8–10 minutes, until the mix begins to change colour and becomes a deep amber colour. Resist the urge to stir, but gently swirl the pan from time to time to distribute the heat. Remove from the heat and carefully stir in the cream and rum. If the mixture seizes up, return the pan to a low heat and stir the mix until smooth. Set aside for about 30 minutes in the pan, then drizzle liberally over the cakes, allowing the icing to drip unevenly down the sides.

Blackberry and star anise friands

These look splendid when iced – destined for top ranking on any tiered cake stand – but also work un-iced, in the cookie tin, for grabbing on a whim. They'll lose their slightly chewy edge after the first day or so, but still taste great. Blueberries or raspberries can be used instead of the blackberries. Don't use strawberries, though: they are too watery.

MAKES 12

180g unsalted butter, plus an extra 10g, melted, for brushing
60g plain flour, plus extra for dusting
200g icing sugar
120g ground almonds
1½ tsp ground star anise
   (or 3 whole star anise, blitzed
   in a spice grinder and passed
   through a fine-mesh sieve)
⅛ tsp salt
150g egg whites (from 4 large eggs)
finely grated zest of 1 small orange
   (1 tsp)
18 whole blackberries (about 120g),
   cut in half lengthways

ICING (OPTIONAL)
60g blackberries (about 8), plus
   an extra 24 small blackberries,
   to garnish
¾ tbsp water
1 tsp lemon juice
165g icing sugar

We use a regular muffin tin here, but all sorts of moulds work: large muffin tins, mini-muffin tins, rectangular or oval moulds (as shown in the photo).

Un-iced, these will keep for up to 4 days. If the weather is warm, store them in the fridge and zap them in the microwave for a few seconds (literally 3 seconds!) to restore their buttery moisture. They can also be frozen for up to 3 months, then thawed in the fridge and warmed through in a 170°C/150°C Fan/Gas Mark 3 oven for 5 minutes; this will restore their crisp edges, as well. Once iced, they're best eaten on the same day.

1   Preheat the oven to 220°C/200°C Fan/Gas Mark 7. Brush the 12 holes of a regular muffin tin with the melted butter and sprinkle all over with flour. Tap the tray gently to ensure an even coating of the flour, then turn upside down to remove the excess. Place in the fridge to chill while you make the batter.

2   **To brown the butter,** place in a small saucepan and cook over a medium heat until melted. Continue to cook until the butter is foaming, gently swirling the pan from time to time, to allow the solids to brown more evenly. You will see dark brown sediments begin to form on the sides and bottom of the pan. Continue to allow the butter to bubble away until it turns a rich golden brown and smells of toasted nuts and caramel. Remove the pan from the heat and let it stand for 5 minutes, to allow the burnt solids to collect at the bottom of the pan. Strain through a fine-mesh (or muslin-lined) sieve, discarding the solids. Allow the browned butter to cool slightly before using. It should still be warm when folding into the mix later: if it is too hot, it will 'cook' the egg whites; if it is too cool, it will be difficult to incorporate into the mix.

3   While the butter is cooling, sift the flour, icing sugar, ground almonds, star anise and salt into a bowl. Place the egg whites in a small bowl and use a whisk or fork to froth them up for a few seconds – you do not need to whisk them completely. Pour the egg whites into the sifted dry ingredients and stir until they are incorporated. Add the orange zest and browned butter and mix until the batter is smooth. ››

4   Remove the muffin tin from the fridge and fill the moulds just over two-thirds of the way up the sides. Place three halved blackberries on top, cut side down, and bake for 10 minutes. Reduce the temperature to 210°C/190°C Fan/Gas Mark 6 – starting with a high oven temperature and then bringing it down is the way to achieve the lovely brown crust you want – turn the tray around in the oven for even cooking, and continue to cook for another 8 minutes, until the edges of the friands are golden brown and the centres have a slight peak and spring back when gently prodded. Set aside to cool before removing them from their moulds: you might need to use a small knife to help you release the sides.

5   **If you are icing the cakes,** place 60g of blackberries in a small bowl with the water and lemon juice. Use a fork to mash them together, then pass the mixture through a fine-mesh sieve to extract as much fruit juice as possible: you should get about 60ml. Sift the icing sugar into a medium bowl, pour in the blackberry juice and combine to make a light purple runny icing: it should just be thick enough to form a thin glaze on the tops of the cakes. Spoon the icing over the cakes, spreading it to the edges so that it runs down the sides. Do this on a rack, if you can, as icing them on a plate or sheet of paper means that the icing will pool at the bottom. Place 2 small blackberries on each friand, set aside for 20 or 30 minutes to set, then serve.

Coffee and walnut financiers

Financiers, like the little blocks of gold they're named after, typically come in the shape of a rectangle. We like to make them in straight, high-sided popover tins, as we have here, so that the icing can trickle down the sides.

These tins are not widely available, however, so we have adjusted the recipe to work in either a regular muffin or a mini-muffin tin. As mini-muffins, they provide the perfect end to a meal, to accompany your coffee.

Financiers are similar to friands, another little French cake whose elegance and svelteness somehow betrays quite how much (burnt) butter is built into their being. It's this 'beurre noisette' that gives financiers their rich and nutty flavour.

MAKES 12 (USING A REGULAR MUFFIN TIN) OR 24 (USING A MINI-MUFFIN TIN)

The batter can be made and kept in the fridge for up to 2 days.

Once baked, financiers are best eaten on the same day, but these will keep for up to 2 days in a sealed container, even after icing. The icing will set a little but the taste won't be affected.

80g walnut halves, plus an extra
   12–24 halves to garnish
120g unsalted butter, cut into 2cm
   cubes, plus extra for greasing
220g icing sugar
90g plain flour, plus extra for dusting
1 tsp baking powder
¼ tsp salt
80g ground almonds
230g egg whites (from 6 large eggs)
1 tbsp instant coffee granules,
   dissolved in 70ml boiling water
1½ tsp finely ground espresso coffee
   (such as Lavazza)

ICING
250g icing sugar
2½ tsp instant coffee granules
35ml hot full-fat milk
15g liquid glucose

1   Preheat the oven to 170°C/150°C Fan/Gas Mark 3. Spread the walnuts out on a baking tray and roast for 10 minutes. Remove from the oven and, when cool enough to handle, roughly chop them into 0.5–1cm pieces. Set aside until ready to use.

2   To make the batter, start by browning the butter. Place the butter in a small saucepan and cook over a medium heat until melted. Continue to cook until the butter is foaming, gently swirling the pan from time to time, to allow the solids to brown more evenly. You will see dark brown sediments begin to form on the sides and bottom of the pan. Continue to allow the butter to bubble away until it turns a rich golden brown and smells of toasted nuts and caramel. Remove the pan from the heat and let it stand for 5 minutes, to allow the burnt solids to collect at the bottom of the pan. Strain through a fine-mesh (or muslin-lined) sieve, discarding the solids. Allow the browned butter to cool slightly before using. It should still be warm when folding into the mix later: if it is too hot, it will 'cook' the egg whites; if it is too cool, it will be difficult to incorporate into the mix. ›

3   While the butter is cooling, sift the icing sugar, flour, baking powder and salt into a medium bowl. Add the almonds and whisk to combine. Place the egg whites in a mixing bowl and use a whisk or fork to froth them up a little – you will not need to whisk them completely. Pour the egg whites and dissolved coffee granules into the dry ingredients and stir until just combined. Add the browned butter and mix until the batter is thick, shiny and smooth. Fold in the walnuts and ground coffee, then cover with cling film – making sure that it actually touches the surface of the batter – and transfer to the fridge for at least 2 hours.

4   Preheat the oven temperature to 200°C/180°C Fan/Gas Mark 6. Butter the moulds of your chosen muffin tin and dust with flour. Tap away any excess flour, then spoon the batter into each mould, filling them three-quarters full. Bake for about 25 minutes if using a regular muffin tin, or 14 minutes for a mini-muffin tin, or until the tops are a little cracked and a skewer inserted into the centre comes out clean.

5   **Make the icing** while the cakes are in the oven. Sift the icing sugar into a medium bowl and add the remaining ingredients. Mix until smooth and set aside: don't worry if there are undissolved coffee granules in the icing – these look good!

6   Remove the tin from the oven and set aside for 5 minutes, before gently tapping it against your work surface to encourage the cakes to fall out. If there are any stubborn bits sticking to the tin, use a butter knife to gently ease them out. Place the financiers on a wire rack to cool completely. To serve, spread the icing on top and finish with a walnut half, a dusting of icing sugar and a little finely ground espresso powder if you like.

Flourless chocolate 'teacakes'

Our 'teacakes' – unlike the more bread-like teacakes, dense with raisins – are light, airy and gluten-free. They work with a cup of afternoon tea, but are also rich enough to satisfy as a dessert, with a decorative shard of almond praline.

We were introduced to water ganache by Colleen Murphy during her many years with the company. It might sound like a contradiction in terms – a ganache without cream?! – but it's something we're really keen on, both for its stability – it doesn't lose its shine in the way that a cream-based ganache can – and also for the smooth and direct 'pure chocolate' hit it brings.

Don't be tempted to skip the resting stage before the cake is baked: it's really important to allow the ground almonds to fully absorb the liquids, as this is what makes the cakes as moist as can be.

MAKES 6 'TEACAKES' (USING INDIVIDUAL BUNDT TINS)
OR 12 REGULAR MUFFINS (USING A MUFFIN TIN)

160g unsalted butter, cubed, plus
  an extra 20g, melted, for brushing
200g dark chocolate (70% cocoa
  solids), roughly chopped
160g caster sugar
1 tsp instant coffee granules, dissolved
  in 1 tsp boiling water
25ml Amaretto
160g ground almonds
5 large eggs, yolk and whites separated
¼ tsp salt

WATER GANACHE
85g dark chocolate (70% cocoa solids),
  roughly chopped into 2cm pieces
35g caster sugar
35g liquid glucose
60ml water
scraped seeds of ½ vanilla pod
35g unsalted butter, at room
  temperature, cut into 2cm cubes

You can make these in 6 individual bundt tins, or in a regular muffin tin.

The ganache can be kept at room temperature (covered with cling film which is touching the surface of the ganache) for up to 4 days. It can also be kept in the fridge for up to 2 weeks, and then brought back to room temperature before spreading.

Un-iced, the cakes will keep in a sealed container for up to 4 days. Once iced, they are best eaten on the day of serving, but will keep for up to 2 days: the icing will lose a bit of its sheen, but the taste will be unaffected.

1   **To make the 'teacakes',** place the butter and chocolate in a large heatproof bowl over a pan of simmering water, making sure the base of the bowl isn't touching the water. Whisk the mixture and, when melted, remove the bowl from the heat. Add half the sugar, along with the coffee, Amaretto, almonds and egg yolks. Stir to combine and set aside.

2   Place the egg whites and salt in the bowl of an electric mixer with the whisk attachment in place. Whisk on a high speed for about 1 minute, until soft peaks form. Slowly add the remaining sugar and continue to whisk for about 3–4 minutes, until you get a light and dry mix.

3   Spoon one dollop of the egg white into the chocolate and fold to combine before gently folding in the remainder. Set aside, at room temperature, for an hour to rest.

4   Preheat the oven to 180°C/160°C Fan/Gas Mark 4. Brush the base and sides of the bundt or muffin tins liberally with melted butter: allow the excess to drain away by placing them upside down on some kitchen paper. »

5   Once the cake mix has rested, spoon or pipe it into the 6 moulds (or 12, if making in the muffin tin), filling them three-quarters full. Place the moulds on a baking tray in the centre of the oven and bake for 20–25 minutes, rotating the tray halfway through, until the cakes are cooked and a skewer inserted into the centre of a cake comes out with just a few crumbs attached (not wet batter). Remove from the oven and allow the cakes to sit for 10 minutes before inverting the moulds on to a wire cooling rack. Set aside until completely cool and then gently tap out the cakes.

6   **To make the ganache,** place the chocolate in a medium bowl and set aside. Put the sugar and glucose in a small saucepan and place over a medium-low heat. Stir to combine and, when the sugar has melted, increase the heat to medium and bring to the boil, stirring gently from time to time. Continue to boil for about 7 minutes, until the colour is a pale amber. Remove from the heat and carefully pour in the water. Don't worry if the mix seizes: just return the pan to the heat, add the scraped vanilla seeds and stir gently and continuously until it returns to the boil. Remove from the heat and wait for a minute before pouring the water-caramel over the chocolate. Allow to stand for 5 minutes, then whisk to combine. Add the butter, a couple of cubes at a time, whisking after each addition. Continue until all the butter has been added, whisking to combine until the mix is smooth and shiny.

7   Spread some water ganache over the top of each cake, allowing it to gently dribble down the sides. Set aside to cool and let the ganache set before serving.

Lemon and semolina syrup cakes

Syrup cakes remind Yotam of his childhood in Jerusalem, where syrup-soaked cakes – perfumed with orange blossom, rose water or a smack of citrus – were everywhere. So moist as to be positively drenched, these go very well as they are with morning coffee, afternoon tea, or served after a meal with some yoghurt, soured cream or crème fraîche.

The thin slice of lemon sitting on top of the cakes provides an extra citrus hit that we love, but we also know that our tolerance for eating lemon (in all forms) is higher than that of others. Some love it, some don't – a problem solved by the fact that it can easily be removed before eating, if desired.

MAKES 8

These keep well for 3 days in an airtight container.

120g unsalted butter, at room temperature, plus extra for greasing
135g caster sugar
1½ lemons (the whole lemon is finely grated to give 1 tsp zest, and squeezed to give 20ml lemon juice; the ½ lemon is very thinly sliced into 8 rounds)
100g ground almonds
2 large eggs, lightly beaten
70g fine semolina
½ tsp baking powder
⅛ tsp salt

SYRUP
60ml lemon juice
50g caster sugar

1   Preheat the oven to 180°C/160°C Fan/Gas Mark 4. Grease 8 moulds of a regular muffin tin and line each mould with squares of baking parchment so that it rises 2cm up the sides.

2   Place the butter, sugar and lemon zest in an electric mixer with the paddle attachment in place. Beat on a high speed for about 3 minutes, until light and fluffy, then add the ground almonds. Mix for a minute before gradually adding the eggs. Reduce the speed to low and add the semolina, baking powder and salt. Mix for 30 seconds, until incorporated, then pour in the lemon juice. Divide the mixture between the muffin cases and place a slice of lemon on top of each cake.

3   Bake for 25–30 minutes, until the cakes are golden brown on top, the lemon slices are starting to caramelize and a skewer inserted into the centre of a cake comes out clean.

4   **Make the syrup** while the cakes are baking. Put the lemon juice and sugar in a small saucepan and bring to the boil over a medium-low heat. Stir to dissolve the sugar and simmer for 2–3 minutes. Remove from the heat and, as soon as the cakes come out of the oven, brush or spoon the syrup liberally over the top. Set aside to cool before lifting them out of the muffin tin: keep each cake in its parchment paper when serving, though – they look lovely as they are.

Roma's doughnuts with saffron custard cream

This recipe is adapted (so much so as to be unrecognizable from the original!) from a clipping Helen's mother-in-law, Roma Kausman, tore from the *Jerusalem Post* in 1973. Roma used to make doughnuts – sufganiyots – at Hanukkah, but we can't think of any celebration at which a sugar-coated doughnut is not welcome, to remind everyone how perfectly sweet life can be.

We know you're not going to make these every day – they're a lot of work – but much of the time is spent waiting for the dough to prove. We have put the dough in the fridge overnight after the first prove to reduce the amount of time you'll need to wait for it to prove on the day you're planning to fry and eat the doughnuts. But all the effort you put in will be rewarded, we promise. And you'll then be able to say that you made your very own doughnuts!

Proving the doughnuts on small squares of baking parchment is important: they will deflate if you try to lift them with your fingers, and the paper will help you to transfer them to the oil without having to touch them. And yes, the paper also goes into the oil: it feels strange to do this, but trust us (or actually trust Peter Gordon, from whom we first learnt the technique). Once the doughnuts start frying, the paper naturally separates and can then be fished out with tongs.

If you are looking for shortcuts, the saffron custard can be replaced by a more traditional strawberry jam. The brandy can also be skipped, if you like: it adds a lovely subtle flavour, but there's enough going on, flavour-wise, if you don't have a bottle around and open.

MAKES 10
—

You will need a piping bag to pipe the custard filling.

The saffron custard can be made up to 2 days in advance (whip it with the cream just before serving) and kept in the fridge. The dough must be started a day in advance as it is kept in the fridge overnight.

Once fried, the doughnuts are best eaten on the same day.

DOUGHNUTS
130g strong bread flour
130g plain flour, plus extra for dusting
20g caster sugar
2 tsp fast-action (or easy-bake) dried yeast
¼ tsp salt
25g unsalted butter, melted
finely grated zest of 1 small orange (1 tsp)
1 large egg yolk
70ml full-fat milk, warmed through until tepid
70ml tepid water
1 tsp brandy (optional)
about 1 litre sunflower oil, for frying
—

SAFFRON CUSTARD CREAM
160ml full-fat milk
⅛ tsp saffron threads
2 large egg yolks
50g caster sugar
1 packed tbsp cornflour (10g)
scraped seeds of ¼ vanilla pod
25g unsalted butter, cut into small pieces
80ml double cream

CARDAMOM SUGAR
80g caster sugar
1 tsp ground cardamom (see pages 351–2 for how to make your own)

1   **To make the doughnuts,** place both flours in the bowl of an electric mixer with the sugar, yeast and salt. Use a hand-held whisk to combine, then add the dough hook attachment. Add the melted butter, orange zest and egg yolk and mix on a medium-low speed for about 30 seconds. Combine the milk, water and brandy, if using, in a small jug and then, with the machine still running, gradually pour this into the flour mix. When all of the liquid has been added, increase the speed to medium-high and mix for 3–4 minutes, scraping down the sides of the bowl if you need to, until the mixture is smooth and elastic.

2   Tip the dough on to a lightly floured work surface and knead gently – adding a little more flour if necessary – until smooth and no longer sticky. Place in a lightly oiled bowl, cover with cling film and set aside in a warm, draught-free place until the dough has doubled in size: this can take between 1 and 4 hours, depending on the temperature of your kitchen. When the dough has doubled in size, knock it down with your fist, cover with cling film and place in the fridge overnight.

3   **To make the custard,** place the milk and saffron threads in a small saucepan. Heat gently until the milk is just coming to a simmer and bubbles are beginning to form around the sides. In the meantime, combine the egg yolks with the sugar, cornflour and vanilla seeds in a small bowl and whisk together to form a paste. When the milk is just coming to a simmer, slowly whisk half of it into the egg yolk mixture (it helps to have a damp cloth underneath the bowl to steady it while you whisk with one hand and pour with the other), before whisking this back into the remaining hot milk. Cook over a medium-low heat for about 5 minutes, whisking continuously, until very thick and smooth. When you lift some of the mix out of the pan it should hold on to the whisk for a few seconds before falling off in one big blob. Remove from the heat and whisk in the butter, one piece at a time, until fully combined and smooth. Transfer the custard to a clean bowl or jug, cover with cling film – you want it to be actually touching the surface to prevent a skin forming – and set aside in the fridge until completely chilled. The custard keeps well in the fridge for a couple of days, so it's a good idea to make this the day before the doughnuts are made.

4   Cut out 10 squares of baking parchment measuring 10 x 10cm and arrange on two large baking trays. Once the dough has been in the fridge overnight, tip it on to your work surface, roll roughly into a log and then cut the log into 10 pieces, each weighing approximately 45g. Shape each into a round ball – this is best done by placing each piece on the work surface, cupping your hand over it and then applying some pressure while you roll it around into a smooth sphere. Place each ball on one square of baking parchment. Cover the tray loosely with oiled cling film and set aside somewhere warm to rise to almost double the size. Again, this can take anywhere between 45 minutes and 4 hours, depending on the temperature of the room.

5   **To make the cardamom sugar,** mix together the sugar and cardamom in a wide bowl and set aside.

6   When the doughnuts are ready to fry, fill a medium pan (about 18cm wide) with enough oil so that it rises 5cm up the sides of the pan. Heat the oil to 180°C. To test that the oil is ready, either use a deep-fry thermometer, or drop a small piece of bread into the pan: if it rises straight to the surface and turns golden brown in about 1 minute, it is hot enough.

7   Lifting the balls on the baking parchment, gently drop three balls at a time into the oil, paper side up (the paper is dropped into the oil too). Fry in batches for 3 minutes – turning over halfway through – until golden brown on both sides. As they cook, the paper will slide away and, as it does, use tongs to lift it out and discard. Use a slotted spoon to lift the doughnuts out as they cook. Drain them briefly on kitchen paper before rolling them in the cardamom sugar. They can now either be eaten hot, as they are, or set aside until barely warm before being piped with the saffron custard cream (or jam: see introduction).

8   When ready to fill the doughnuts, finish making the custard filling by placing the double cream in a medium bowl and, using a hand-held whisk, whisk until soft peaks form. Add the cooled custard and very lightly whisk together until just combined.

9   Push a small knife through one side of the doughnut, twisting gently to create a little tunnel through the centre. Fill a piping bag with the custard and pipe about a tablespoon into each one.

Chocolate Guinness cakes with Baileys Irish Cream

The recipe in Nigella Lawson's wonderful book, *Feast*, inspired our version of these cakes. We have amplified the Irish element in her original recipe by piping Baileys-infused mascarpone cream into the middle of the cakes. Thanks to Daniel Karlsson for this idea. This is then followed by a light drizzle of chocolate ganache, followed by shavings of chocolate! It sounds extravagant, we know, but it's actually a really easy cake to make, all whisked together in one bowl.

The secret to making a really shiny chocolate ganache is to use a food processor, as we do here.

We like to make these in eight mini-loaf tins, 9.5 x 6.5cm at the top and 7 x 4cm at the bottom. If you use these you'll need a piping bag to insert the Baileys cream. Alternatively, you could use an 18cm round springform tin. If you do this, just line the round tin regularly (rather than allowing a 2cm overhang). You'll also need to increase the baking time to 40 minutes. When the cake is cool, slice it in half horizontally, spread the Baileys cream over the bottom layer and sandwich back together.

The ganache can be stored at room temperature, providing it's not too warm, for 3 days, or kept in the fridge for up to 2 weeks. Without the cream filling, the cakes will keep for up to 3 days in an airtight container at room temperature.

Once the cakes have been assembled, they must be kept in the fridge and eaten within a day.

SERVES 8

120ml Guinness
120g unsalted butter, cubed, plus extra for greasing
30g Dutch-processed cocoa powder
200g caster sugar
65g soured cream
1 large egg
2 tsp vanilla extract
130g plain flour
¼ tsp salt
1 tsp bicarbonate of soda
5g chocolate (70% cocoa solids), shaved with a peeler (this is about a square of chocolate, but it's hard to shave such a small amount, so just shave it off the block you have)

BAILEYS CREAM

125g mascarpone
45ml Baileys Irish Cream
40g icing sugar, sifted

CHOCOLATE GANACHE

100g dark chocolate (70% cocoa solids), chopped into 2cm pieces
100ml double cream
1½ tsp golden syrup
1½ tsp unsalted butter, softened

1   Preheat the oven to 195°C/175°C Fan/Gas Mark 5. Grease and line the long side and the base of eight small loaf tins with a strip of parchment paper. Allow a 2cm overhang on each side to help you lift out the cakes later on.

2   Place the Guinness and butter in a medium saucepan over a medium heat. Stir gently until the butter has melted, taking care that it does not come to the boil. Sift the cocoa powder and sugar together into the pan and whisk into the mix, then transfer to a medium bowl.

3   In a separate bowl, whisk together the soured cream, egg and vanilla, then pour this into the Guinness mix, whisking as you do so. Sift the flour, salt and bicarbonate of soda together into a bowl, then whisk this into the mixture until smooth and combined. Pour the batter into the tins and bake for 20 minutes or until a skewer inserted into the centre of the cake comes out clean. Remove from the oven and allow to cool for 10 minutes before gently easing them out, using the parchment paper overhang to help you. Gently run a knife around the unlined edges if they are stuck, then place on a wire rack to cool completely. ››

4   **To make the Baileys cream,** whisk together the mascarpone and Baileys using an electric hand-held whisk, if you have one, or by hand. Add the icing sugar and continue to beat on a low speed until the mixture is combined. Increase the speed to medium-high and whisk until the cream is thick enough to spread. Keep in the fridge until ready to serve.

5   When the cakes are completely cool, make a cut in each cake by running a small paring knife down its centre, leaving 2cm uncut at either end. Transfer the cream to a piping bag fitted with a 1½cm wide nozzle. Gently ease the piping bag into the opening of the cut side of each cake and pipe in the cream until it starts to ooze out.

6   **To make the chocolate ganache,** place the chocolate pieces in a food processor, blitz until fine and set aside.

7   Put the cream and golden syrup in a small pan and place over a medium-high heat. As soon as bubbles begin to appear – just before it comes to the boil – remove from the heat. Get the food processor running again, with the chocolate still inside, and pour in the hot cream in a steady stream. Process for about 10 seconds, then add the butter. Continue to process until the mixture is shiny and smooth.

8   You can also make the ganache by hand: just make sure the chocolate is chopped fairly finely before you scald the cream and golden syrup and pour it over the chocolate. Stir everything together with a wooden spoon until almost melted, then add the butter. Stir again until the ganache is smooth.

9   Whether you make it in a machine or by hand, use a rubber spatula to scrape the ganache into a bowl and cover with cling film. Set aside until it has set to the consistency you want, then use it to ice the cake: if you want a thin layer to spread over the cakes, it can be poured over while liquid so that you get an even, light and shiny coating. For a thicker ganache with a spreading consistency, leave it for about 2 hours at room temperature before using a spatula or knife to ice the cakes. Spoon about one tablespoon over each cake: you want it to cover the cut with the cream oozing out. Decorate with chocolate shavings and serve.

Cakes

—

There's something a little bit magic and a big bit satisfying about baking a cake. Starting with just a few basic building blocks – flour, eggs, butter, sugar, a raising agent – the number of directions you can take from there is inspiring.

You'll find cakes for all occasions here: easy loaf cakes for everyday baking, and cakes you'll save for special occasions; booze-filled cakes to serve to adults after supper, and pink-iced cakes to make your kid's day. We have cakes you'll need to eat on the day of making, and others that will be happy to stick around for the week. We have round cakes, loaf cakes, bundt cakes, rolled cakes, long cakes, tall cakes, light cakes, dense cakes, cakes which are all (secretly) about the icing, and cakes which stand alone. And we have cakes free from gluten, and cakes which – though not free from sugar – are packed with lots of naturally sweet ingredients like root vegetables and tropical fruit.

That's a quick outline of the main routes we head down. Here, in more detail, are some of the attractions you'll pass on the way.

CAKES FOR EVERYDAY BAKING, CAKES FOR SPECIAL OCCASIONS › Simple loaf cakes such as our Lemon and Poppy Seed Cake (see page 187) and Tessa's Spice Cake (see page 186) are perfect for everyday baking. Eminently sliceable and in no need of elaborate icing, these are cakes which can sit around for a good few days, ready to eat alongside a cup of tea. Cakes packed with root vegetables – the Beetroot, Ginger and Soured Cream Cake (see page 130) and the Parsnip and Pecan Cake with Aniseed and Orange (see page 128), for example – have a similarly long shelf life. Again, they're perfect for everyday baking for the week ahead.

Some cakes, on the other hand, are to be saved for a special occasion. Layered cakes such as the (aptly named) Celebration Cake (see page 193), the Louise Cake with Plum and Coconut (see page 173), the Pineapple and Star Anise Chiffon Cake (see page 179) and the Pistachio and Rose Water Semolina Cake (see page 165) are all, in their own way, labours of love. This is perfectly apt, though, as why would you want to make a cake for someone you don't adore?

CAKES FOR TEA TIME, CAKES FOR DESSERT (AND CAKES FOR BREAKFAST) › Of course, it is always possible to simplify the special, or to make the simple special – we can all scrub up for the occasion when we want to! A simple Take-home Chocolate Cake (see page 152), for example, can be turned into an impressive dessert when served with a spoonful of espresso cinnamon mascarpone cream; and a Coconut, Almond and Blueberry Cake (see page 151), intended for tea time, can be converted into dessert when served warm with a drizzle of cream.

The opposite is also true. A showstopper such as the Pineapple and Star Anise Chiffon Cake (see page 179), adorned with pineapple flowers you've made yourself, will still go down very well when served unadorned; and the Pistachio and Rose Water Semolina Cake (see page 165) will still be a treat without the crystallized petals. While strewing a cake with hand-crystallized flowers might be as close to a declaration of love as it's possible for a cake to get, no one is going to think you love them any less without the flowers.

We had lots of fun working out whether cakes made for tea time could work just as well after supper, or whether cakes made for weddings could also work on a wet weekend. In the process, we stumbled across the fact that the Rhubarb and Strawberry Crumble Cake (see page 148) – conventionally served after a meal – also tastes uncommonly good eaten for breakfast, along with some thick Greek yoghurt.

CAKES FOR BIG KIDS, CAKES FOR SMALL KIDS › The pairing of booze and fruit is one so winning that we find it hard to resist. Prunes and Armagnac, grappa and grapes, rum and raisins, wine and plums: soaking dried fruit or cooking fresh fruit with alcohol brings a depth of flavour and degree of moisture to a cake that we absolutely love. Cakes such as the Grappa Fruit Cake (see page 141) or the Rum and Raisin Cake with Rum Caramel Icing (see page 124) might not be the ones to focus on when you're baking for your child's party. And cakes with lots of coffee or distinct spices such as anise or ground cardamom – the Coffee and Cardamom Pound Cake (see page 181), for example – might also not be the stuff of six-year-old dreams. But for those to whom cake is more than just a vehicle for icing and candles, these are cakes to get seriously excited about.

Between pink-icing-kiddie-heaven and booze-soaked-adult-heaven, there are many cakes to please all. Belinda's Flourless Coconut and Chocolate Cake (see page 190) is particularly popular with all the family, as are the Louise Cake with Plum and Coconut (see page 173) and the Rhubarb and Strawberry Crumble Cake (see page 148).

Kit

We've tried not to go too bonkers with the number of tins we use, but this also had to be balanced against the amount of fun there is to be had by baking cakes in all shapes and sizes: round, square, loaf, bundt, chiffon, rolled into the shape of a barrel . . . The day that cakes are no longer fun to make, look at and eat would, we think, be a sad day indeed.

Each recipe will specify the recommended style of cake tin, and we have, where we can, suggested alternatives when a specialist tin is called for. Bundt tins can be substituted with round cake tins, for example, or round tins used instead of square. In some cases, however, the specific cake tin is really important. The Vineyard Cake (see page 134) and the Pineapple and Star Anise Chiffon Cake (see page 179), for example, must be made in a chiffon cake tin (also known as an angel food cake tin); the shape and design of the tin is not just for fun here: it affects the way the cakes are baked and cooled and the cakes don't really work without it. The same is true of springform tins. These are often called for when a cake needs to be removed from a tin without inverting it. Lots of our cakes have lovely things on top of them, and turning them out on to a rack to cool (as you'd have to do if a tin was not springform) would mean that all this crumble and topping would get lost.

Rum and raisin cake with rum caramel icing

Going to the ice cream parlour is something of a tradition for Helen and her eldest son, Sam. They either share a tall sundae or go their separate ways down the cup or cone route. Sam's choice varies from week to week, but Helen always goes for a single scoop of rum and raisin. This, along with her affection for the rum-soaked retro classic rum baba, was the inspiration behind this cake.

SERVES 8–10

200g raisins
120ml dark rum
300g plain flour, plus extra for dusting
1 tsp baking powder
1 tsp bicarbonate of soda
½ tsp ground cinnamon
¼ tsp salt
250g unsalted butter, at room temperature, plus extra for greasing
250g light brown muscovado sugar

1 tsp vanilla extract
2 large eggs
200g soured cream

RUM CARAMEL ICING
60g unsalted butter
80g light brown muscovado sugar
3 tbsp milk
1 tbsp dark rum
100g icing sugar, sifted

We make this in a 23cm bundt tin; if you don't have the bundt tin, you can use a 23cm round springform tin: it won't look quite as pretty, but will still work well.

The raisins need to be prepared the day before you start baking, so that they are nice and plump from soaking up all the booze.

Iced or un-iced, this cake will keep for 2–3 days in an airtight container.

1   The day before you bake the cake, place the raisins and rum in a large container or jar for which you have a lid. Give it a good shake and set aside to macerate. Whenever you walk past the container or jar, give it a shake.

2   Preheat the oven to 190°C/170°C Fan/Gas Mark 5. Grease and flour a 23cm round bundt tin.

3   Sift the flour, baking powder, bicarbonate of soda, cinnamon and salt together into a medium bowl and set aside.

4   Place the butter, sugar and vanilla extract in the bowl of an electric mixer with the paddle attachment in place. Beat on a medium-high speed until smooth and lightened. Add the eggs, one a time, beating well after each addition. Reduce the speed to low and, with the machine still running, add the flour mix alternately with the soured cream, beginning and ending with the flour mix to stabilize the mixture and prevent it from curdling. Finally, add the soaked raisins and rum and mix on a low speed, just to combine. Scrape the mix into the bundt tin, smoothing the top, and bake for about 50 minutes, or until a skewer inserted into the centre of the cake comes out clean. Remove the cake from the oven and set aside for 15 minutes in the tin before inverting on to a cooling rack to cool completely.

5   **Make the icing** when you are ready to serve. Place the butter in a small saucepan and melt over a low heat. Add the sugar and cook for 1 minute, stirring continuously, until the mix comes together. Add the milk, increase the heat and bring to a boil. Remove the pan from the heat, add the rum, mix well and set aside to come to room temperature. When cool, beat in half of the icing sugar using a wooden spoon. Once incorporated, add the remaining half and beat until thick and smooth. Spread the rum and caramel icing over the top of the cake, letting it run slowly down the sides.

Prune cake with Armagnac and walnuts

SERVES 12

This looks best made in a 23cm bundt tin, but a 23cm round springform tin also works well. If you make it in the round tin, you'll need a little more crumble than for the bundt tin; we've listed both sets of quantities below.

The prunes need to be prepared the day before you start baking, to allow them time to soak. The crumble can be made up to 3 days in advance and stored in an airtight container.

This is at its absolute best eaten warm, fresh from the oven or on the day of making. Don't worry if you can't eat it all, though: it will keep well for up to 3 days in an airtight container. You'll just need to warm it through for 5 minutes (wrapped loosely in foil) in an oven set to 180°C/160°C Fan/Gas Mark 4 before serving.

250g pitted prunes, quartered
100ml Armagnac (or brandy)
finely grated zest of 1 orange (1½ tsp)
300g plain flour, plus extra for dusting
1 tsp baking powder
1 tsp bicarbonate of soda
½ tsp salt
200g unsalted butter, at room temperature, plus extra for greasing
200g caster sugar
1 tsp vanilla extract
2 large eggs

230g crème fraîche, removed from the fridge 30 minutes before needed
icing sugar, for dusting

CRUMBLE
(THE BRACKETED WEIGHTS ARE FOR THE 23CM ROUND CAKE TIN; THE SALT REMAINS THE SAME IN BOTH)

40g soft light brown sugar (or 60g)
2 tsp ground cinnamon (or 1 tbsp)
40g walnut halves (or 60g), roughly chopped into 0.5cm pieces
⅛ tsp salt

1   Place the prunes in a bowl with the Armagnac (or brandy) and orange zest. Cover the bowl with cling film and leave at room temperature overnight to soak, stirring a few times.

2   Preheat the oven to 200°C/180°C Fan/Gas Mark 6. Grease and flour a 23cm bundt or 23cm round springform tin and set aside.

3   **To make the crumble,** combine all the crumble ingredients in a small bowl and set aside.

4   Sift the flour, baking powder, bicarbonate of soda and salt together into a bowl and set aside.

5   Place the butter and sugar in the bowl of an electric mixer with the paddle attachment in place. Beat on a medium-high speed until light and fluffy. Add the vanilla and eggs, one at a time, beating well after each addition and scraping down the sides of the bowl to ensure even mixing. Reduce the speed to low and add the flour mix alternately with the crème fraîche, beginning and ending with the flour mix to stabilize the mixture and prevent it from curdling. Remove the bowl from the machine and, using a rubber spatula, fold in the soaked prunes along with their syrupy alcohol.

6   Spoon half of the cake batter into the tin and sprinkle over the nut crumble. Follow this with the remaining batter and bake for 50–55 minutes, or 60–65 minutes for the round springform tin, or until a skewer inserted into the centre of the cake comes out clean. Remove from the oven and allow to rest for 10 minutes in the tin. If using a bundt tin, invert it on to a cake plate, or simply lift it out of the springform tin on to a plate. Dust with icing sugar, if serving warm, or set aside to come to room temperature before dusting and serving.

RUM AND RAISIN CAKE WITH RUM CARAMEL ICING

PRUNE CAKE WITH ARMAGNAC AND WALNUTS

Parsnip and pecan cake with aniseed and orange

Yotam has always been sceptical about cakes made with root vegetables. There have been a number of attempts over the years to lure him over to the beetroot, parsnip and carrot side, but it wasn't until this cake that the conversion process began and he started to see what the naturally-sweet-inherently-moist fuss was all about.

This cake is the happy outcome of a disagreement over what constitutes the perfect carrot cake. Yotam thinks a carrot cake should be 'light and fluffy', Helen thinks it should be 'dense and fruity'. Never the twain should meet on this all-important of matters, so Helen took the diplomatic route of letting the carrots be and working on a parsnip cake instead. We are both, thankfully, agreed on the suitability of the 'dense and fruity' result.

It makes sense that parsnips work so well here, as they're from the same family as carrots: the umbelliferae. Parsnips are at their sweetest and juiciest in the winter months – when the starch has converted to sugar – so this cake is best made then.

SERVES 8–10

———

150g pecan halves

3 large parsnips, peeled and coarsely grated, avoiding the core if old and woody (450g)

100g currants

finely grated zest of 1 large orange (1 tbsp)

3 large eggs

225g caster sugar

280ml sunflower oil, plus extra for greasing

190g plain flour

1 tsp ground cinnamon

1½ tsp baking powder

1½ tsp bicarbonate of soda

1 tsp ground nutmeg

1 tsp ground aniseed (or 1 tsp finely ground fennel seeds)

¾ tsp salt

———

ICING

300g cream cheese, at room temperature

150g icing sugar, sifted

125ml double cream

1½ tsp ground aniseed

finely grated zest of 1 small orange (1 tsp)

The icing can be made up to 2 days ahead and stored in the fridge. You will just need to quickly whip it again before using.

Un-iced, the cake keeps well for up to 3 days in an airtight container or wrapped in aluminium foil. Once iced, the cake needs to be eaten on the same day.

1   Preheat the oven to 170°C/150°C Fan/Gas Mark 3. Grease and line a 23cm round cake tin with baking parchment.

2   Spread the pecans out on a baking tray and roast for 10 minutes. Remove from the oven and, when cool enough to handle, roughly chop and place in a large bowl. Set aside until completely cool before adding the parsnips, currants and orange zest.

3   Increase the oven temperature to 210°C/190°C Fan/Gas Mark 6.

4   Place the eggs and sugar in the bowl of an electric mixer with the whisk attachment in place. Beat on a high speed for about 2 minutes, until thick and creamy. With the machine still running, slowly and steadily pour in the oil until it is all combined. Sift the flour, cinnamon, baking powder, bicarbonate of soda, nutmeg, aniseed and salt together into a bowl, then add these to the mixer. Mix to combine, then turn off the machine before folding in the nuts, parsnips, currants and zest.

5   Pour into the tin and bake for about 60 minutes, or until a skewer inserted into the centre comes out clean. Keep a close eye on it after 55 minutes or so, as the cake can go from being still wet in the centre to fully cooked within just a few minutes: you might need to cover the tin with aluminium foil for the last 5 or 10 minutes if it is taking on too much colour. Remove from the oven and set aside until completely cool before removing the cake from the tin.

6   **To make the icing,** place the cream cheese in the bowl of an electric mixer with the paddle attachment in place. Mix on a high speed for 1 minute until smooth, then add the icing sugar to the mixer along with the cream. Continue to mix for 1–2 minutes, until thick, before adding the aniseed and orange zest. Mix until just combined, then transfer to the fridge until ready to use (up to 2 days). On the day of serving, use a palette knife to spread the icing over the top of the cake, gently swirling it as you go.

Beetroot, ginger and soured cream cake

Esme, Yotam's test kitchen colleague, was so convinced by this particular cake that she decided to triple the recipe and slip it in as the middle tier to her wedding cake (chocolate on the bottom tier, for those interested, traditional fruit cake up top).

The addition of the vitamin C tablet helps preserve and 'set' the colour of the beetroot in the cake. It's something Yotam does to preserve the colour of quince in his savoury cooking and the same method works very well here. As you slice the cake open, the streaks of magenta-coloured beetroot will make you smile.

SERVES 6—8

75g walnut halves
200g plain flour
150g caster sugar
2 tsp baking powder
¼ tsp bicarbonate of soda
¼ tsp salt
2 medium raw red beetroot, peeled and coarsely grated (250g)
finely grated zest of 1 large orange (1 tbsp)
100g stem ginger, finely chopped
2 large eggs
60g soured cream
125ml sunflower oil

1 large vitamin C tablet (1500mg), crushed with a pestle and mortar or the back of a spoon to form a fine powder (optional)

ICING
150g cream cheese, at room temperature
60g icing sugar, sifted
70ml double cream
6cm piece of fresh ginger, grated into a fine-mesh sieve placed over a bowl, and the flesh squeezed to extract all the juices (about 20ml)

Use a microplane to grate the ginger, if possible; grating the ginger so finely will really help when trying to extract the juice.

Un-iced, the cake will keep for 3 days at room temperature in an airtight container. Once iced, the cake is best eaten on the same day and any leftovers kept in the fridge for a couple of days. As always, bring it back to room temperature before eating.

1   Preheat the oven to 180°C/160°C Fan/Gas Mark 4. Grease and line a 20cm round cake tin and set aside.

2   Spread the walnuts out on a baking tray and roast for 10 minutes. Remove from the oven and chop into 1cm pieces, then set aside. Increase the oven temperature to 195°C/175°C Fan/Gas Mark 5.

3   Place the flour, sugar, baking powder, bicarbonate of soda and salt in a large mixing bowl and whisk to combine and aerate. Add the beetroot, orange zest, walnuts and stem ginger, but do not stir.

4   Place the eggs and soured cream in another small bowl and whisk to combine. Add the oil and crushed vitamin tablet, if using, and whisk again. Pour over the beetroot and flour mix and, using your hands or a large spatula, mix thoroughly to combine.

5   Pour the mix into the cake tin and bake in the middle of the oven for 50–55 minutes, or until a skewer inserted into the centre of the cake comes out clean. Remove from the oven and set aside for 30 minutes before removing from the tin and setting aside on a wire rack until completely cool. The baking parchment can be left on or removed as you like: the advantage of leaving it on is that the sides will not dry out if you are not eating it straight away.

6   **To make the icing,** place the cream cheese in the bowl of an electric mixer
with the paddle attachment in place and beat for about 10 seconds, until smooth (the
amount of time it takes to become smooth will vary, depending on the consistency
of your cream cheese – see pages 352-3). Add the icing sugar and beat until well
incorporated. Add the cream and beat for about 1 minute, until the icing is thick and
smooth. Add the ginger juice, beat for a final few seconds, then use a palette knife to
spread over the top of the cake, and serve.

Apple and olive oil cake with maple icing

This is such a popular staple on the Ottolenghi cake counter that we've allowed it to make a guest appearance from the pages of the first *Ottolenghi: The Cookbook*. As with all good revival tours, it's bigger and better than ever, second time around.

If you want to do without the maple icing, you can: a dusting of icing sugar also works well. Bear in mind, though, that those customers who return again and again to the same apple and olive oil cake confess that, secretly, the icing is the reason they order it in the first place.

SERVES 10

100g sultanas
275ml water
350g plain flour
½ tsp ground cinnamon
1½ tsp bicarbonate of soda
1½ tsp baking powder
½ tsp salt
3 large Bramley apples (800g)
    (use Granny Smiths, as an alternative)
200g caster sugar
150ml extra virgin olive oil
2 large eggs, lightly beaten,
    plus 2 extra egg whites
scraped seeds of ½ vanilla pod
finely grated zest of 1 lemon (1 tsp)

MAPLE ICING
100g unsalted butter, at room
    temperature, plus extra for greasing
100g soft light brown sugar
85g maple syrup
220g cream cheese

The olive oil gives the cake a depth of flavour and moisture and also means that it lasts a long time (the flavour actually improves after a day or two). Wrapped in cling film, the cake will keep in the fridge (un-iced) for up to a week. Bring it back to room temperature and ice it on the day of serving.

1   Preheat the oven to 180°C/160°C Fan/Gas Mark 4. Grease and line the base and sides of a 23cm round cake tin with baking parchment. The paper should rise 2–3cm above the sides of the tin. Set aside.

2   Place the sultanas and 200ml of water in a medium saucepan. Simmer over a low heat until all the water has been absorbed, then set aside.

3   Sift the flour, cinnamon, bicarbonate of soda, baking powder and salt together into a bowl and set aside. Peel and core the apples, then cut into 2–3cm dice and set aside in a separate bowl.

4   Place the sugar, olive oil, whole eggs, vanilla seeds and lemon zest in the bowl of an electric mixer with the paddle attachment in place. Beat on a medium speed for about 6–7 minutes, until the mix is light in colour, doubled in size and has thickened a little. Don't be tempted to increase the speed of the machine when mixing: this will create air bubbles, which you don't want. Remove the bowl from the machine and use a large spatula to fold in the apples, sultanas and the remaining 75ml of water. Add the sifted dry ingredients and gently fold to combine.

5   Place the egg whites in a separate clean bowl and whisk to form soft peaks: there's only a small amount of egg white here so you might need to do this by hand. Gently but thoroughly fold the egg whites into the cake mix, then scrape the batter into the tin. Level the top with a spatula and bake for 55 minutes (slightly longer if you are using Granny Smiths, as they don't lose their shape as quickly as Bramleys), or until a skewer inserted into the centre of the cake comes out clean. Remove from the oven and set aside to cool in the tin.

6   **Make the icing** while the cake is cooling. Place the butter, sugar and maple syrup in the bowl of an electric mixer with the paddle attachment in place. Beat until light and airy, then add the cream cheese, a quarter at a time. Continue to beat for about 2 minutes, until smooth and thick.

7   When the cake is completely cool, use a large serrated knife to cut it in half horizontally. Spread half the icing over the bottom layer of the cake, then place the other layer back on top. Spoon the remaining icing on top – leave the sides un-iced so that the icing in the middle can be seen – and serve.

Vineyard cake (aka Cleopatra cake)

This cake originally came from Yotam's friend Kit Williams (who herself found it in *Gourmet* magazine) during her time at Baker & Spice. We then adapted it for Valentine's day and called it 'Cleopatra cake', on account of the large bunch of grapes needed for the recipe!

The list of ingredients may seem unlikely in a cake – the olive oil, the sweet fortified wine – but do give it a try. It's not every cake that gets a whole bottle of wine poured into it, and the result – with its intensity of flavour – is really rather special.

SERVES 12

———

500g plain flour, plus extra for dusting
2 tsp baking powder
½ tsp bicarbonate of soda
¾ tsp salt
340g caster sugar
175g unsalted butter, at room temperature, plus extra for greasing
75ml extra virgin olive oil
finely grated zest of 2 lemons (2 tsp)
finely grated zest of 1 medium orange (2 tsp)
scraped seeds of ½ vanilla pod

4 large eggs
450ml Carte Or Muscat de Beaumes de Venise wine, at room temperature
100g seedless red grapes, washed and halved lengthways

TOPPING

70g unsalted butter, at room temperature
70g caster sugar
100g seedless red grapes, washed and halved lengthways

———

1 Preheat the oven to 210°C/190°C Fan/Gas Mark 6. Grease and lightly flour a 25cm round, 10cm deep angel food cake or chiffon tin, tapping away any excess flour.
2 Sift the flour, baking powder, bicarbonate of soda and salt together into a bowl and set aside.
3 Place the sugar in the bowl of an electric food mixer with the paddle attachment in place. Add the butter, olive oil, lemon zest, orange zest and vanilla seeds and mix for 2 minutes, on a medium-high speed, until smooth and fluffy. Add the eggs, one at a time, beating well after each addition. Reduce the speed to low and add a third of the flour mix, followed by half of the wine. Repeat with the remaining flour and wine, finishing with the final third of flour and continuing to mix on a low speed. Once combined, pour into the prepared cake tin and scatter 100g grapes evenly on top. Place in the oven and bake for 20 minutes.
4 **Make the sugar crust topping** while the cake is in the oven. Place the butter and sugar in a small bowl and beat with a wooden spoon to form a thick paste. When the cake has been in the oven for 20 minutes, quickly but gently remove it and dot the sugar crust evenly over the top, breaking it into small pieces as you go. Scatter 100g grapes evenly over the top and return it to the oven. Immediately lower the oven temperature to 180°C/160°C Fan/Gas Mark 4 and continue to bake for another 35–40 minutes, or until a skewer inserted into the centre of the cake comes out clean. Remove from the oven and set aside to cool for 30 minutes before removing from the tin. The cake can either be served straight away or stored in an airtight container.

This cake can only be made in an angel food cake or chiffon tin. The cake is so large that it's only this kind of tin – with the hole built into the middle – that will enable an even bake. Bundt tins will not work because you want the sugar crust and grapes to remain on top when the cake is served, which would not be possible as the bundt tin is inverted.

The cake will keep for up to 5 days in an airtight container at room temperature.

(NF)

Tin can cake part I
Butternut, honey and almond

Part-bread, part-cake, this tin loaf is the first of what we think of as our boy scout or girl guide trilogy: we were not in the woods when they were baked and the fire was not homemade, we know, but there's something timeless and wholesome about loaves baked in a regular tin can. The end result keeps (and freezes) well, so, homemade fire or not, you can at least take it with you to sustain you on a long walk in the woods.

Traditionally, these are made in cylindrical log tins which are about 8cm wide and 17cm high. They used to be more widely available than they are these days. You occasionally see them on eBay, but they're generally considered novel and difficult to come by. Our alternative – regular 400g tin cans – works very well. Baking in a tin gives the loaves such a great shape – so wonderfully sliceable, into thick rounds to share out, like all good scouts should.

You need to open the tins by working with the opener perpendicular to them so that it cuts a slice off the top without leaving a lip. Save the contents in another container for future use, then wash and dry the empty tins. Tins with a ring-pull will leave a little lip which will make it harder to slide the cake out of the tin when it's baked. If you only have tins with a ring-pull, that's fine: just flip them over and open them from the base with a tin opener, as described. *Using a tin opener will make the exposed edges of the tin sharp, so take a lot of care when lining the tins with baking parchment.*

MAKES 2 TIN LOAVES OR 1 LARGER LOAF (USING A REGULAR 900G LOAF TIN)

¼ of a small butternut squash, peeled and cut into roughly 4cm pieces (100g)

125g unsalted butter, at room temperature, cubed; plus a little extra, melted, for brushing; plus extra to serve

100g caster sugar

finely grated zest of 1 small orange (1 tsp)

25g runny honey

1 large egg, beaten

100g raisins

50g toasted flaked almonds

160g self-raising flour

⅛ tsp salt

60ml full-fat milk

You'll need an extra-long skewer (bamboo satay sticks are perfect, if you have them) for inserting into the centre of the tin loaves to check they are ready. We make these cakes in 400g tin cans, but you can also make one larger loaf if you prefer. Use a 900g loaf tin. Just make sure the parchment lining rises about 5cm above the rim of the tin, so that you have some leverage with which to lift it out.

1   Place the squash pieces in a small saucepan and cover with water. Bring to a simmer over a medium-high heat and cook for about 10 minutes, until soft. Strain, then use a fork to mash the squash to a purée.

2   Preheat the oven to 190°C/170°C Fan/Gas Mark 5.

3   Next prepare the two tin cans (see intro, opposite). To line them with baking parchment, use a brush to lightly butter the inside of the two empty, clean tins. Line the round base by tracing around it and cutting out circles of parchment to fit exactly. Use the long handle of a wooden spoon to help you get the circles of parchment into place: this sounds trickier than it is – you'll just need to take care not to cut yourself on the opened ends of the tins. To line the insides of the tins, measure the circumference and height of the tin and then cut a piece of baking parchment paper about 5cm taller than the tin; a slight overlap of the paper is fine.

4   Place the butter, sugar, orange zest and honey in the bowl of an electric mixer with the paddle attachment in place. Mix for about 3 minutes, until light and creamy, then slowly add the beaten egg, stopping to scrape down the sides of the bowl halfway through. The mixture may look slightly curdled at this stage, but don't worry. Add the cooled butternut purée, raisins and almonds and mix on a low speed, to combine. Sift the flour and salt together into a bowl, then add this in batches to the butternut mix, alternating with the milk. Mix on a low speed until just combined, taking care not to over-mix.

5   Dollop this mixture into the tins so that it rises all the way to the top of the tin, not the paper: you'll need to do this by the spoonful, as the batter is quite thick and the tins are narrow. Place the filled tin cans on a baking tray, sitting upright, and bake for about 45–50 minutes (whether baking in the tin cans or in a larger loaf tin), or until a (long) skewer inserted into the centre comes out dry and clean.

6   Remove the baking tray from the oven and set the loaves aside for 15 minutes to cool in their tins before sliding them out. This is easily done by tipping the tins on their sides (use a tea towel to hold them, as they will still be quite hot) and gently tugging at the overhanging parchment paper. The loaf should slide out with the parchment paper around it. Set aside until completely cool before using a serrated knife to cut them into thick slices. They are great just as they are, or toasted – either way, spread them liberally with butter before serving.

The butternut squash can be cooked up to 2 days in advance and stored in the fridge. Cut open and clean 2 tin cans in preparation (see above).

Once made, the loaves will keep for up to 3 days, wrapped in cling film, or frozen for up to 2 months.

Tin can cake part II
Pineapple, pecan and currant

The pineapple rings should be in their own juice for this (rather than syrup). If you can find it, start with crushed canned pineapple so you won't need to blitz up the rings.

MAKES 3 TIN LOAVES OR 1 LARGER LOAF (USING A REGULAR 900G LOAF TIN)

80g pecan halves

1 x 432g tin pineapple rings, in juice (not syrup)

125g unsalted butter, cubed; plus a little extra, melted, for brushing; plus extra to serve

150g demerara sugar

80g currants

2 large eggs, beaten

320g self-raising flour

¼ tsp salt

¼ tsp ground cloves

1   Preheat the oven to 180°C/160°C Fan/Gas Mark 4.

2   Spread the pecans out on a small baking tray and roast for 8 minutes. Remove from the oven and, once cool enough to handle, chop roughly and set aside. Increase the oven temperature to 190°C/170°C Fan/Gas Mark 5.

3   Drain the juice from the pineapple tin – you should have about 150ml – and place in a medium saucepan. Cut each pineapple slice into four and place in a food processor. Use the pulse button so that it is chopped into fine pieces: you want it to have the consistency of crushed pineapple rather than turning it into a purée. Transfer to the saucepan with the juices, along with the butter and sugar. Place over a medium-low heat until the butter and sugar have melted, then increase the heat to medium-high. Bring to the boil and simmer for 4 minutes. Remove from the heat, stir through the currants and set aside for the mixture to cool to room temperature.

4   Meanwhile, carefully line three tin cans with baking parchment (see page 137).

5   When the mixture is at room temperature, add the beaten eggs and stir to combine. Sift the flour, salt and ground cloves together into a bowl, then fold this into the pineapple mixture along with the chopped roasted pecans. Fold until just combined, taking care not to over-work the mixture.

6   Dollop the cake mix into the prepared tins to about three-quarters of the way up the sides: you'll need to do this by the spoonful, as the batter is quite thick and the tins are narrow. Place the filled tin cans on a baking tray, sitting upright, and bake for about 50 minutes (whether baking in the tin cans or in a larger loaf tin), or until a (long) skewer inserted into the centre comes out dry and clean.

7   Remove the baking tray from the oven and set the loaves aside for 15 minutes to cool in their tins before sliding them out. This is easily done by tipping the tins on their sides (use a tea towel to hold them as they will still be quite hot) and gently tugging at the overhanging parchment paper. The loaf should slide out with the parchment paper around it. Serve warm or cold, sliced with a serrated knife into thick slices and spread liberally with butter.

We make these cakes in 400g tin cans, but you can also make one larger loaf if you prefer. Use a 900g loaf tin. Just make sure the parchment lining rises about 5cm above the rim of the tin, so that you have some leverage with which to lift it out. The batter should rise three-quarters of the way up the tin.

Once made, the loaves will keep in an airtight container for up to 3 days, or wrapped in cling film and frozen for up to 2 months. They do dry up a bit over time, so if you are eating them after the first day or so, they're best toasted.

Cut open and clean 3 tin cans in preparation (see page 136).

Tin can cake part III

Banana, date and walnut

MAKES 3 TIN LOAVES OR 1 LARGER LOAF (USING A REGULAR 900G LOAF TIN)

60g walnut halves

200g Medjool dates, pitted and roughly chopped into 2cm pieces

200g soft light brown sugar

60g unsalted butter, cubed; plus a little extra, melted, for brushing; plus extra to serve

180ml water

½ tsp bicarbonate of soda

1 large egg, lightly beaten

1 medium banana, peeled and mashed (100g)

½ tsp vanilla extract

200g self-raising flour

¼ tsp salt

We make these cakes in 400g tin cans, but you can also make one larger loaf if you prefer. Use a 900g loaf tin. Just make sure the parchment lining rises about 5cm above the rim of the tin, so that you have some leverage with which to lift it out. The batter should rise two-thirds of the way up the tin.

Cut open and clean 3 tin cans in preparation (see page 136).

1   Preheat the oven to 180°C/160°C Fan/Gas Mark 4.

2   Spread the walnuts out on a baking tray and roast for 5 minutes. Remove from the oven and, once cool enough to handle, chop roughly and set aside. Increase the oven temperature to 190°C/170°C Fan/Gas Mark 5.

3   Place the dates, sugar, butter and water in a medium saucepan and heat gently, stirring from time to time, until the sugar has dissolved and the butter has melted. Increase the heat, bring the mixture to the boil, then remove from the heat straight away. Transfer the mixture to a large bowl and set aside to cool to room temperature.

4   Meanwhile, carefully line three tin cans with baking parchment (see page 137).

5   Add the bicarbonate of soda, egg, banana and vanilla to the date mixture and beat with a wooden spoon to combine. Add the walnuts, then sift the flour and salt together into the mix. Stir to combine thoroughly but do not over-mix.

6   Dollop the cake mix into the prepared tins to about two-thirds of the way up the sides: you'll need to do this by the spoonful, as the batter is quite thick and the tins are narrow. Place the filled tin cans on a baking tray, sitting upright, and bake for about 35 minutes, or 40 minutes if making one large loaf, or until a (long) skewer inserted into the centre of the cakes comes out clean.

7   Remove the baking tray from the oven and set the loaves aside for 15 minutes to cool in their tins before sliding them out. This is easily done by tipping the tins on their sides (use a tea towel to hold them as they will still be quite hot) and gently tugging at the overhanging parchment paper. The loaf should slide out with the parchment paper around it. Serve warm or cold, sliced with a serrated knife into thick slices and spread liberally with butter.

Grappa fruit cake

The combination of the dried fruit, citrus and vanilla in this cake is reminiscent of the Italian panettone. The similarity ends there, however, with the addition of the yoghurt and oil, which deliver moisture, richness and a cakey texture.

Use the best grappa you can afford: some of the cheaper varieties taste a bit like paint stripper. If you can't get grappa, then brandy, Grand Marnier or Cointreau all work well. If using the candied citron, vodka also works well.

SERVES 10

We've made this in an 18cm wide brioche tin, but you can also make it in a 20cm square tin, if you prefer. Around Easter we make these in individual brioche moulds as an alternative to hot cross buns; a regular muffin tin also works well.

Iced or un-iced, these keep well for up to 4 days in an airtight container. They do become denser over time, but not unpleasantly so – in fact, we actually prefer them a day or two after they are made. The icing won't look as fresh as it does on day one – it becomes a bit wrinkly – but tastes absolutely fine.

unsalted butter, for greasing
50g sultanas
50g currants
30ml good-quality grappa (or one of the alternatives listed above)
70g eggs (2 small eggs), lightly beaten
125g caster sugar
scraped seeds of ½ vanilla pod
60g Greek yoghurt
75ml sunflower oil
finely grated zest of 1 lemon (1 tsp)
35g good-quality mixed peel (or candied citron or orange peel), plus extra to garnish
120g plain flour, plus extra for dusting
½ tsp baking powder
⅛ tsp salt

ICING
120 icing sugar, sifted
1 tbsp lemon juice
1½ tsp grappa (or one of the alternatives listed above)

1   Grease and flour a large brioche or square tin, or the smaller individual tins, and set aside. Preheat the oven to 195°C/175°C Fan/Gas Mark 5.

2   Place the sultanas and currants in a small bowl, pour over the grappa and set aside for 10 minutes.

3   Place the eggs, sugar and vanilla seeds in a large bowl and whisk to combine. Add the yoghurt and oil and whisk again before folding in the lemon zest, sultanas, currants, grappa and mixed peel.

4   Sift the flour, baking powder and salt into the wet mix, stir through to combine, then spoon into the tin. It should rise three-quarters of the way up the sides if making it in one larger tin, or about two-thirds of the way up the sides if making it in smaller tins. Bake for 55 minutes, or about 16 minutes if making in smaller tins, or until a skewer inserted into the centre of the cake comes out clean. Remove from the oven and leave to cool for 30 minutes.

5   **To make the icing,** place the icing sugar, lemon juice and grappa in a bowl and whisk until smooth.

6   Transfer the slightly warm cake(s) from the mould(s) and on to a wire rack. Spread the icing over the top, letting it trickle down the sides and top with chopped candied peel. Serve warm, or set aside to cool and store in an airtight container.

GRAPPA FRUIT CAKE

Lemon and blackcurrant stripe cake

We had a momentary wobble as the recipes for *Sweet* were coming together that there was not enough colour. Yotam ran off to his local grocers to get as many bright berries as he could, and the remit of the week was: colour, colour, colour! This tall, conical showstopper-of-a-cake is one of the happy outcomes. It starts its life, simply, as a flat sponge in a baking tray. Rolled up and covered in silky buttercream, it looks rather like a barrel. Cut into it, however – revealing the stripes! – and it looks like a whole lot of vertically inclined (and very colourful) fun.

See page 349 for the importance of timing when cooking with sugar: this is useful to understand before making the buttercream.

SERVES 8–10 (IT'S NOT A WIDE CAKE – JUST 14CM – BUT IT'S HIGH)

The buttercream can be made up to 3 days in advance and stored in the fridge or freezer: just bring it back to room temperature and quickly whip it in the electric mixer to restore its fluffiness before spreading.

Although the cake is best eaten on the day it's made, any leftovers will be fine the following day if stored in the fridge. As always, bring it back to room temperature before serving.

8 large eggs, whites and yolks
   separated
140g caster sugar, plus an extra 20g
1 tbsp lemon juice (grate the zest
   before juicing)
80g plain flour
⅛ tsp salt
finely grated zest of 1 small lemon
   (¾ tsp)
icing sugar, for dusting

BLACKCURRANT (OR MIXED BERRY) PURÉE
300g blackcurrants (or mixed berries),
   fresh or frozen and defrosted,
   plus an extra 40g to garnish
60g caster sugar

**BLACKCURRANT (OR MIXED BERRY)
BUTTERCREAM**
85g golden syrup (or corn syrup)
120g caster sugar
scraped seeds of ½ vanilla pod
4 large egg yolks
300g unsalted butter, cut into
   3cm cubes, softened
100g berry purée (see above)

1   Preheat the oven to 200°C/180°C Fan/Gas Mark 6. Line a shallow 40 x 32cm baking tray with baking parchment and set aside.

2   Place the egg yolks in the bowl of an electric mixer with the whisk attachment in place. Add 140g sugar and the lemon juice and beat on a medium-high speed for about 3 minutes, until pale and thick. Transfer the mixture to a large mixing bowl and sift the flour and salt directly over the egg mixture in two batches, folding through the mix with a rubber spatula after each addition. Sprinkle the lemon zest on top and set aside.

3   Place the egg whites in a clean bowl of an electric mixer with the whisk attachment in place. Whisk on a medium-high speed until soft peaks form, then slowly drizzle in the extra 20g sugar. Continue to whisk until firm peaks form, then gently fold a third of the egg whites into the egg yolk mixture until incorporated. Finally, fold in the remaining egg whites until combined, then scrape the mixture into the baking tray. Even the top out with a small spatula and bake for 15 minutes, or until the sponge is a light golden brown and a toothpick inserted into the centre comes out clean. Remove from the oven and place on a wire rack to cool in the tray for 5 minutes before dusting the top lightly with icing sugar. Place a clean tea towel on top of the sponge, then flip it over so that the sponge is now lying on top of the tea towel. Carefully peel away the paper and trim the very edges of the sponge. Be careful not to cut away too much: you really just want to straighten out the edges. ››

4   Now, starting at the shorter edge of the sponge, carefully roll it up (along with the tea towel). This is to 'train' the cake, ready for rolling up again later. After about 20 minutes, or when the sponge is no longer warm, unroll the sponge. With the short end facing towards you, measure and cut three equal strips parallel to the long edge, each just under 11cm wide. (If you have a pizza cutter, this is a really easy way to cut the strips.) Cover with a clean tea towel and set aside.

5   **For the purée,** place the blackcurrants or berries and sugar in a medium saucepan and place over a medium-low heat. Warm through for 4–5 minutes, until the blackcurrants or berries have softened and the sugar has dissolved. Transfer to a food processor and blitz to form a purée. Strain through a fine sieve set over a bowl to catch the purée: you need 150g, so save any extra in the fridge to spoon over yoghurt.

6   **To make the buttercream,** place the golden syrup, caster sugar and vanilla seeds in a medium saucepan. Place over a low heat and stir until all the sugar dissolves: this is your sugar syrup.

7   In the meantime, place the egg yolks in the bowl of an electric mixer with the whisk attachment in place. Beat on a medium-high speed until thick and pale lemon in colour. Leave the machine on while you check the sugar syrup: when all the sugar has melted, stir again, increase the heat to medium and simmer until bubbles begin to appear. Swirl the pan gently and continue to simmer until there are large bubbles all over the surface of the syrup. Remove the pan from the heat and carefully pour the hot syrup in a slow, steady stream down the edge of the mixing bowl into the beating yolks. When all the syrup has been added, increase the mixer speed to high and continue to whisk the mixture for about 10 minutes, until the outside of the bowl is no longer warm. Gradually add the butter, one cube at a time, allowing it to be incorporated into the mix before adding the next. When all the butter has been added, scrape down the bowl and continue to whisk for another minute, until the buttercream is very smooth and light. Add 100g blackcurrant (or mixed berry) purée and mix on a medium speed until fully incorporated.

8   **To assemble the cake,** spread each of the strips of sponge with about 80g blackcurrant buttercream: this should leave you with about 300g to ice the top and sides of the cake later. Take one strip of sponge and, starting with the short end, roll it up. Once this strip is rolled, position the exposed end at the beginning of the next strip and keep rolling. Again, once this is rolled – the cylinder will be getting wider now – position the exposed end at the beginning of the last strip and continue to roll. You now have a rolled cylindrical cake! (Imagine, for a moment, if you lined up the three strips end to end to create one very long strip. Then imagine rolling that very long strip up, from one end to the other. You should end up with a coiled barrel shape.) Turn the cylinder on to the serving plate so that it is standing on one of its flat ends.

9   Spread the remaining buttercream all over the top and sides of the cake, smoothing with a spatula to create an even surface. Dribble the remaining 50g of blackcurrant (or mixed berry) purée on top of the cake and top this with the blackcurrants reserved for garnish. Set aside for at least 1 hour at room temperature (or in the fridge if it is a very warm day) before serving.

Rhubarb and strawberry crumble cake

SERVES 12

CRUMBLE
120g unsalted butter, melted
150g soft light brown sugar
190g plain flour
30g desiccated coconut
¼ tsp salt

FRUIT
250g rhubarb (2 or 3 medium sticks),
    cut into 1cm slices
250g strawberries, hulled and sliced
    0.5cm thick
25g soft light brown sugar
30g tapioca flour (or cornflour)
2 tsp lemon juice
scraped seeds of ½ vanilla pod
⅛ tsp salt

CAKE
185g plain flour
¾ tsp baking powder
¼ tsp salt
160g unsalted butter, at room
    temperature, cubed
220g icing sugar
3 large eggs
1 tsp vanilla extract

We make this in a 23cm round tin,
but use a 23cm square tin if that is
what you have. Either way, just make
sure it is springform or a tin with a
removable base.

Once assembled, the cake will keep
for 2 days, wrapped in cling film
or stored in an airtight container.
The fruits may discolour a little, but
this won't affect the taste.

1   Preheat the oven to 200°C/180°C Fan/Gas Mark 6. Lightly grease and line
a 23cm square or round springform tin (or cake tin with a removable base) with
baking parchment and set aside.

2   **For the crumble layer,** place all the ingredients in a large bowl and use your
hands or a wooden spoon to mix: you need to work the mixture quite a lot to get
evenly moist, large crumbs. The consistency will be damper and more pebbly than
you might be expecting, but this is what you want. Set aside.

3   **For the fruit layer,** place all the ingredients in a medium bowl, toss gently
to combine and set aside.

4   **To make the cake,** sift the flour, baking powder and salt together into a bowl
and set aside. Place the butter and icing sugar in the bowl of an electric mixer with
the paddle attachment in place. Beat for about 3 minutes on a medium-high speed,
until light and fluffy. Add the eggs, one at a time, beating well after each addition.
Add the vanilla extract, followed by the dry ingredients and beat until combined.
Turn the machine off as soon as everything is combined, then pour into the lined
cake tin, using a drop spatula or the back of a spoon to even out the surface.
Next, spoon over the fruit mixture and sprinkle evenly with the crumble mixture.

5   Transfer to the oven and bake for about 70 minutes, until the cake is golden
brown on top and a skewer inserted into the centre comes out with just a few
moist crumbs attached. Have a look at the cake 15 or 20 minutes before the end
of cooking: if it looks like it is getting too dark on top, cover the tin with aluminium
foil for the remainder of the cooking, to prevent it taking on any more colour.
Set the cake aside until completely cool before removing from the tin and
transferring to a cake platter to serve.

Coconut, almond and blueberry cake

Take the word 'cake' out of the title here and this pretty much reads like a list of superfoods. All food is super to us, though, particularly when the word cake is added! The cake is a variation of Belinda's Flourless Coconut and Chocolate Cake (see page 190), with the addition of some flour to offset the juiciness of the blueberries. It's super simple and wonderfully moist. It's also versatile, as happy to be served warm for dessert, with some double cream poured over, as it is at room temperature when it's time for tea.

SERVES 10–12

This will keep for up to 3 days in an airtight container or wrapped in aluminium foil. It also freezes well for up to a month.

180g ground almonds
60g desiccated coconut
250g caster sugar
70g self-raising flour
¼ tsp salt
4 large eggs
200g unsalted butter, melted, then set
   aside to come to room temperature

1½ tsp vanilla extract
finely grated zest of 2 lemons (2 tsp)
200g fresh blueberries
20g flaked almonds

1   Grease and line a 23cm round cake tin. Preheat the oven to 180°C/160°C Fan/ Gas Mark 4.

2   Place the almonds, coconut, sugar, flour and salt in a large mixing bowl and whisk to aerate and remove the lumps.

3   Place the eggs in a separate medium bowl and whisk lightly. Add the melted butter, vanilla extract and lemon zest and whisk again until well combined. Pour this into the dry mix and whisk to combine. Fold in 150g blueberries, then pour the mixture into the tin. Sprinkle the last of the blueberries on top, along with the flaked almonds, and bake for 50–55 minutes, or until a skewer inserted into the centre of the cake comes out clean. Keep a close eye on it towards the end of cooking: the relatively large number of eggs in the mix means that it can go from still being a little bit liquid in the centre to being well cooked in just a few minutes.

4   Set aside for 30 minutes before inverting out of the tin, removing the baking parchment and placing the cake the right way up on a serving plate. It can either be served warm with cream or set aside until cool.

Take-home chocolate cake

The recipe for this first appeared in an article written about Helen when she ran her café, the Mortar & Pestle, in Melbourne. Rather intimidatingly for Helen, the headline for the article was: 'World's Best Chocolate Cake'. Nothing like setting the bar high in terms of expectation! All these years on, though, it still stands the test of time.

It could actually be called lots of things: 'world's easiest cake', possibly, requiring nothing more than one large bowl to make it all in. Or 'most versatile cake', given that it can be served un-iced, with just a light dusting of cocoa powder, or dressed up to the nines, as we have done here, with a thin layer of chocolate ganache and served with espresso cinnamon mascarpone cream.

In the shops, however, it just goes by the name 'take-home chocolate cake'. This is because we make it as a smaller cake (as seen in the photo) to be shared by four people after a meal. The name lives on though, even in the recipe for our larger version here. The cake keeps so well that customers would still be able to take home a whole cake, even if there were only four people at the first sitting.

SERVES 12

250g unsalted butter, at room temperature, cut into 2cm cubes, plus extra for greasing
200g dark cooking chocolate (70% cocoa solids), chopped into 2cm pieces
1½ tsp instant coffee granules, dissolved in 350ml boiling water
250g caster sugar
2 large eggs, lightly beaten
2 tsp vanilla extract
240g self-raising flour
30g Dutch-processed cocoa powder, plus 1½ tsp extra for dusting
¼ tsp salt

CHOCOLATE GANACHE (OPTIONAL)
200g dark chocolate (70% cocoa solids), broken or chopped roughly into 2cm pieces
200ml double cream
1 tbsp golden syrup
1 tbsp unsalted butter, softened

ESPRESSO CINNAMON MASCARPONE CREAM (OPTIONAL)
375ml double cream
190g mascarpone
scraped seeds of ½ vanilla pod
2½ tsp finely ground espresso coffee
¾ tsp ground cinnamon
2½ tbsp icing sugar

The ganache can be stored at room temperature, providing it's not too warm, for 3 days, or kept in the fridge for up to 2 weeks. It can also be frozen, although it will lose a bit of its shine when defrosted.

Iced or un-iced, the cake will keep well for 4–5 days in an airtight container.

1   Preheat the oven to 170°C/150°C/Gas Mark 3. Grease a 23cm round cake tin and line with baking parchment, then set aside.

2   Place the butter, chocolate and hot coffee in a large heatproof bowl and mix well until everything is melted, combined and smooth. Whisk in the sugar by hand until dissolved. Add the eggs and vanilla and whisk again until the mix is thoroughly combined and smooth. Sift the flour, cocoa powder and salt together into a bowl and whisk this into the melted chocolate mix. The batter here is liquid, but don't think you have missed something: this is how it should be. Pour the mixture into the prepared cake tin and bake for 60 minutes, or until the cake is cooked and a skewer inserted into the centre comes out clean or with just a few dry crumbs attached. The top will form a crust and crack a little, but don't worry, this is expected. Leave the cake to cool for 20 minutes before removing from the tin, and set aside until completely cool. ››

3   **For the ganache,** place the chocolate pieces in a food processor, blitz until fine and set aside.

4   Put the cream and golden syrup into a small pan and place over a medium-high heat. As soon as bubbles begin to appear – just before it comes to the boil – remove from the heat. Get the food processor running again, with the chocolate still inside, and pour in the hot cream in a steady stream. Process for about 10 seconds, then add the butter. Continue to process until the mixture is shiny and smooth.

5   You can also make the ganache by hand: just make sure the chocolate is chopped fairly finely before you scald the cream and golden syrup and pour it over the chocolate. Stir everything together with a wooden spoon until almost melted, then add the butter. Stir again until the ganache is smooth.

6   Whether you make it in a machine or by hand, use a rubber spatula to scrape the ganache into a bowl and cover with cling film, with the cling film actually touching the top of the ganache. Set aside until it has set to the consistency you want, then use it to ice the cake: if you want a thin layer to spread over the cake, it can be poured over while liquid so that you get an even, light and shiny coating. For a thicker ganache with a spreading consistency, leave it for about 2 hours at room temperature before using a spatula or knife to ice the cake.

7   **If making the espresso cinnamon mascarpone cream,** place all the ingredients in the bowl of an electric food mixer with the whisk attachment in place. Beat for 1–2 minutes until soft peaks form.

8   Divide the cake between plates and spoon the mascarpone cream alongside, if using.

Apricot and almond cake with cinnamon topping

We have used apricots here, but other stoned fruit – plums or peaches, for example – work well if apricots are not in season and you don't want to use tinned. Just make sure the pieces of fruit are not too heavy or large, as you don't want them to sink.

The topping has a way of cooking quite irregularly – buckling here and there on top and sometimes even 'seeping' into the batter below – but don't worry if this happens: it's all part of the cake's rustic charm.

SERVES 10

CINNAMON TOPPING
60g unsalted butter
100g caster sugar
2 tsp ground cinnamon
⅛ tsp salt
2 large eggs, lightly beaten

CAKE
85g unsalted butter, at room temperature
200g caster sugar
2 large eggs

finely grated zest of 1 small lemon (¾ tsp)
1 tsp vanilla extract
¼ tsp almond extract
220g self-raising flour
⅛ tsp salt
160g soured cream
35g ground almonds
8 large apricots (500g), halved and stoned, or 20 tinned apricot halves (500g drained weight)

You don't want to invert the cake here (because of the fruit baked on top), so a springform or other cake tin with a removable base is a must. We've used a round cake tin, but a square tin – with similar dimensions and a removable base – also works well.

Once baked, the cake can be kept in an airtight container for up to 3 days. Warm it in the oven for 10–15 minutes at 200°C/180°C Fan/Gas Mark 6 before serving, if desired.

1   **To make the topping,** melt the butter in a small saucepan and add the sugar, cinnamon and salt. Stir to combine, then remove from the heat. Allow to cool for 5 minutes, stir through the beaten eggs and set aside.

2   Preheat the oven to 195°C/175°C Fan/Gas Mark 5. Grease a 23cm round springform tin and line with baking parchment.

3   **To make the cake,** place the butter and sugar in the bowl of an electric mixer with the paddle attachment in place. Beat on a medium-high speed until light and fluffy, then add the eggs, one at a time, beating well after each addition and scraping down the sides of the bowl a few times. Add the lemon zest, vanilla and almond extract and mix to combine. Sift the flour and salt into a bowl, reduce the speed of the mixer to low and add the dry ingredients to the creamed mix, alternating in batches with the soured cream, so that you begin and end with the flour. Mix to combine, then spoon or scrape the batter into the tin. Smooth over with a spatula or the back of a spoon and sprinkle the ground almonds over the top. Arrange the apricot halves on top, cut side facing up, starting around the outside edge of the tin and working towards the centre, then spoon the cinnamon topping over and around the apricots.

4   Bake for about 1 hour, or until a skewer inserted into the middle of the cake comes out clean (although the topping might still be a bit sticky). Keep an eye on it towards the end of cooking, as it can go from under-cooked to over-cooked very quickly. Set aside for 20 minutes in the tin to cool before removing and serving warm, with some cream alongside.

Pistachio roulade with raspberries and white chocolate

Our technique of 'training' the roulade here (see page 348) is a neat little trick, if you don't know it already. Once you've cracked it (or not, in the case of your sponge), you'll feel like a roulade-making pro.

SERVES 10

The white chocolate cream can be prepared a day in advance and kept in the fridge; remove it from the fridge about 30 minutes before you want to use it, so that it softens up a little.

Once assembled, the cake is best eaten on the same day, although any leftovers will keep in the fridge for up to a day. Allow it to rest at room temperature for 30 minutes before serving.

70g shelled pistachio kernels, plus an extra 15g, roughly chopped
4 large eggs, whites and yolks separated
130g caster sugar
2 tbsp hot water
80g self-raising flour
⅛ tsp salt
⅛ tsp almond extract
20g icing sugar
300g fresh raspberries

WHITE CHOCOLATE CREAM
200g white chocolate buttons, or 200g block of white cooking chocolate, roughly chopped into 1cm pieces
75g unsalted butter, soft but not oily
280g cream cheese
270ml double cream
⅛ tsp almond extract

1   Preheat the oven to 200°C/180°C Fan/Gas Mark 6. Grease a 35 x 30cm shallow baking tray and line with baking parchment.

2   Place 70g of pistachios in the small bowl of a food processor (or use a spice grinder) and grind until fine but not oily: don't worry if there are some medium-sized pieces in the mix, these will not affect the cake. Set aside until needed.

3   Place the egg yolks and sugar in the bowl of an electric mixer with the whisk attachment in place. Mix for about 4 minutes, until thick and creamy. Transfer the mixture to a large bowl and add the hot water, dribbling it down the sides of the bowl. Sprinkle over the ground pistachios and gently fold to combine: don't worry if it's not well mixed at this stage.

4   Sift the flour and salt together into a bowl, then sift again into the egg yolk and pistachio mixture. Fold to combine.

5   Beat the egg whites in a clean bowl of an electric mixer with the whisk attachment in place. Whisk to form soft peaks, then fold into the pistachio mix, a third at a time, along with the almond extract. Scrape the batter into the tray and bake for 15–18 minutes, or until the cake springs back when lightly touched in the centre. Remove the cake from the oven and set aside for 5 minutes.

6   Sift half the icing sugar evenly over the surface of the cake and cover with a clean tea towel. Place a wire rack on top, then flip the cake over, so that the wire rack is now underneath the tea towel and cake. Lift off the tray, carefully peel away the paper and lightly dust the top of the cake with the remaining icing sugar.

7   With one of the short ends of the sponge facing towards you, roll up the still-warm cake with the tea towel inside. Allow the cake to rest for 10 minutes, still rolled up in the tea towel (this 'trains' the cake for the final roll), then unroll the cake and set aside to come to room temperature. Don't worry if the ends of the cake curl up a little or if the surface has some cracks in it: this often happens. ››

8   **Make the chocolate cream** while the cake is cooling. Place the chocolate in a bowl set over a pan of simmering water, making sure the base of the bowl is not touching the water. Stir from time to time until melted, then remove from the heat and set aside to cool slightly. Place the butter in the bowl of an electric mixer with the paddle attachment in place. Beat on a medium-high speed for 30 seconds, until smooth, then add the cream cheese. Beat well to combine, then add the melted chocolate. Continue to beat until smooth before adding the double cream and almond extract. Beat on a medium-high speed until the mixture forms soft waves.

9   When ready to assemble, use a small spatula to spread about two-thirds of the white chocolate cream evenly over the surface of the cake. Leave a border of about 2cm without any cream at the short end of the cake furthest away from you. Place all but twelve of the raspberries evenly on top of the cream, then roll the cake up as you did before, this time without the tea towel inside. Using a long spatula or fish slice, transfer the cake to a long platter. Use a small spatula or butter knife to spread the remaining cream all over the cake, smoothing it out as you go. Place the remaining raspberries along the centre of the cake, and sprinkle with the extra pistachio nuts.

Tropical fruit cake

This is an exceptionally moist cake – almost unusually so, with its bounty of pineapple and banana and the addition of oil. It's known as a 'hummingbird cake' in Australia, New Zealand and Canada, and is traditionally iced with a plain cream cheese icing, but we've added mango purée here: it's not that the cake needs any help – you can eat it without any icing at all, if you like – but we love the chrome-yellow colour it brings to the cake and the way it complements the tropical fruits inside. Piled high with fresh fruit on top, this is an unexpectedly refreshing cake.

Canned pineapple is a fine alternative to fresh, if you prefer. Drain your chunks or slices and proceed, as per the recipe, to chop them in the food processor.

The cream cheese icing can be made a day ahead. In fact, it needs to be refrigerated for at least 2 hours to firm up before covering the cake, so it's good to get ahead.

Un-iced, the cake will keep for around 3 days in an airtight container. Once iced, it is best eaten on the same day. Leftovers can be kept in the fridge for a day or two: just bring the cake back to room temperature before serving.

SERVES 8

—

1 medium pineapple, peeled and core removed: 300g of the flesh should be cut into 3–4cm chunks for the cake, 50g of the flesh should be cut into 2–3cm chunks for the garnish
2 large eggs
1 tsp vanilla extract
100g soft light brown sugar
100g caster sugar
160ml sunflower oil
2 ripe bananas, peeled and mashed (150g)
45g desiccated coconut
225g plain flour
1 tsp bicarbonate of soda
½ tsp ground cinnamon
½ tsp ground ginger
½ tsp ground cardamom
½ tsp salt

ICING

¼ of a large ripe mango, peeled and roughly chopped (50g)
65g unsalted butter, at room temperature
100g cream cheese
75g icing sugar, sifted

TO GARNISH

½ banana, cut into roughly 1cm pieces (50g)
⅓ of a large ripe mango, flesh cut into long, thin strips (70g)
50g pineapple flesh (see above)
scooped out seeds of 1 passionfruit
20g flaked coconut

—

1   Preheat the oven to 200°C/180°C Fan/Gas Mark 6. Grease and line the base and sides of a 20cm round springform tin with baking parchment and set aside.

2   Place 300g of pineapple flesh in a food processor and use the pulse button to crush the fruit: it should be finely chopped but not become a purée. If starting with fresh pineapple, tip the finely chopped flesh into a medium saucepan and place over a medium heat. Bring to a simmer, cook for 4–5 minutes (taking care that it does not boil vigorously, as this will cause too much of the liquid to evaporate), then transfer to a large mixing bowl (large enough to mix the whole cake in later) to cool. If you are starting with canned pineapple you can skip this boiling stage.

3   Place the eggs, vanilla, soft brown sugar and caster sugar in the bowl of an electric mixer with the whisk attachment in place. Whisk together for about 3 minutes, until creamy, then, with the machine on a medium speed, pour in the oil in a slow and steady stream until combined. Add this to the bowl of cooled pineapple along with the mashed bananas and desiccated coconut. Stir to combine. ››

4 Sift the flour, bicarbonate of soda, spices and salt together into the wet mix and use a large rubber spatula to fold until just combined. Pour into the cake tin and bake for about 40 minutes, until nicely browned. Reduce the oven temperature to 180°C/160°C Fan/Gas Mark 4 and continue to cook for 10–15 minutes, or until a skewer inserted into the centre comes out clean. Remove the cake from the oven and leave to cool in its tin for about an hour on a wire rack. Turn out on to a serving platter, carefully remove the paper, then set aside to cool completely.

5 **To make the icing,** place the mango flesh in the small bowl of a food processor and blitz to form a fine purée. Tip out into a small bowl and set aside. Add the butter and cream cheese to the food processor – there is no need to wash the bowl – and process until smooth. Add the icing sugar, pulse to combine, then add the mango purée. Pulse again until evenly mixed and scrape into a bowl. Keep in the fridge, covered, for at least 2 hours – it needs this time to thicken – before icing the cake.

6 When ready to serve, use a small spatula or knife to spread a thick layer of the mango icing all over the top and sides of the cake. Place all the fruit for garnish in a small bowl, mix gently, then spoon it into the centre of the cake: you want it to be piled up in the middle, rather than spread evenly over the top. Finish by pressing the flaked coconut into just the sides of the cake, and serve.

Pistachio and rose water semolina cake

Making this cake is a labour of love, but that's only appropriate, we think, for a cake adorned with rose petals. If you want to save time, however, you can do without the petals or use shop-bought dried rose petals: the cake and cream are both special enough for those you feed to know you love them. If you are going all-out with the roses, red or pink petals is a matter of preference: the red petals will turn a deep purple once candied.

SERVES 10–12

The cake keeps well for up to 5 days in an airtight container. The rose petals should be sprinkled over just before serving.

3 cardamom pods
150g shelled pistachio kernels, plus an extra 20g, finely chopped, to serve
100g ground almonds
170g fine semolina
1¼ tsp baking powder
¼ tsp salt
300g unsalted butter, at room temperature, cubed, plus extra for greasing
330g caster sugar
4 large eggs, lightly whisked
finely grated zest of 1 lemon (1 tsp), plus 1 tbsp lemon juice
2 tbsp rose water (not rose essence, see pages 355-6)
½ tsp vanilla extract

CREAM
200g Greek yoghurt
200g crème fraîche
1 tbsp icing sugar
1 tbsp rose water

SYRUP
100ml lemon juice
80ml rose water
100g caster sugar

CRYSTALLIZED ROSE PETALS (IF USING)
1 large egg white
10g pesticide-free red or pink rose petals (about 40 medium rose petals)
25g caster sugar

1   Preheat the oven to 100°C/80°C Fan/Gas Mark ¼. Line a baking tray with baking parchment, and grease a 23cm springform cake tin and line with baking parchment.

2   **To crystallize the rose petals,** if doing so, whisk the egg white by hand until frothy, then, using a small pastry brush or paintbrush, very lightly paint over both sides of each petal with the egg white: do this in two or three small batches, brushing and then sprinkling lightly over both sides with the sugar. Shake off the excess sugar and lay the petals on the lined baking tray. Place in the oven for 30 minutes, until dry and crunchy, then set aside to cool.

3   Increase the oven temperature to 180°C/160°C Fan/Gas Mark 4.

4   Use the flat side of a large knife to crush the cardamom pods and place the seeds in the small bowl of a food processor: you'll have just under ¼ teaspoon of seeds. The pods can be discarded. Add the pistachios and blitz until the nuts are finely ground – the black cardamom seeds won't really grind down – then transfer to a bowl. Add the ground almonds, semolina, baking powder and salt. Mix together and set aside. ››

5   Place the butter and sugar in the bowl of an electric mixer with the paddle attachment in place. Beat on a medium-high speed until fully combined, but take care not to over-work: you don't want to incorporate a lot of air into the mix. With the machine still running, slowly add the eggs, scraping down the sides of the bowl a few times and making sure that each batch is fully incorporated before adding the next. The mix will curdle once the eggs are added, but don't worry: this will not affect the end result.

6   Remove the bowl from the machine and add the dry ingredients, folding them in by hand and, again, taking care not to over-mix. Next fold in the lemon zest, juice, rose water and vanilla and scrape the batter into the tin. Level with a palette knife and bake for about 55–60 minutes, or until a skewer inserted into the centre of the cake comes out clean but oily.

7   **Make the cream** while the cake is in the oven. Place all the ingredients for the cream in a bowl and use a hand-held whisk to whip everything together for about 2 minutes, until thick. Keep in the fridge until ready to serve.

8   **Start to make the syrup** about 10 minutes before the cake comes out of the oven: you want it to be warm when the cake is ready. Place all the ingredients for the syrup in a small saucepan over a medium heat. Bring to the boil, stirring so that the sugar dissolves, then remove from the heat: don't worry that the consistency is thinner than you might expect, this is how it should be.

9   As soon as the cake comes out of the oven, drizzle all of the syrup over the top. It is a lot of syrup, but don't lose your nerve: the cake can take it! Sprinkle over the finely chopped pistachios and set the cake aside in its tin to come to room temperature. Remove from the tin and scatter the rose petals over the cake. Serve with a generous spoonful of cream alongside.

Festive fruit cake

We sell this cake at Christmas and Easter time in the shop. It's also a good base for a wedding (or any other festive) cake. The very small amount of ground almonds in the batter helps to bind it, as well as adding to the shelf life. The inclusion of alcohol is not traditional in an Easter cake, but we find the combination of dried fruit and booze very hard to resist. Get the best-quality dried fruit you can for this: it makes all the difference.

SERVES ABOUT 20

This can be made in either an 18cm square or 20cm round cake tin. A blowtorch is handy here, to scorch the top of the marzipan alternatively, you can put the cake under a hot grill.

The fruit needs to be macerated for 24–48 hours before baking. The cake itself needs to sit for at least a day before decorating and serving, however, the flavours will develop over time, so ideally make it a week in advance and store in an airtight container.

Once iced, the cake will keep for up to 3 months in an airtight container.

200g plain flour
15g ground almonds
⅓ tsp bicarbonate of soda
¾ tsp mixed spice
¾ tsp ground cinnamon
⅓ tsp nutmeg
¼ tsp salt
150g unsalted butter, at room temperature, cut into 2cm cubes, plus extra for greasing
120g soft dark brown sugar
finely grated zest of 1 lemon (1 tsp)
finely grated zest of 1 small orange (1 tsp)
15g black treacle or molasses
25g fine-cut or no-peel orange marmalade
2 large eggs, beaten, plus 1 extra egg, lightly beaten, for folding through at the end
35ml brandy
35ml dark rum

FRUIT MIX
140g currants
380g raisins
120g ready-to-eat, soft dried apricots, tough stems removed and roughly chopped
5 Medjool dates, pitted and roughly chopped (75g)
75g pitted prunes, roughly chopped
75g glacé cherries, roughly chopped
100g best-quality mixed peel (or candied orange peel)
75ml dark rum
75ml brandy

TOPPING
60g fine-cut or no-peel orange marmalade (if you only have thick cut, just finely chop the pieces of orange)
300g golden marzipan (25–30% almonds)

1   **To make the fruit mix,** place all the fruit in a large container with a lid. Pour over the rum and brandy and mix well. Cover and leave at room temperature for 24–48 hours, shaking the container every few hours.

2   Preheat the oven to 160°C/140°C Fan/Gas Mark 3. Grease an 18cm square or 20cm round cake tin and line the base and sides with two layers of parchment paper. Allow for enough paper so that it rises over and above the top edge of the tin by 5cm. Having two layers will insulate the cake from the heat of the metal tin so that the sides don't cook too quickly. Set aside until needed.

3   **To make the cake,** place the flour, ground almonds, bicarbonate of soda, spices and salt in a medium bowl. Use a hand whisk to stir until any lumps in the almonds are broken up. ››

4   Place the butter, sugar and both zests in the bowl of an electric mixer with the paddle attachment in place. Beat on a medium-high speed for 2–3 minutes, until pale and well combined. Add the treacle and marmalade and mix to combine. Add the 2 eggs gradually, mixing well after each addition, until fully incorporated, scraping down the sides of the bowl. Reduce the speed to low and slowly add the dry ingredients. Mix until just combined, then add the macerated fruit. Gently mix, then remove the bowl from the mixer. Use a wooden spoon to fold through the last egg.

5   Spoon the cake mix into the prepared tin and use a spatula to make a slight dip in the centre of the batter to ensure an even top on the cake once it is cooked. Bake for between 2 hours and 2 hours 15 minutes, or until a skewer inserted into the centre of the cake comes out clean (cover with foil if the cake looks like it is taking on too much colour).

6   Mix together the brandy and rum in a bowl and set aside. As soon as the cake comes out of the oven, brush the alcohol over the top until it's all soaked in. Set aside until completely cool and store in an airtight container (for 1 week, ideally) before decorating.

7   **For the topping,** spread all but ½ teaspoon of the marmalade over the top of the cake to form a thin layer. On a work surface which has been lightly sprinkled with icing sugar, roll out the marzipan to 0.5cm thick. Use the base of the cake tin to cut out a square or circle the same size as the cake and lay this on top of the cake. Gently press to seal it to the marmalade, then use the remaining marzipan to make twelve small balls, about 5g each. Dip the base of the balls in the remaining marmalade and stick them on to the cake, three balls in each corner; if you are making a round cake, put three balls in the middle of the cake and space the remaining balls around the edge of the cake.

8   If you have a blowtorch, lightly scorch the top of the cake and balls to give the marzipan some colour. Alternatively, you can place the cake under a hot grill for a few minutes: just keep a close eye on it so that it doesn't take on too much colour.

Flourless chocolate layer cake with coffee, walnuts and rose water

This started life as a roulade. Having no flour in it, though, it was so delicate that, rather than rolling into neat layers, it kept cracking into three more-or-less even layers. It looked so great in its deconstructed form that we decided to convert it into a layer cake. Don't despair if something doesn't go according to plan A in the kitchen – plan B can be even better! The pairing of the coffee with rose water might seem a bit odd but, actually, Turkish delight is commonly eaten alongside strong black coffee.

As always with nuts – but particularly with walnuts – taste your batch before you start baking. The range in quality can be huge and will make or break the taste of the cake. You'll know by just trying one nut whether you're on to a good thing. Don't be put off by the large amount of walnuts required here: there's a lot of richness in the otherwise delicate sponge and cream which the nuts balance out.

SERVES 8

CAKE
120g walnut halves

6 large eggs, whites and yolks
    separated

215g caster sugar

215g dark cooking chocolate
    (70% cocoa solids), roughly chopped
    or broken up

2½ tsp instant coffee granules

50ml hot water

CARAMELIZED WALNUT TOPPING
30g caster sugar

40g walnut halves, roughly chopped

ROSE WATER CREAM
380ml double cream

2½ tbsp icing sugar

1½ tbsp rose water (not rose essence,
    see pages 355-6)

The cake is best eaten on the day it is made. Any leftovers can be stored in the fridge, wrapped in cling film, where it will keep for up to 2 days. Remove from the fridge at least 30 minutes before serving, so that it is not fridge-cold.

1   Preheat the oven to 180°C/160°C Fan/Gas Mark 4. Grease a 35 x 25cm Swiss roll tin and line with baking parchment, then set aside.

2   Spread 120g walnuts out on a baking tray and roast for 8 minutes. Set aside to cool, then roughly chop and set aside until assembling the cake. Increase the oven temperature to 200°C/180°C Fan/Gas Mark 6.

3   **To make the cake,** place the yolks in the bowl of an electric mixer with the whisk attachment in place. Beat on a medium-high speed and, with the machine still running, gradually add the sugar. Continue to beat until the mixture is thick, lighter in colour and trebled in volume.

4   While the yolks are beating, place the chocolate pieces in a large heatproof bowl set over a pan of simmering water, making sure the base of the bowl is not touching the water. Place the coffee granules in a small cup and dissolve in 50ml hot water. Add the coffee to the chocolate and stir gently (it will seize up if you stir too often or too vigorously) until the chocolate has completely melted. Turn off the heat and fold the yolk and sugar mix into the chocolate mixture in three batches.

5   Place the egg whites in a clean bowl of an electric mixer with the whisk attachment in place. Whisk on a high speed until stiff peaks form, then fold gently into the chocolate mix. Scrape the mixture into the tin, spreading over the surface so that it is even. Bake for 20 minutes, until cooked through and a skewer inserted into the centre comes out clean, then set aside to cool completely. ››

6   **To caramelize the walnuts,** line a small baking tray (with a lipped edge) with baking parchment. Place the sugar and 40g walnuts in a small sauté or frying pan and cook over a medium-high heat until the sugar begins to melt and turn a pale amber colour. Use a spatula to stir the walnuts and sugar together, so that the walnuts are evenly coated. Continue to cook for another 5 minutes, until the caramel is a dark amber and the walnuts are golden brown. Remove from the heat and pour on to the lined tray. Set aside to cool, then roughly break any clumps of walnuts into smaller pieces. You can make these in advance and store them in an airtight container.

7   **Make the rose water cream** once the cake is cool. Place all the ingredients for the cream in the bowl of an electric mixer with the whisk attachment in place. Whip until soft peaks form, then set aside in the fridge until ready to assemble the cake.

8   Turn the cooled cake out on to a chopping board and remove the tin and paper. Place a second chopping board on top of the cake and flip it back over, so that the crust side of the cake is facing upwards. Trim about 0.5cm off the short edges of the cake, then cut the sponge into three even pieces, each about 25 x 11cm. Carefully transfer one piece of cake on to a serving platter and spread one-third of the rose water cream evenly over the surface of the cake. Sprinkle half the roasted walnuts over the cream and place another layer of sponge on top. Repeat with the cream and remaining walnuts, then place the final layer of sponge on top. Dollop and spread the remaining cream on top of the cake. Sprinkle the caramelized walnuts on top of the cream and serve.

Louise cake with plum and coconut

This is inspired by (but completely different to!) the 'Louise' cake: a hugely popular tea time treat in New Zealand. More of a slice than a cake, it's traditionally made with a thin cakey bottom, a spread of raspberry jam in the middle and a thin layer of coconut meringue on top. We've kept the layers theme but rung a lot of changes.

We sell this in our shops as a 'summer slice', using the best stone fruits, from peaches to apricots to cherries, depending on what's in season. Whichever fruit you use, it needs to be ripe but not too soft.

SERVES 9

Traditionally, Louise cakes are baked in rectangular tins and cut into fairly thin squares. We've made ours in a high-sided 20cm square tin with a removable base. The resulting slices are about three times the height of the original. We love the height – it makes everyone feel like a kid when presented with a slice – but you can also make it in a 23cm round springform tin instead, if necessary. Wedges are not as neat to cut as squares, but the cake will still work well.

The cake is at its best on the day it's made, but is absolutely fine kept for up to 2 days in an airtight container in the fridge. The plum juice will make the base a bit soggy after day one, but this won't affect the taste.

125g unsalted butter, at room temperature, cut into 2cm cubes
100g caster sugar
finely grated zest of 1 lemon (1 tsp)
3 large egg yolks
125g plain flour
1½ tsp baking powder
¼ tsp salt
20g desiccated coconut
80ml whole milk
1 tsp vanilla extract
5 medium dark red plums, ripe but firm (450g), or peaches, apricots, cherries, etc.

MERINGUE
60g flaked almonds
140g egg whites (from 3½ large eggs)
⅛ tsp salt
185g caster sugar
1 tsp vanilla extract
1 tsp white wine vinegar
1 tsp cornflour

1   Preheat the oven to 170°C/150°C Fan/Gas Mark 3.

2   Spread out the flaked almonds for the meringue on a baking tray and roast for 10 minutes, until they are a light golden brown. Remove from the oven and set aside to cool.

3   Increase the oven temperature to 185°C/165°C Fan/Gas Mark 5. Line the base and sides of a high-sided 20cm square or 23cm round tin (with a removable base) with baking parchment.

4   Place the butter, sugar and lemon zest in the bowl of an electric mixer with the paddle attachment in place. Beat on a medium-high speed, until light and creamy. Add the egg yolks, one at a time, and beat until combined. Sift the flour, baking powder and salt together into a bowl. Add the coconut and stir to combine. With the machine on a low speed, gradually add the dry ingredients to the butter mix, alternating with the milk and vanilla. Scrape the batter into the prepared tin – it will only rise about a fifth of the way up the sides – and smooth the top evenly. Place in the oven and cook for 25 minutes, until the cake is fully cooked and a skewer inserted into the centre comes out clean.

5   Meanwhile, prepare the plums. Slice each plum vertically in half. Discard the stones and slice each half into four segments so that you have eight segments per plum and forty segments in total. If you start with a larger quantity of smaller plums, or another smaller stone fruit like cherries, then just quarter each fruit. ››

6 When the cake is cooked, remove it from the oven and turn the temperature up to 200°C/180°C Fan/Gas Mark 6. Gently lay the plum segments on top of the cake, close together and cut side down. Don't overlap the fruit, though, as this will make the middle layer too watery.

7 **To make the meringue,** place the egg whites and salt in a clean bowl of an electric mixer with the whisk attachment in place. Beat on a medium-high speed for about 1 minute until soft peaks form. Add the sugar, a tablespoon at a time, and continue to whisk on a high speed until the egg whites are stiff and glossy. Add the vanilla, vinegar and cornflour and whisk again until combined. Finally, fold in the toasted flaked almonds.

8 Scrape the meringue into the cake tin, on top of the plums, and spread out evenly over the fruit. Swirl the meringue around so you get rough waves and peaks, then place in the oven. Immediately lower the oven temperature to 180°C/160°C Fan/Gas Mark 4 and bake for 35 minutes, or until the meringue has formed a hard crust and is just beginning to brown. Remove from the oven and allow to cool in the cake tin for at least 30 minutes before pushing up the removable base to release the cake. Peel away the parchment paper, place on a platter, and serve.

Almond butter cake with cardamom and baked plums

When Helen was working as a pastry chef at Donovan's restaurant in Melbourne, there was a seriously VIP reservation: Stephanie Alexander and Maggie Beer – both big names on the Australian food scene – were in for the evening, having supper together. Nervous about what to bake for such a special occasion, Helen pounced upon a fresh batch of Morello cherries, which she decided to serve along with this cake. The dish got the double thumbs-up, so a new recipe – and Helen's day – was made. Fresh Morello cherries are not always easy to come by, so we've switched to baked plums, which work wonderfully well. Use the cherries if you can find them (they also come in jars), but don't be tempted to use regular black cherries: they don't have the flavour or acidity needed for cooking. Poached quince are also lovely.

For notes on the important difference between almond paste and marzipan, see pages 351 and 354.

SERVES 8–10

BAKED PLUMS
650g plums (about 8–10)
100ml dry white wine
80g caster sugar
10 whole cardamom pods, roughly crushed in a pestle and mortar
¼ tsp ground cinnamon
1 long strip of orange peel
100ml water

CAKE
200g almond paste, broken into 4 or 5 pieces

200g caster sugar
250g unsalted butter, at room temperature
finely grated zest of 1 large orange (1 tbsp)
¾ tsp freshly ground cardamom (see pages 351–2)
6 large eggs
⅛ tsp almond extract
140g plain flour
20g cornflour
1½ tsp baking powder
¼ tsp salt

The plums can be baked up to 3 days in advance and warmed through (for 10 minutes at 200°C/180°C Fan/Gas Mark 6) before serving.

The cake will keep for up to 3 days, wrapped in cling film or aluminium foil at room temperature.

---

1   Preheat the oven to 200°C/180°C Fan/Gas Mark 6. Place the plums in an even layer in a small 22 x 16cm ovenproof baking dish and set aside.

2   Place the white wine, sugar, cardamom, cinnamon, orange peel and water in a medium saucepan and bring to the boil. Remove from the heat and carefully pour over the plums. Cover the dish tightly with aluminium foil and bake for 20–40 minutes – the cooking time depends on the size and ripeness of the plums – or until they are soft but still whole: you can check their softness with a skewer. Set aside, covered, until required. The plums can be served warm or at room temperature.

3   Reduce the oven temperature to 180°C/160°C Fan/Gas Mark 4.

4   **To make the cake,** grease and flour a 23cm bundt tin. Place the almond paste in the bowl of an electric mixer with the paddle attachment in place, add the sugar and beat on a medium-low speed for about 3 minutes, for the almond paste to break up. Add the butter, orange zest and ground cardamom and continue to beat. Add the eggs, one at a time, beating well between each addition and scraping down the sides of the beater and bowl from time to time. Add the almond extract and beat to combine. Sift the flour, cornflour, baking powder and salt together into a bowl and add this to the creamed mix, beating on a medium-low speed until just combined.

5   Scrape the mixture into the bundt tin and bake for 50–55 minutes, or until a skewer inserted into the centre of the cake comes out clean. Remove from the oven and set aside to cool in the tin for 15 minutes before inverting on to a cake platter. Serve fresh from the oven, or at room temperature, with the baked plums and juices alongside. Remember that the stone has not been removed from the plums – serving them as they are is part of the rustic nature of the dish – so watch out! If you do want to remove the stones, just break the plums open and do so before serving.

Pineapple and star anise chiffon cake

This cake is as light as it is large – the benefit being, of course, that everyone can have a great big slice and still be able to bounce away from the table. The light and billowy texture is a result of both the lack of butter (in the cake and the icing) and the whisked egg whites being folded (with all their aeration) into the batter just before baking.

The pineapple 'flowers' look great and don't require any fancy kit, but the cake works fine without them if it's a step too far. You've got the pineapple there, though, so we encourage you to give them a try! As an alternative, some julienned strips of orange zest or whole star anise (for decoration, rather than eating) work well.

This is a cake which delivers in all areas: packed with flavour, light as a dream and a complete 'wow' to look at. Get hold of your chiffon cake tin, shape your pineapple slices into flowers, then get your head around the double negatives in the Kit Note. The rest is just a good old-fashioned cake.

SERVES 12

It's very important to use a 23 or 24cm chiffon cake tin with a removable base, and which is not non-stick. Double negatives do funny things to the brain, we know, but it's a really vital point. Once the cake comes out of the oven, the tin is turned upside down before the cake is left to cool. If you have a non-stick tin, the cake will slip down on to the surface of the counter; you want the cake to be stuck to the tin, elevated by the little legs of the chiffon tin. The cake will seep down a little towards the surface – that's fine: it just needs to not be touching it. If your tin does not have little legs, raise it off the surface using a few cups to rest the edge of the tin on. So, to clarify: don't start with a non-stick tin (start with a not non-stick one!) and don't grease it. It's crucial for the success of the cake.

The flowers can be made a day in advance and kept in a cool, dry place until needed: don't store them in an airtight container or they will go soft.

Un-iced, the cake will keep for up to 3 days, wrapped in foil or in a very large airtight container. Once iced, it's best eaten on the same day.

1 large pineapple (about 1.2kg), peeled and core removed: two-thirds of the flesh roughly chopped (400g net) for the cake; the other third, unchopped (200g), is used for the pineapple flowers
225g self-raising flour
240g caster sugar, plus an extra 50g for the egg whites
1½ tsp ground star anise (or 3 whole star anise, blitzed in a spice grinder and passed through a fine-mesh sieve), plus extra to garnish
½ tsp salt
125ml sunflower oil
130g egg yolks and 300g egg whites, separated (from 7 or 8 large eggs)
finely grated zest of 2 large oranges (2 tbsp)
scraped seeds of ½ vanilla pod
1¼ tsp cream of tartar

ICING
300g icing sugar ('pure' icing sugar is best here, if you can get hold of it – see page 356), sifted
60ml pineapple juice (from the large pineapple above)

DRIED PINEAPPLE FLOWERS
30g caster sugar
30ml water
⅓ of a large pineapple (see above), sliced widthways as thinly as you can without tearing the slices: a serrated bread knife works well. Ideally, you'll get 10–12 slices, about 1–2mm thick

1   Preheat the oven to 200°C/180°C Fan/Gas Mark 6.

2   Place the 400g chopped pineapple in a food processor and blitz to form a fine purée. Transfer to a medium saucepan and bring to the boil over a medium-high heat. Simmer for 3 minutes, then remove from the heat. Reserve 200g of the purée for the cake and set aside to cool. Strain the remaining 200g through a fine-mesh sieve placed over a bowl to get the 60ml you need for the icing. If you fall short of 60ml, just make it up with water or orange juice. ››

3   Place the flour, 240g of sugar, ground star anise and salt in a large mixing bowl and whisk to combine and aerate. Make a well in the centre and add the 200g of pineapple purée, sunflower oil, egg yolks, orange zest and vanilla seeds. Whisk the eggs and liquids together before gently drawing in the dry ingredients to form a smooth batter.

4   Place the egg whites in the bowl of an electric mixer with the whisk attachment in place. Beat on a high speed for about 30 seconds, until frothy, then add the cream of tartar. Continue to beat until soft peaks form, then gradually sprinkle in the extra 50g sugar. Continue to beat for about 5 minutes, until stiff, glossy peaks form. Use a large whisk or rubber spatula to gently but thoroughly fold the meringue into the batter, until the mixture is well combined and there are no streaks of meringue visible.

5   Pour the batter into the ungreased chiffon cake tin (see Kit Note on page 179 for the importance of not greasing the tin) – the mixture should reach up to 3–4cm from the top of the tin – and bake for 50 minutes, or until a skewer inserted into the centre of the cake comes out clean. Cover with aluminium foil for the last 25 minutes or so, if it looks as though your cake is taking on too much colour. Remove from the oven and immediately invert the tin: don't worry if the removable base slips down a little when the cake is turned over: the cake will still stay suspended because the tin is not greased. Set aside for at least 1 hour, in its tin, until completely cool. Reduce the oven temperature to 120°C/100°C Fan/Gas Mark ½.

6   **To make the icing,** place the sifted icing sugar into a bowl and add the 60ml pineapple juice. Stir with a wooden spoon until smooth and set aside.

7   **To make the pineapple flowers,** place the sugar and water in a small saucepan over a medium heat and heat gently until the sugar has dissolved. Increase the heat to high, boil hard for 30 seconds, then remove from the heat. Lightly brush both sides of the pineapple slices with the warm syrup, then lay them on a wire rack placed over a parchment-lined baking tray. Place the tray in the oven and bake for 1–2 hours (the cooking time varies hugely depending on how ripe the pineapple is), until the slices are golden and completely dry but still have some malleability.

8   Remove the trays from the oven and immediately shape the slices either over the moulds of an egg carton or inside the moulds of a muffin tin, to form little cups. Set aside to cool as they are – sitting on top of or inside their moulds – to firm up.

9   When the cake is cooled, turn the tin the right way round again and, using a long metal spatula, loosen the cake from the sides and base of the tin, as well as the central tube (you might need a long, thin knife to help you with this). Invert the cake back on to a serving plate. Drizzle the icing over the top and sides and place the pineapple flowers randomly all over the cake. Sprinkle with star anise and serve.

Coffee and cardamom pound cake

These next two (companion) recipes are adapted from the 'Perfect Pound Cake' recipe in Rose Levy Beranbaum's *Cake Bible*. As it really is a perfect pound cake – moist and close-textured – it's hard to do anything other than follow Rose's exact method. We diverge on one point, though: while Rose says that the cake doesn't work in a large tin, we find that baking it in a bundt tin – where the tube in the middle enables the heat to distribute evenly through the cake as it bakes – works just fine.

We've gone for two versions here: this one has a more 'adult' flavour, with the coffee and cardamom, while the other, based on the Neapolitan ice cream theme, is more family-friendly.

This is best served once completely cool, to allow the flavours to develop. In an ideal world you'd make it in the morning and serve it about six or eight hours after baking. We know that the difference between the ideal and the reality is often great, however, so don't lose sleep over a few hours here and there.

Un-iced, the cake will keep at room temperature for up to 3 days, wrapped in cling film. It can also be frozen for up to 3 months. Once iced, it's best eaten on the same day.

NF

SERVES 10–12

90ml full-fat milk, at room temperature, plus an extra 20ml for the coffee
6 large eggs, at room temperature
2 tsp vanilla extract
200g self-raising flour
100g plain flour, plus extra for dusting
½ tsp salt
300g caster sugar
300g unsalted butter, soft but not oily, diced, plus extra for greasing
1½ tsp freshly ground cardamom (see pages 351–2)
1½ tbsp instant coffee granules
2 tsp Dutch-processed cocoa powder

ICING

1½ tbsp instant coffee granules
45ml full-fat milk, warmed
240g icing sugar, sifted
30g unsalted butter, softened

1   Preheat the oven to 195°C/175°C Fan/Gas Mark 5. Grease and flour a 23cm bundt tin and set aside.

2   **For the cake,** place the milk, eggs and vanilla extract in a medium bowl and lightly whisk, just to combine.

3   Sift the flours and salt directly into the bowl of an electric mixer with the paddle attachment in place, then add the sugar and mix on a low speed for 30 seconds. Add the butter and half of the egg mixture and continue to mix until the dry ingredients are incorporated. Increase the speed to medium and beat for 1 minute. Scrape down the sides of the bowl, then gradually add the remaining egg mixture, in two batches, making sure the first batch is fully incorporated before adding the next. Don't worry if your batter looks slightly split: it's due to the large proportion of eggs in the mix, but it won't affect the final result. ››

4   Scrape down the sides of the bowl and divide the mixture between two bowls. Add the ground cardamom to one bowl and fold to combine. Warm the extra 20ml of milk in a small saucepan, then place in a small bowl with the coffee granules and cocoa powder. Stir until the coffee dissolves and the consistency is that of thick but pourable milk. Combine this with the cake mixture in the second bowl.

5   Spoon the two mixtures into the prepared tin in four alternate blocks, two of each colour, then use a skewer or small knife to make a zigzag-shaped swirl once through the mix, to create a marble effect. Do not be tempted to overdo the swirling as you will lose the effect of the marbling.

6   Bake for 40–45 minutes, or until a skewer inserted into the centre of the cake comes out clean. Remove from the oven and set aside for 10 minutes. The cake tends to dome in the oven, so if this happens and you want a perfectly flat base (the top will become the bottom once it's inverted), just slice off the top to flatten it out before turning the cake out on to a wire rack to cool completely.

7   **To make the icing,** combine the coffee and warm milk in a small mixing bowl. Add the icing sugar to the coffee mixture, together with the soft butter. Whisk until smooth and thick, then spoon all over the cooled cake, so that it drips unevenly down the sides. Allow the icing to set slightly before serving.

COFFEE AND CARDAMOM POUND CAKE AND NEAPOLITAN POUND CAKE (FOR THE FAMILY) ›

Neapolitan pound cake (for the family)

We've gone for the classic Neapolitan colours – brown, white and pink – with a pink icing. It's basically heaven for the birthday party of a six-year-old, but a plain white or cream icing also works well if you want to tone down the pink vibe.

The degree of pinkness (or any-colour-ness) will vary depending on the brand of food colouring you choose. You'll need anything from a whole tube (if you have a very basic liquid gel) to ⅛ teaspoon (if you are starting with concentrated gel). Always start with a little and take it from there: it's much easier to keep adding, rather than trying to take away (which would be impossible!).

SERVES 10

90ml full-fat milk, at room temperature, plus an extra 20ml for the cocoa paste
6 large eggs, at room temperature
1 tbsp vanilla extract
200g self-raising flour
100g plain flour, plus extra for dusting
½ tsp salt
300g caster sugar
300g unsalted butter, soft but not oily, diced, plus extra for greasing
2 tbsp Dutch-processed cocoa powder
a drop or two of pink or any other food colouring (preferably gel or paste)

ICING

45ml full-fat milk, warmed
260g icing sugar, sifted
30g unsalted butter, soft
½ tsp vanilla extract
a drop or two of pink food colouring (preferably gel or paste)

Un-iced, the cake will keep at room temperature for up to 3 days, wrapped in cling film. It can also be frozen for up to 3 months. Once iced, it's best eaten on the same day.

1   Preheat the oven to 200°C/180°C Fan/Gas Mark 6. Grease and flour a 23cm bundt tin and set aside.

2   **For the cake,** place the milk, eggs and vanilla extract in a medium bowl and lightly whisk, just to combine.

3   Sift the flours and salt directly into the bowl of an electric mixer with the paddle attachment in place, then add the sugar and mix on a low speed for 30 seconds. Add the butter and half of the egg mixture and continue to mix until the dry ingredients are incorporated. Increase the speed to medium and beat for 1 minute. Scrape down the sides of the bowl, then gradually add the remaining egg mixture, in two batches, making sure the first batch is fully incorporated before adding the next. Scrape down the sides of the bowl, then divide the batter equally between three separate small bowls.

4   Warm the extra 20ml milk in a small saucepan, then place in a small bowl with the cocoa powder. Stir to form a smooth and very thick paste, then combine this into one of the bowls of cake batter and set aside. Tint the second bowl of cake batter with the pink food colouring, adding a drop or two at a time until it is the colour you want. Leave the third and remaining bowl of batter as it is.

5   Spoon the three mixtures into the prepared tin in six alternate blocks, two of each colour, then use a skewer or small knife to make a zigzag-shaped swirl once through the mix, to create a marble effect. Don't be tempted to overdo the swirling as you will lose the effect of the marbling.

6   Bake for 40–45 minutes, or until a skewer inserted into the centre of the cake comes out clean. Remove from the oven and set aside for 10 minutes (the cake will start to shrink from the sides only after it's removed from the oven). The cake tends to dome in the oven, so if this happens and you want a perfectly flat base (the top will become the bottom once it's inverted), just slice off the top to flatten it out before turning the cake out on to a wire rack to cool completely.

7   **To make the icing,** combine the warm milk and icing sugar in a small mixing bowl. Add the butter and vanilla and whisk until smooth, then add a drop or two of pink food colouring (depending on how bright you want to go) and mix well. Spoon all over the cooled cake, so that it drips unevenly down the sides. Allow the icing to set for a few minutes before serving.

Tessa's spice cake

This is a simple spiced pound cake, but one that is seriously moist, with a lovely fine crumb. There's enough going on, spice-wise, that we've restrained ourselves when it comes to an icing and left it unadorned. The loaf's straight sides and the sprinkle of icing sugar – all part of accentuating its simplicity – make a slice the perfect accompaniment to a cup of tea.

Mixed spice is not hard to get hold of in the UK, but pumpkin spice or quatre épices are both good substitutes, if you're looking for an alternative. Quatre épices is a little bit hotter and less sweet than the others, so you might want to use a pinch less. Tessa's original recipe called for Chinese five-spice powder, which is even stronger and more savoury than the quatre épices. Basically, the cake is something of a blank canvas, there for you to heighten or soften the spices as you like.

With thanks to Tessa Faulkner for this recipe.

SERVES 10–12
—

180g unsalted butter, at room temperature
160g soft dark brown sugar
160g soft light brown sugar
finely grated zest of 1 large orange (1 tbsp)
3 large eggs
120g soured cream

1 tbsp vanilla extract
1 tsp mixed spice (or quatre épices)
225g plain flour
¾ tsp salt
½ tsp bicarbonate of soda
1 tsp malt vinegar (or apple cider vinegar)
icing sugar, for dusting

—

The cake will keep well for up to 5 days in a sealed container.

1   Preheat the oven to 190°C/170°C Fan/Gas Mark 5. Grease a regular 900g loaf tin and line with baking parchment, then set aside.

2   Place the butter, brown sugars and orange zest in the bowl of an electric mixer with the paddle attachment in place. Cream until lightened and smooth but not too fluffy: you don't want to aerate the cake too much.

3   In a separate bowl, whisk together the eggs by hand. Add the soured cream and vanilla and whisk again until smooth.

4   Sift the mixed spice, flour and salt together into a separate bowl and set aside.

5   In alternate batches, and with the machine on a medium-low speed, add a third of the egg and soured cream mixture to the creamed mix, followed by a third of the sifted dry ingredients. Continue with the second and third batch, continuing to mix until combined. Stir the bicarbonate of soda with the vinegar in a small bowl: it will fizz up a little, but that's fine. Add this to the mixture and as soon as everything is combined, turn off the machine. Don't worry if the mixture starts to split at this point: it will still cook up well. Scrape the mixture into the loaf tin and bake for 50–55 minutes, or until a skewer inserted into the centre of the cake comes out clean.

6   Remove the cake from the oven on to a wire rack for about 15 minutes to cool slightly before inverting on to a cake plate. Set aside until completely cool, then dust with icing sugar. This cake is best served at room temperature, as the flavour of the spice becomes more pronounced.

Lemon and poppy seed cake (National Trust version)

However ambitious and discerning Helen's palate, this light lemon cake is the one she'd take with her to a desert island if she could only choose one. It's much simpler than many of the other cakes she loves, but it's the one she returns to again and again. There's something safe and reassuring about it which would comfort as the waves came crashing down around the island.

It's why we've called it, affectionately, our 'National Trust' cake. However unpredictable the weather, however disastrous the outing, however much fun has not really been had on the family day out, there's something wonderfully reassuring about the predictability of the cake you'll have in the café, along with a cup of tea. It's one of life's great certainties.

SERVES 8 (USING A REGULAR LOAF TIN) OR 9 (USING MINI-LOAF TINS)

You can make this in a regular 900g loaf tin, as we do here, or, if you have them, nine mini-loaf tins (9 x 6 x 4 cm) also work well. If you are making the mini-loaves, you'll just need to reduce the baking time to 25 minutes.

This will keep for 3 days in an airtight container.

3 large eggs
225g caster sugar
120ml double cream
75g unsalted butter, cubed,
   plus extra for greasing
10g poppy seeds
finely grated zest of 3 lemons (1 tbsp)

170g plain flour
1¼ tsp baking powder
¼ tsp salt

GLAZE
100g icing sugar, sifted
2 tbsp lemon juice

1   Preheat the oven to 180°C/160°C Fan/Gas Mark 4. Grease the loaf tin and line with baking parchment, then set aside.

2   Place the eggs and sugar in the bowl of an electric mixer and whisk on a medium-high speed for about 2 minutes, until pale and frothy. Add the cream and continue to whisk for about 2 minutes, until the mixture has combined, thickened a little and turned pale.

3   In the meantime, melt the butter in a small saucepan over a low heat, add the poppy seeds and lemon zest and set aside.

4   Sift the flour, baking powder and salt together into a bowl, then use a rubber spatula to fold this into the egg mixture before folding through the butter, poppy seeds and zest.

5   Spoon the mixture into the cake tin so that it rises three-quarters of the way up the sides. Place the tin on a baking tray and cook for about 50 minutes or until a skewer inserted into the centre of the cake comes out clean.

6   **Make the glaze** by whisking the icing sugar with the lemon juice in a bowl. Pour this over the top of the cake as soon as it comes out of the oven, spreading it over the top so that it sinks in and creates a nice glaze. Set aside to cool for 30 minutes before removing from the tin. Leave to come to room temperature before serving.

TESSA'S SPICE CAKE

LEMON AND POPPY SEED CAKE (NATIONAL TRUST VERSION)

Belinda's flourless coconut and chocolate cake

Every month or so we gather in the test kitchen with our pastry chefs. It's an open forum, with the chefs presenting their offerings, which we then taste and discuss. It's always exciting, as ideas are constantly being improved and implemented. This cake was a product of one of those meetings, brought to the table by Franceska Venzon, herself inspired by Belinda Jeffery's version of the cake. We've played around with the shape – baking it in a loaf tin – and added a chocolate ganache, but the base is all Belinda's.

There's something about a cake showcasing its flourless-ness or gluten-free nature which can often make it sound a little bit worthy. Unfairly so, in a case like this, where the feeling of eating it is the very opposite of 'free-from': it's utterly buttery and decadent.

SERVES 8
—

200g unsalted butter, at room
   temperature, plus extra for greasing
250g caster sugar
60g desiccated coconut
scraped seeds of 1 vanilla pod
¼ tsp salt
4 large eggs
180g ground almonds

WATER GANACHE
60g cooking chocolate (70% cocoa
   solids), roughly chopped into
   1cm pieces
25g caster sugar
25g liquid glucose
3 tbsp water
scraped seeds of ¼ vanilla pod
25g unsalted butter, at room
   temperature, cut into 2cm cubes

This can either be made in a regular 900g loaf tin or in a 23cm round springform tin.

This will keep well for up to 5 days in an airtight container. It can be eaten on the day of making, but we think it tastes even better served at room temperature the following day.

1   Preheat the oven to 180°C/160°C Fan/Gas Mark 4. Grease the base and sides of the 900g loaf tin or 23cm round springform tin and line with baking parchment, then set aside.

2   Place the butter, sugar, desiccated coconut, vanilla and salt in an electric mixer with the paddle attachment in place. Beat on a medium-high speed, until pale and fluffy: about 3 minutes. Add the eggs, one at a time, beating well after each addition. Reduce the speed to low, add the ground almonds and mix until just combined.

3   Scrape the mixture into the cake tin and bake for either 40 minutes if using the loaf tin, or 50 minutes if using the round tin, or until the cake is golden brown on top and a skewer inserted into the middle comes out clean. Remove the cake from the oven and set aside to cool in the tin before inverting on to a serving plate. Set aside until completely cool.

4 **Make the water ganache** when you are ready to serve. Place the chocolate in a medium bowl and set aside. Put the sugar and glucose in a small saucepan and place over a medium-low heat. Stir to combine and, when the sugar has melted, increase the heat to medium and bring to the boil, stirring gently from time to time. Continue to boil for about 7 minutes, until the colour is a pale amber. Remove from the heat and carefully pour in the water. Don't worry if the mix seizes: just return the pan to the heat, add the scraped vanilla seeds and stir gently and continuously until it returns to the boil and the sugar has melted again. Remove from the heat and wait for a minute before pouring the water-caramel over the chocolate. Allow to stand for about 3 minutes, then whisk to combine. Add the butter, a couple of cubes at a time, whisking after each addition. Continue until all the butter has been added, whisking to combine until the consistency is that of golden syrup.

5   Spread the ganache over the top of the cake, letting a little run down the sides.

Celebration cake

All cakes are cause for a certain degree of celebration, but certain celebrations are cause for a cake with layers! This is the cake we make for our customers' big parties: birthday parties, wedding celebrations, anniversaries, and all sorts. It's enormous, it's delicious, and it's great for parties as you prepare everything well in advance. It's also, incidentally, gluten-free, held together not by flour, not even by ground nuts, but by the magic of beaten egg whites, sabayon and the chilling effect of the freezer.

Decorate it as you like: we tend to go for a degree of restraint in our presentation, smoothing out the top layer of icing with a palette knife and adding a little bit of icing-sugar-dusted fruit to each corner of the cake. It's a bit of a blank canvas for you to do what you like with, though: more fruit or some nuts, for example, always look good.

SERVES 20–25 (IT'S NOT CALLED A CELEBRATION CAKE FOR NOTHING!)
—

We use three 35 x 25cm Swiss roll tins for this cake, but it's fine to use one: you'll just need to bake the sponge layer in three separate batches – the mixture is happy to sit around and wait. If you have three Swiss roll tins with slightly different dimensions, this is also fine: the individual layers can be trimmed to size once they're out of the freezer.

Both the sponge and ganache need to be made at least a day ahead for the sponge to freeze and the ganache to set. The sponge can be made and frozen up to 2 weeks before assembling; the ganache is fine for up to 3 days in the fridge, then gently warmed over a pot of simmering water to soften before using.

Ideally, the cake should be eaten on the day it is assembled. Leftovers are delicious the next day: they just don't look all that great. If assembling a few hours in advance, keep the cake in the fridge and bring it out half an hour before serving, to come to room temperature.

440g dark cooking chocolate (70% cocoa solids), broken into 2cm pieces
250g egg yolks (from 12 or 13 large eggs)
440g caster sugar
400g egg whites (from 10 large eggs)
1 tbsp brandy
500ml double cream
200g blueberries, plus an extra 8 to garnish
200g blackberries, plus an extra 12 to garnish

200g strawberries, hulled and thinly sliced lengthways, plus a few extra slices to garnish
200g raspberries, plus an extra 8 to garnish
icing sugar, for dusting (optional)

GANACHE
300g white chocolate, broken into 2cm pieces
300ml double cream

—

1   Preheat the oven to 190°C/170°C Fan/Gas Mark 5. Grease three 35 x 25cm Swiss roll trays and line with baking parchment (or just one, see Kit Note).

2   **To make the cake,** place the chocolate in a large heatproof bowl set over a pan of simmering water, making sure the base of the bowl is not touching the water. Stir occasionally until melted, then remove from the heat and set aside to cool slightly.

3   Place the egg yolks and sugar in the bowl of an electric mixer with the whisk attachment in place. Mix for about 3 minutes, until thick and pale, then gently fold into the melted chocolate. Stir until almost combined and set aside.

4   Place the egg whites in a clean bowl of an electric mixer with the whisk attachment in place. Beat on a high speed, until soft peaks form, then gently fold into the chocolate. Lastly, fold through the brandy, then divide the mix between the three Swiss roll tins (or pour a third of the mix into your one tray, if you're cooking in three batches). Use a spatula to even out the top(s) and place in the oven. Bake for 15 minutes, until firm to touch and a skewer inserted into the sponge comes out clean. Set aside to cool. ››

5   Once all the cakes are cooled, place a baking tray or chopping board (that fits in your freezer and which you won't mind being without for 24 hours) over one of the trays and flip the whole thing over, so the board is now sitting underneath the cake. Remove the tray and the paper – do this carefully, to prevent the cake sticking to the paper and tearing – and place a clean sheet of baking parchment on top of the cake. Flip the second layer of cake so that it is sitting on top of the first, and then again, carefully remove the paper before replacing it with a clean layer of parchment. Repeat with the third layer, then wrap the whole thing – baking tray or chopping board and all – firmly in cling film. Freeze for at least 24 hours.

6   **To make the ganache,** place the white chocolate in a medium bowl and set aside. Put the cream into a medium, heavy-based, saucepan and place over a medium-low heat. Cook until just starting to simmer, then pour over the chocolate. Allow to sit for 3 minutes, for the chocolate to soften, then gently stir until the chocolate is melted and fully combined. Cover with cling film and refrigerate overnight (or up to 3 days).

7   Assemble the cake on the day it is going to be eaten. Place the ganache in the bowl of an electric mixer with the whisk attachment in place. Add 500ml of double cream and whip on a medium-high speed for about 30 seconds, until thick and only just pourable: it shouldn't go quite as far as whipped cream, as it will firm up as you spread it. Keep a close eye on it, as it can over-whip very quickly.

8   Mix the berries, apart from those for the garnish, in a large bowl and set aside.

9   Just before assembling the cake – you need to do this at the very last minute as the layers need to be frozen stiff to work with – remove the layers from the freezer. If you have worked with Swiss roll trays with slightly different dimensions, now is the time to trim them so that they are all the same size. Do this one layer at a time (rather than attempting to cut them all at once, stacked on top of one another).

10   Place one layer of sponge on your serving platter and spread a third of the ganache-cream on top, taking it right up to the edges. Scatter half the berries on top, again taking them right to the edges of the cake. Place the second layer of sponge on top of the first and repeat with the cream and fruit. Top the cake with the final layer of sponge and spread the remaining cream on top, either smoothed out with a palette knife or with a wavy pattern. Scatter the fruit reserved for garnish in each corner of the cake and dust the fruit lightly with icing sugar, if using. From here you can either add some more garnish, if you like, or perhaps a piped message of celebration on top of the icing.

Cheesecakes

—

We often talk about breaking recipes down to their component parts to help with getting organized and getting ahead. Nowhere is this more applicable than in the making of cheesecakes, whose layers are so completely distinct: the base (which can always be made well in advance), the filling (which often needs to be made in advance so that it has time to chill and set), and the topping (which is the one thing that usually has to be kept on the to-do list until the day of serving). Within these three parallel objectives there's a lot of room for play.

THE BASE › Most of our cheesecake bases are biscuit-based and crunchy: the contrast between this and the chilled, set, creamy filling is always a winning formula. A couple of the cakes follow a different path, however: the Roasted Strawberry and Lime Cheesecake (see page 221) is sponge-soft and the Baked Ricotta and Hazelnut Cheesecake (see page 209) has no base at all.

THE FILLING › The filling for all cheesecakes will always be, well, rich. Cream cheese often plays a starring role, of course, but surprise yourself with our Baked Ricotta and Hazelnut Cheesecake (see page 209). It is very different – completely opposite, in fact – to what you might be expecting, served warm from the oven rather than set and chilled from the fridge.

THE TOPPING › This is where you can really go to town. We've had our own fun with all sorts of options: crunchy coconut, meringue kisses, and a great big bunch of fruit options – cranberry compote, baked apricots, roasted strawberries and caramelized pineapple – to cut through the richness of the cake. Play around and try things out here: your cakes will work with all sorts of alternatives.

OUR TINS, TIPS AND TRICKS › We often prefer to make lots of small cheesecakes rather than one large one. The inherent decadence of cheesecake is somehow heightened further when you have an entire (mini) cake to yourself. To make the Passionfruit Cheesecake with Spiced Pineapple (see page 207), the Lime Meringue Cheesecakes (see page 201) and the Baked Ricotta and Hazelnut Cheesecake (see page 209), you'll need a set of 8cm round, bottomless rings. A muffin tin will also work for the ricotta cakes, if you are looking for an alternative. Otherwise, a 23cm round springform cake tin (or any tin with a removable base) is used for many of the larger cakes.

Timing-wise, don't cut corners. Cheesecakes need to bake for a long time in a low oven. They need a long time to cool and they often need a long time to set. The reason they're so precious is that they don't respond well to swift changes in temperature. If you were to try and speed up the cooling process by taking the cheesecake out of the oven and transferring it to the fridge, for example, it would quite literally fall apart at the seams and develop a big crack. This need not be a disaster – it won't affect the taste and you can often cover the crack with a topping – but it's always pleasing to bake a crack-free cake. Start with room temperature ingredients and follow our cake-cooling instructions exactly: we leave the cake in the oven once it's baked, propping the oven door slightly open with a wooden spoon.

Although a lot of people bake their cheesecakes in a water bath (bain-marie) – where the individual cake or cakes sit in a larger tray, which is filled with warm water before going into the oven – this is not a technique we're huge fans of. The rationale behind the water bath is that because the temperature of the water cannot rise above 100°C, the cheesecake will cook evenly, resulting in a smooth, creamy texture. While this makes sense in theory, we find that it can be rather messy, and sometimes even dangerous (try carrying a tray full of hot water across the kitchen and discovering – doh! – you've forgotten to leave the oven door open). And however much we've mummified our tins in foil, we also find that, more often than not, the water will somehow seep in and result in a disappointingly soggy crust. The long, slow bake and the long, slow cooling period is the method we prefer.

Lime meringue cheesecakes

Part lime-meringue-pie, part classic-cheesecake, these make for an impressive dessert. It's one to save for a special occasion – there is a fair bit of work – but, as with lots of cakes with more than one layer, they are not quite as epic a feat as they first seem. Being able to make two out of the three layers the day before you are serving – the base layer and the cheesecake – helps, leaving just the meringue to make on the day itself. Decadent and rich, but light in texture, these are a big hit with citrus fans.

We use a Swiss meringue for these cheesecakes (as opposed to French or Italian meringue, see page 347), so the texture is chewy and marshmallow-like. Beyond the heat treatment the egg whites and sugar receive before they are whipped, there's no extra baking, so it's important to ensure they are very warm, ideally reaching the temperature of 71°C on a sugar thermometer.

MAKES 8

In addition to the sugar thermometer, you would ideally use a blowtorch to brown the meringue, as this produces the best results. If you don't have one, place the cakes under a grill until browned. We like to make these as individual cakes, in 8cm round cake rings; slightly smaller rings are fine if that's what you have (you'll just make an extra cake as a result), but don't be tempted to use larger rings: part of the attractiveness of these cakes is their height, and you will lose this if they are too wide. You will also need a piping bag with a 1cm tip for piping the meringue 'kisses'.

The base can be made a day in advance and stored in the fridge. The cheesecakes (without the meringue topping) can be made a day in advance and refrigerated overnight. The nut topping can be made up to 5 days in advance and stored in an airtight container.

Once the meringues have been browned, they are best eaten within 3 or 4 hours. Any leftover cakes can be kept in the fridge for a day: the meringue will have softened, but they'll still taste good.

BASE
60g Brazil nuts
140g digestive biscuits, roughly broken
20g desiccated coconut
70g unsalted butter, melted, plus extra for greasing

FILLING
280g cream cheese
1 x 410g tin condensed milk
120g egg yolks (from 6 large eggs)
200ml freshly squeezed lime juice (you'll need the zest from 2 of the limes before juicing)
finely grated zest of 2 limes (2 tsp)

TOPPING (OPTIONAL)
15g coconut chips
25g Brazil nuts, thinly sliced (don't worry if they break up a bit when sliced: they'll still be fine)
20g soft dark brown sugar
½ tsp lime juice

MERINGUE
100g egg whites (from about 2½ large eggs)
180g caster sugar
⅛ tsp salt

1   Preheat the oven to 170°C/150°C Fan/Gas Mark 3. Lightly grease the sides of eight individual 8cm wide cake rings, and line the sides with baking parchment – you want the paper to rise 4cm above the top of the ring – then place on a large baking tray which is also lined with baking parchment.

2   **For the base,** spread the Brazil nuts out on a baking tray and roast for about 12 minutes, until lightly golden. Set aside to cool before placing in the small bowl of a food processor. Blitz until finely chopped, then add the biscuits to the food processor. Blitz to form fine crumbs and tip into a small bowl. Add the coconut and melted butter and use your hands to mix well. Place 2 heaped tablespoons of crumbs in the base of each ring, using your hands to press them into the base. Even out the crust with the back of a spoon or the base of a glass and set aside in the fridge.

3   **To make the filling,** place the cream cheese in the bowl of an electric mixer with the paddle attachment in place. Mix on a medium-low speed until creamy, then add the condensed milk and egg yolks. Continue to mix until smooth, scraping down the sides occasionally, before adding the lime juice. Mix to incorporate, then strain the mixture into a large jug. Add the lime zest and pour the mixture into the prepared rings so that it rises three-quarters of the way up the sides. ››

4   Bake for 20 minutes, until the cheesecakes have just set. Remove from the oven and allow to cool completely before covering lightly with cling film and placing in the fridge for at least 4 hours or overnight.

5   **To make the topping,** put the coconut and Brazil nuts into a small saucepan and place over a medium heat. Toast for about 3 minutes, stirring frequently, until a light golden brown. Add the sugar and lime juice and cook for 1 minute, until melted and well combined. Tip on to a parchment-lined tray and set aside to cool.

6   **Make the meringue** on the day of serving. Using a pan large enough to allow the bowl of your electric mixer to sit on top, pour enough water into the pan so that it rises a quarter of the way up the sides. Bring to the boil. Place the egg whites, sugar and salt in the bowl of the electric mixer with the whisk attachment in place and whisk to combine. Reduce the heat so that the water is just simmering, then place the bowl on the pan, making sure the water doesn't touch the base of the bowl. Whisk the eggs continuously for 5 minutes by hand, until they are very warm (you want the eggs to reach a temperature of 71°C on a thermometer – see introduction), then transfer back to the electric mixer. Whisk for about 5 minutes on a high speed, until the meringue is stiff and cool. Transfer the meringue to a piping bag fitted with a 1cm tip.

7   Carefully remove the rings and paper collars from the cheesecakes, then pipe meringue 'kisses' on top. You will have more meringue to play with than you need here, but it's better to have spare, in this instance, than go without your kisses.

8   Using a blowtorch, heat the meringue so that parts of it turn a golden brown. Alternatively, place the tray of cheesecakes under a hot grill for about 1–2 minutes: you'll need to watch them constantly to make sure they don't burn. Sprinkle over the coconut topping – you might have a couple of tablespoons left over to snack on – and serve.

White chocolate cheesecake with cranberry compote

All the sweetness comes from the white chocolate here, so use the best-quality chocolate you can find: you'll really taste the difference. The cranberry compote, spooned on top, provides a sharp and welcome counterpoint, but the cake also works without it if you are looking for a shortcut. Some fresh berries served alongside – strawberries, raspberries or blackberries – would be perfect.

SERVES 10–12

The compote will keep for up to 5 days in the fridge, and also freezes well. The cheesecake must be made at least the day before you plan to serve it, and kept in the fridge.

Once assembled, the cake will keep well for 3–4 days in the fridge.

BASE
70g whole raw almonds, skin on
180g digestive biscuits
100g unsalted butter, melted,
    plus extra for greasing

FILLING
600g good-quality white chocolate:
    500g roughly broken; 100g chopped
    into 1cm pieces (or use white
    chocolate chips)
500g cream cheese
4 large eggs, lightly beaten
300g soured cream
finely grated zest of 1 small orange
    (1 tsp)
scraped seeds of ½ vanilla pod

CRANBERRY COMPOTE
150g fresh (or frozen and defrosted)
    raspberries
180g fresh (or frozen and defrosted)
    cranberries
110g caster sugar
65ml orange juice

1   Preheat the oven to 180°C/160°C Fan/Gas Mark 4. Lightly grease the base and sides of a 23cm round springform tin and line with baking parchment.

2   Spread the almonds out on a baking tray and roast for 10 minutes, then set aside to cool. Transfer to a food processor and pulse just a few times – you want the almonds to be in roughly 0.5cm pieces rather than turning to powder – then transfer to a separate bowl.

3   Reduce the oven temperature to 170°C/150°C Fan/Gas Mark 3.

4   Put the digestives into a food processor and blitz until fine: you want the consistency to be that of dried breadcrumbs. Add to the bowl of almonds, along with the melted butter, and use your hands or a wooden spoon to combine. Spoon the crumbs into the tin, pressing them firmly into the base. Even out the crust with the back of a spoon or the base of a glass and set aside in the fridge.

5   **To make the filling,** place the roughly broken white chocolate in a heatproof bowl set over a pan of simmering water (make sure the base of the bowl is not touching the water), stirring from time to time. Once the chocolate has melted, turn off the heat, remove the bowl from the pan of hot water and set aside for 5 minutes to cool slightly, stirring occasionally. ››

6   Place the cream cheese in the bowl of an electric mixer with the paddle attachment in place. Beat on a medium-high speed until smooth. Reduce the speed to medium-low and gradually add the eggs, followed by the soured cream, orange zest and vanilla seeds. Add the melted chocolate – it should be tepid rather than warm, as you don't want the white chocolate chips to melt when they are added later – and beat on a medium-low speed until combined. Finally, stir in the finely chopped white chocolate (or white chocolate chips) and pour the mixture into the chilled base. Smooth over the top and place on a baking tray.

7   Bake for about 1 hour, or until the middle of the cheesecake has a slight wobble when you gently shake the pan. Turn off the oven but leave the cheesecake inside for an hour, with the oven door propped open with a wooden spoon. Remove from the oven and cool completely before wrapping in cling film and chilling in the fridge for at least 4 hours, or preferably overnight, until the cheesecake is cold and firm.

8   **For the compote,** place the raspberries in the small bowl of a food processor and process to form a liquid – don't use a blender here as it will blitz the seeds as well as the fruit and give the purée a slightly bitter taste. Pass through a fine-mesh (or muslin-lined) sieve to remove the seeds, which can be discarded. You should have around 75ml of purée.

9   Stir together the cranberries, sugar and orange juice in a medium saucepan. Place on a medium-low heat until the sugar has dissolved. Increase the heat and gently boil for 8–10 minutes, until most of the cranberries have burst and the mixture is thick. Remove the pan from the heat and stir in the raspberry purée. Transfer to a bowl, place some cling film directly on top of the compote and set aside to cool. The compote will thicken to an almost jelly-like consistency but will break up readily when stirred before you spoon it on top of the cake.

10   When ready to serve, release the springform tin and remove the baking parchment. Slide the cheesecake on to a serving plate and spoon over the cranberry compote. Use a warm knife (dip the blade in hot water and wipe dry before using) to cut slices and serve at once.

SWEET

Passionfruit cheesecake with spiced pineapple

We have regular meetings at which all our pastry chefs – there are about 15 – come together in the test kitchen to share their ideas. Everyone arrives bearing their sweet offerings, which are then passed around the table and closely scrutinized. This cheesecake was brought to one of those meetings by Céline Lecoeur: it received unanimous praise from everyone at the table. And our customers – who made it an instant bestseller – agreed.

For details on where to get hold of strained passionfruit pulp, see page 355. The alternative is to scoop out the pulp of about a dozen passionfruit, place it in a food processor and blitz. Don't worry about the numerous seeds releasing their bitter flavours as they're crushed: they're so slippery that they just whizz around and around the processor rather than breaking down.

MAKES 8 (USING 8CM RINGS), OR ONE LARGE CAKE SERVES 10

We like to make these as individual cakes, in 8cm round cake rings. Alternatively, you could make one large cake in a 23cm round springform tin. Baking and resting times in the oven are listed in the recipe for both options.

The cheesecakes must be made the day before serving, to allow the filling to chill and set overnight (the pineapple topping is best made and added on the day of serving).

Once assembled, the cakes are best eaten on the same day. Leftovers will keep for up to 2 days in the fridge; they just won't look as perfect as on day one.

BASE

40g flaked almonds, lightly crushed in your hand
130g digestive biscuits, roughly broken
½ tsp ground cinnamon
½ tsp ground star anise (about 2 whole star anise, finely ground in a spice grinder)
80g unsalted butter, melted, plus extra for greasing

FILLING

140g strained passionfruit pulp (see page 355), or the blitzed pulp of about 12 medium passionfruit (see introduction)
750g cream cheese
200g caster sugar
80g soured cream
3 large eggs, plus 3 extra large egg yolks, lightly whisked

SPICED PINEAPPLE

1 small pineapple (700g), peeled, core removed and flesh cut into roughly 1.5cm cubes
¼ tsp ground cinnamon
¼ tsp ground star anise (about 1 whole star anise, finely ground in a spice grinder)
½ vanilla pod, sliced in half lengthways and seeds scraped
65g caster sugar
1 tbsp lemon juice
1 tbsp water
pulp and seeds from 2 medium passionfruit

1   Preheat the oven to 170°C/150°C Fan/Gas Mark 3. Lightly grease the sides of eight individual 8cm wide cake rings, and line the sides with baking parchment – you want the paper to rise 1cm above the top of the ring – then place on a large parchment-lined baking tray. If using a large springform tin, grease and line the base and sides – again, the paper should rise 1cm above the sides of the tin – place the tin on a baking tray and set aside.

2   Place the almonds on a parchment-lined baking tray and roast for 6 minutes, until golden. Remove from the oven and set aside to cool. ››

3 **For the base,** place the digestive biscuits in a food processor and blitz to form fine crumbs: the consistency should be that of dried breadcrumbs. Tip into a medium bowl and add the almonds, ground cinnamon and ground star anise. Add the melted butter and stir well to combine. Spoon the crumbs into the tins, using your hands to press them into the base. Even out the crust with the back of a spoon or the base of a glass and set aside in the fridge for around 30 minutes to chill.

4 If making your own passionfruit pulp, strain the blitzed pulp through a fine-mesh (or muslin-lined) sieve, discarding the seeds. You should have about 140ml of pulp. Set aside.

5 Place the cream cheese and sugar in the bowl of an electric mixer with the paddle attachment in place. Beat on a medium speed until smooth, then add the soured cream and mix until just combined. Reduce the speed to medium-low and, with the machine still running, pour in the whisked eggs and yolks in a steady stream. Mix thoroughly, then add the passionfruit pulp and gently combine. Pour the filling into the chilled crumb-lined cake tins: it should rise to the top of the rings or about 2cm from the top if making one large cake. Bake for 25 minutes, or 55–60 minutes if making one large cake, until the edges are set but the centre remains slightly wobbly when the tray is gently shaken. Turn off the oven but leave the cheesecakes inside for 30 minutes, or 1 hour for the large cake, with the door propped open with a wooden spoon. Remove from the oven and set aside to cool completely, before wrapping the tray in cling film and refrigerating overnight: the cheesecake is very soft so will not cut without chilling.

6 On the day of serving, preheat the oven to 200°C/180°C Fan/Gas Mark 6. Place the pineapple cubes in a medium bowl with the cinnamon, star anise and vanilla pod and seeds. Toss well and spread out on a parchment-lined tray. Bake in the oven for 15 minutes, until lightly roasted, then set aside.

7 To make the 'dry' caramel (see page 349), place the sugar in a medium sauté pan over a medium-high heat. It will seem as though nothing is happening until suddenly a small section around the edge will begin to melt and turn brown. It may even smoke a little, but don't worry and don't stir: continue to heat, tilting the pan often and swirling gently so that the sugar continues to melt and brown evenly until the caramel is the colour of golden syrup. As soon as the caramel is ready, remove the pan from the heat and carefully pour in the lemon juice and water. It will splutter and spit, so take care. Swirl again over the heat to melt the caramel if the addition of the lemon juice has hardened it. Bring to the boil, stir and reduce for about 30–60 seconds to form a thick syrup, then add the pineapple cubes. Stir to combine and set aside to cool.

8 When ready to serve, run a small knife around the base of the tins, releasing the biscuit base, and gently push the cheesecakes up and out of their moulds. Remove the paper and transfer to a serving platter. Spoon the caramelized pineapple and syrup on to the centre of the cheesecakes, then spoon the passionfruit pulp and seeds on top of that. Serve immediately.

Baked ricotta and hazelnut cheesecake

Unlike most other cheesecakes, this doesn't need to be made ahead of time in order to chill and set. In fact it tastes best served a little warm. It's not what people expect from a cheesecake – there's no crunchy base and it's served warm from the oven – but in Italy, where they certainly know how to 'do' ricotta, nearly all cheesecakes are like this: more of a warm, moist cake (although you can serve it from the fridge, if you like).

With thanks to Laura Jane Stewart, pastry chef at our Ledbury shop, for this recipe.

MAKES 10 (USING 8CM RINGS), 18 (USING A REGULAR MUFFIN TIN) OR ONE LARGE CAKE

We like to make these as individual cakes, in 8cm round cake rings. Alternatively, you could use a regular muffin tin, or you could make one large cake in a 23cm round springform tin. Instructions for all options are listed in the recipe.

The ganache can be made in advance and kept at room temperature for up to 4 days, or in the fridge for up to 2 weeks. If keeping it in the fridge, you'll need to warm it over a pan of simmering water to return it to a spreadable glaze.

Un-iced, these will keep for 3 days in an airtight container in the fridge. You'll need to take the chill off them, so take them out of the fridge a good 30 minutes or so before serving. Once iced, they are best eaten straight away.

300g blanched hazelnuts
35g plain flour
160g chocolate (70% cocoa solids), roughly chopped
100g ground almonds
225g unsalted butter, at room temperature, roughly cubed, plus extra for greasing
250g caster sugar
6 large eggs, whites and yolks separated
400g ricotta cheese
2 tsp vanilla extract
¼ tsp salt

WATER GANACHE
100g dark chocolate (70% cocoa solids), roughly chopped into 2cm pieces
40g caster sugar
40g liquid glucose
70ml water
scraped seeds of ¼ vanilla pod
40g unsalted butter, at room temperature, cut into 2cm cubes
icing sugar, to serve

1   Preheat the oven to 180°C/160°C Fan/Gas Mark 4.

2   Lightly grease the sides of ten individual 8cm wide cake rings, and line the sides with baking parchment – you want the paper to rise 2cm above the top of the ring – then place on a large baking tray which is also lined with baking parchment. Once the rings have been filled with the cake mix they cannot be moved, so arrange them on the tray as you want them to be baked. If using a muffin tin, line the base of the moulds with a circle of baking parchment and grease the sides; if using a large springform tin, grease and line the base and sides – again, the paper should rise 2cm above the sides of the tin – place the tin on a baking tray and set aside.

3   Spread the hazelnuts out on a baking tray and roast for 10 minutes, until they have taken on just a little bit of colour. Remove from the oven and set aside until completely cool (if you blitz them when they are warm, they will turn to an oily paste). Roughly chop 50g of the cooled nuts and set these aside – they will be used to garnish – and place the remainder in the bowl of a food processor, along with the flour. Blitz until fine, then tip into a medium bowl. Place the chocolate in the food processor, blitz to form large crumbs and add these to the hazelnuts and flour. Add the ground almonds, mix together and set aside: the texture is a bit rustic here, which is what you want. ››

4   Increase the oven temperature to 190°C/170°C Fan/Gas Mark 5.

5   Place the butter and sugar in the bowl of an electric mixer with the paddle attachment in place. Beat on a medium-high speed for about 3 minutes, until light and creamy. Add the egg yolks, one at a time, beating well after each addition. Reduce the speed to low, add the chocolate, nut and flour mix and continue to mix until just combined. Remove the bowl from the machine and stir in the ricotta, vanilla and salt. Transfer the cake mix to a separate large bowl and set aside.

6   Wash and dry the bowl of the electric mixer very well before adding the egg whites to it. Whisk the whites on a medium-high speed until stiff, then use a large spatula to fold the egg whites, in two or three batches, into the cake mix. Scrape the mixture into the cake tins, filling them to the top of each ring. Bake for 30–35 minutes if you are using the individual cake rings, 20 minutes if using a muffin tin, or about 60 minutes if making it in one large tin, rotating the tray halfway through, until golden brown and a skewer inserted into the middle comes out more or less clean: it might have a few crumbs attached but should not be wet. Remove from the oven and set aside to cool completely. Remove them from their tins, peel away the paper and set aside. If you are making one large cake and it is a bit cracked on top, don't worry: rustic is fine here and the chocolate ganache will cover it completely.

To make the ganache, place the chocolate in a medium bowl and set aside. Put the sugar and glucose in a small saucepan and place over a medium-low heat. Stir to combine and, when the sugar has melted, increase the heat to medium and bring to the boil, stirring gently from time to time. Continue to boil for about 5 minutes, until the colour is a pale amber. Remove from the heat and carefully pour in the water. Don't worry if the mix seizes: just return the pan to the heat, add the scraped vanilla seeds and stir gently and continuously until it returns to the boil. Remove from the heat and wait for a minute before pouring the water-caramel over the chocolate. Allow to stand for 5 minutes, then whisk to combine. Add the butter, a couple of cubes at a time, whisking after each addition. Continue until all the butter has been added, whisking to combine until the mix is smooth and shiny. Remove from the heat.

7   Dust the cakes with icing sugar, then spoon over the ganache, covering only one half of the cakes with the topping if you like. Let the ganache drip down the sides. Sprinkle over the reserved chopped hazelnuts and serve.

Fig, orange and mascarpone cheesecake

Recipes are like stories, passed on from one person to another. The details and emphases change, but tribute should always be paid to the original source. Ever-mindful of paying tribute where it's due, Helen thought she'd first seen a version of this cake years ago in an *Australian Women's Weekly* magazine. Not content to simply acknowledge the publication and move on, Helen bought no less than five old *Women's Weekly* books and magazines before she finally tracked down the old reference. Hat tipped, we were then happy to take hold of the recipe and re-tell it in our own way.

This is a rich cheesecake, but one with a lighter texture than most, thanks to the whisked-up, air-filled egg whites which are folded through the mix just before baking. It will rise up a little like a soufflé, then deflate when cool.

We like to serve the cake as it is, simple and unadorned, but you can play around with the decoration, if you like: finely julienned strips of orange zest look great on top of the cheesecake and echo the juice within; or if you can get hold of any large fig leaves, these are also fun to sit the cake on top of when serving.

SERVES 12

BASE
100g digestive biscuits

80g walnut halves, finely chopped

60g unsalted butter, melted, plus extra for greasing

250g soft dried figs, tough stalk removed, sliced into 0.5cm strips

250ml freshly squeezed orange juice

1 cinnamon stick

⅛ tsp ground cloves

FILLING
500g cream cheese

500g mascarpone

250g caster sugar

finely grated zest of 1 large orange (1 tbsp)

4 large eggs, whites and yolks separated

2 tsp vanilla extract

The base can be made 2 days in advance and stored in the fridge.

The cheesecake can be assembled up to 2 days in advance and stored in the fridge.

1   Grease the base and sides of a 23cm round springform tin and line with baking parchment, making sure that the paper rises at least 4–5cm above the rim: the cake rises a lot in the oven.

2   For the base, place the digestive biscuits in a food processor and blitz to form fine crumbs: the consistency should be that of dried breadcrumbs. Place in a medium bowl and add the walnuts and melted butter. Use your hands or a large spoon to combine: the mixture should be the consistency of wet sand. Spoon the crumbs into the tin, using your hands to press them into the base, then place in the fridge for at least 20 minutes to firm up.

3   Place the figs, orange juice, cinnamon stick and ground cloves in a medium saucepan over a medium heat. Bring to a simmer and cook for 15–20 minutes, until most of the liquid has evaporated but the mixture is still moist. Set aside to cool, remove the cinnamon stick, then spread over the biscuit base. Return to the fridge while you prepare the filling.

4   Preheat the oven to 180°C/160°C Fan/Gas Mark 4.

5   Place the cream cheese in the bowl of an electric mixer with the paddle attachment in place. Beat on a medium speed for 1 minute, until smooth, before adding the mascarpone, sugar, orange zest, egg yolks and vanilla extract. Continue to beat until all the ingredients are incorporated and the mixture looks smooth and creamy, scraping down the paddle and sides of the bowl from time to time, if you need to.

6   Place the egg whites in a separate clean bowl and whisk (either by hand or with an electric whisk) until firm peaks form. Fold a third into the cream cheese mixture, followed by the remaining two-thirds, then pour the filling over the chilled fig and biscuit base.

7   Place on a baking tray and bake for 75–80 minutes, until the cheesecake is a light golden brown at the edges and the centre is only just firm. Turn off the oven but leave the cheesecake inside for an hour or so, with the door propped open with a wooden spoon. Allow it to come to room temperature before wrapping in cling film and keeping in the fridge for at least 4 hours.

8   When ready to serve, release the springform tin, remove the baking parchment and transfer to a cake platter. The cheesecake is best served chilled, straight from the fridge, and cut with a warm knife (dip the blade in hot water and wipe dry before using).

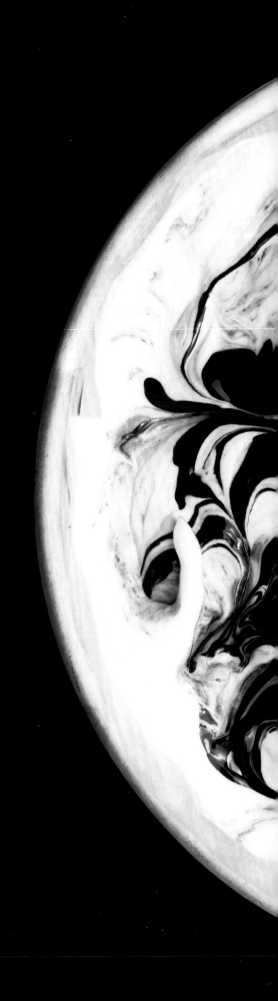

CHOCOLATE BANANA RIPPLE CHEESECAKE

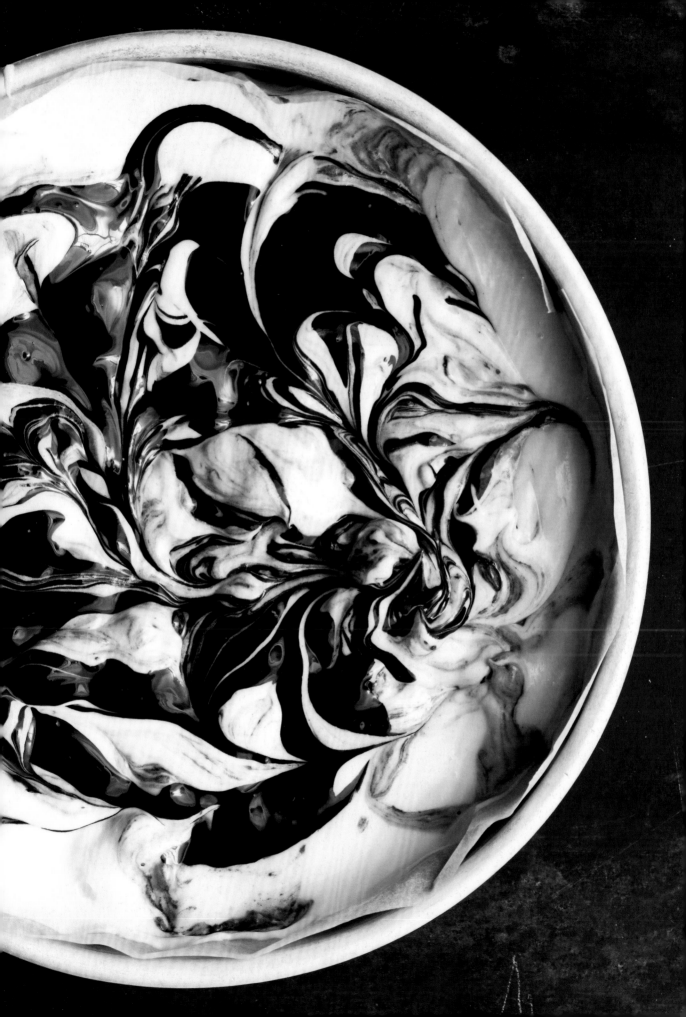

Chocolate banana ripple cheesecake

If you are going to do it, you might as well do it. Take even a couple of the words in this recipe's name and you have something approximating a dessert. Take all four and you have yourself about as serious a tea time or end-of-meal treat as you can imagine.

SERVES 10–12

BASE

30g walnut halves

200g digestive biscuits

2 tbsp cocoa powder

50g demerara sugar

100g unsalted butter, melted, plus extra for greasing

2–3 large ripe bananas, peeled and sliced on the diagonal into 1cm thick pieces (260g)

BANANA GANACHE

125g dark chocolate (70% cocoa solids), roughly chopped into 1cm pieces

25ml full-fat milk

50ml double cream

1 large ripe banana, peeled and mashed (100g)

FILLING

375g white chocolate chips (or 375g white chocolate, roughly chopped into 1cm pieces)

375g cream cheese

3 large eggs, lightly beaten

220g soured cream

1 tsp vanilla extract

The biscuit crumb base can be made and pressed into the cake tin up to 2 days in advance and stored in the fridge. The ganache can also be made 2 or 3 days in advance, stored in the fridge, and gently warmed over a pot of simmering water to soften before swirling. The whole cake needs to be made at least 4 hours before serving and then kept in the fridge to firm up. Ideally, make it the day before you are going to serve it so that it can chill overnight.

Once assembled, the cake is best stored in the fridge and eaten within 3 days.

1   Preheat the oven to 180°C/160°C Fan/Gas Mark 4. Grease the base and sides of a 23cm round springform tin and line with baking parchment.

2   Spread the walnuts out on a baking tray and roast in the oven for 6 minutes. Set aside to cool, then chop roughly into 0.5cm pieces.

3   **For the base,** place the digestive biscuits in a food processor and blitz to form fine crumbs. Tip into a medium bowl and add the cocoa powder, sugar and chopped walnuts. Add the melted butter and stir well to combine. Spoon the crumbs into the tin, using your hands to press them into the base. Even out the crust with the back of a spoon or the base of a glass and set aside in the fridge.

4   Reduce the oven temperature to 170°C/150°C Fan/Gas Mark 3.

5   **To make the banana ganache,** place the chopped chocolate in a medium heatproof bowl. Heat the milk and cream in a small pan, and just as it comes to the boil, pour it over the chocolate. Allow to stand for 1 minute before stirring gently with a rubber spatula so that the chocolate melts: you might need to heat it a little more if it hasn't all melted. Stir in the mashed banana and set aside to cool.

6   **For the filling,** place the chopped white chocolate in a small bowl set over a pan of simmering water (make sure the base of the bowl is not touching the water), stirring from time to time. Once the chocolate has melted, turn off the heat, remove the bowl from the pan of hot water and set aside to cool slightly, stirring occasionally.

7   Place the cream cheese in the bowl of an electric mixer with the paddle attachment in place. Beat on a medium-high speed until smooth, then reduce the speed to medium. Gradually add the eggs, scraping down the sides of the bowl once or twice, followed by the soured cream and vanilla. Add the melted white chocolate – don't worry if it's slightly tepid rather than completely cool – and beat on a medium-low speed until combined.

8   Arrange the sliced bananas evenly over the crumb base in a single layer. Pour the cheesecake filling carefully over the bananas, then, using a small spoon, gently dollop the banana ganache on top of the filling. Using a knife (like a butter knife), gently swirl the ganache and cream cheese together by repeatedly drawing a figure '8' through the mixture to create a marbled look. Place the cheesecake on a baking tray and bake for 60–70 minutes, until the outside of the cheesecake is set but the centre is still slightly soft to touch. Turn off the oven but leave the cheesecake inside, with the door closed, for 1 hour. Remove from the oven and set aside until completely cool, then wrap the whole thing carefully in cling film and chill in the fridge for at least 4 hours or preferably overnight, until the cheesecake is completely firm.

9   When ready to serve, release the springform tin, remove the baking parchment and transfer to a cake platter. Set aside for 15 minutes before serving.

Apricot and Amaretto cheesecake

This is the cheesecake to round off a dinner party. Some will have this instead of a glass of Amaretto; others will see it as the perfect excuse to bring the bottle to the table. Whichever way the party goes, there's an in-built synergy here, with the sweet Amaretto liqueur (made from a base of apricot kernels and bitter almonds) complementing the roasted apricots and flaked roasted almonds.

SERVES 10–12

The biscuit crumb base can be made and pressed into the cake tin up to 2 days in advance and stored in the fridge. The cheesecake can be made up to 3 days in advance and stored in the fridge (the topping should only be added on the day of serving).

Once assembled, the cake is best eaten on the same day. Leftovers will keep for up to 2 days in the fridge; they just won't look as perfect as on day one.

BASE

70g flaked almonds
180g digestive biscuits
100g unsalted butter, melted
350g fresh apricots, cut in half
   and stone removed

FILLING

840g cream cheese
170g caster sugar
scraped seeds of ½ vanilla pod
finely grated zest of 1 large orange
   (1 tbsp)
5 large eggs, lightly beaten
85g soured cream
70ml Amaretto

TOPPING

15g flaked almonds
400g fresh apricots, cut in half
   and stone removed
1 tbsp caster sugar
1 tbsp water
1 tbsp Amaretto

1   Preheat the oven to 170°C/150°C Fan/Gas Mark 3. Lightly grease the base and sides of a 23cm round springform tin and line with baking parchment.

2   Spread all the almonds (for the base and topping) out on a baking tray and roast for 10 minutes, or until they are a light golden brown. Set aside 15g for the topping.

3   **For the base,** place the digestive biscuits in a food processor and blitz to form fine crumbs: the consistency should be that of dried breadcrumbs. Tip into a medium bowl and add the almonds and melted butter. Use your hands or a large spoon to combine: the mixture should be the consistency of wet sand. Spoon the crumbs into the tin, using your hands to press them into the base. Even out the crust with the back of a spoon or the base of a glass and set aside in the fridge.

4   Increase the oven temperature to 210°C/190°C Fan/Gas Mark 6.

5   Spread the apricots for the base out on a baking tray, cut side up, and roast for 25 minutes (or a little longer, if they were very firm to begin with), until they are soft but still holding their shape. Set aside to cool.

6   Reduce the oven temperature to 170°C/150°C Fan/Gas Mark 3.

7   **For the filling,** place the cream cheese, sugar, vanilla seeds and orange zest in the bowl of an electric mixer with the paddle attachment in place. Beat on a medium speed until smooth. Gradually add the eggs, followed by the soured cream, and beat until combined; you might need to scrape down the sides of the bowl once or twice. Finally, add the Amaretto and mix until combined. ››

8   Remove the cheesecake base from the fridge and arrange the roasted apricots evenly over the bottom, cut side down. The apricots should fit quite snugly without overlapping or leaving gaps. Gently pour the cheesecake filling over the apricots and then place on a baking tray. Cook for 1 hour, or until the sides of the cheesecake are set but the middle has a wobble when shaken very gently. Turn off the oven but leave the cheesecake inside for another hour, with the door propped open with a wooden spoon, before placing in the fridge for at least 3 hours or overnight to chill and set completely.

9   On the day of serving, preheat the oven to 210°C/190°C Fan/Gas Mark 6. Spread the apricots out on a baking tray, cut side up, and roast for 25 minutes (or a little longer, if they were very firm to begin with), until they are soft but still holding their shape. Sprinkle the apricots with the sugar, water and the Amaretto. Return to the oven and bake for another 10 minutes, until the apricots are moist and syrupy. Remove from the oven and set aside to cool.

10   When ready to serve, release the springform tin, remove the baking parchment and transfer to a cake platter. Spoon the roasted syrupy apricots into the centre of the cake, sprinkle over the reserved toasted almonds and serve.

Roasted strawberry and lime cheesecake

The sponge cake base of this cheesecake was inspired by (and adapted from) a recipe used by the legendary Junior's Cheesecake in Brooklyn. It's a natural partner to the strawberries and a welcome change from the biscuit base more commonly associated with cheesecakes. The sponge is twice baked: first by itself, as a very shallow cake, and again when the cream cheese mixture goes on top. We love this base, but alternatives work just as well, if you'd prefer something nutty and crunchy and quick to prepare: try the base from the Apricot and Amaretto Cheesecake (see page 219), with or without the flaked almonds.

SERVES 12–16

The cheesecake can be made up to 3 days in advance and kept in the fridge (the strawberries should only be roasted and added on the day of serving).

Once assembled, the cake is best eaten on the same day. Leftovers will keep for up to 3 days in the fridge, but they won't look as perfect, as the strawberries will leak.

BASE
65g plain flour
1 tbsp cornflour
¾ tsp baking powder
⅛ tsp salt
2 large eggs, whites and yolks separated
130g caster sugar
scraped seeds of ¼ vanilla pod
finely grated zest of 1 lime (1 tsp), plus 1 tsp lime juice
30g unsalted butter, melted
¼ tsp cream of tartar

FILLING
900g cream cheese
180g caster sugar
scraped seeds of ½ vanilla pod
5 large eggs (290g), lightly beaten (the gram weight is important here, and as eggs vary in size you might need slightly more or less than 5)
90g soured cream
finely grated zest of 3 limes (1 tbsp), plus 1 tbsp lime juice

ROASTED STRAWBERRIES
about 30 large strawberries, hulled (600g)
20g icing sugar, plus an extra 1 tsp, for dusting

1   Preheat the oven to 190°C/170°C Fan/Gas Mark 5. Grease the base and sides of a 23cm round springform cake tin and line with baking parchment.

2   **To make the sponge base,** place the flour, cornflour, baking powder and salt in a bowl and set aside. Place the egg yolks in the bowl of an electric mixer with the whisk attachment in place, and add 100g of the sugar and vanilla seeds. Whisk on a high speed until pale and thickened. Remove the bowl from the mixer and sift the dry ingredients directly on to the eggs. Fold to combine, then add the lime zest, juice and melted butter and mix to incorporate. Transfer to a large bowl and set aside.

3   Wash and dry the bowl for the electric mixer very well and return it to the machine with the whisk attachment in place. Add the egg whites and whisk on a high speed until frothy. Add the cream of tartar, continue to whisk until soft peaks form, then gradually drizzle in the remaining caster sugar. Continue to whisk until firm peaks form. Fold a third of the egg whites into the cake mixture to lighten it, before folding in the rest until fully combined. Scrape the mixture into the prepared cake tin, smooth the top with a small spatula and place in the oven for about 12 minutes, or until the sponge is pale golden and the centre springs back when touched lightly. Remove from the oven and set aside to cool while you prepare the cheesecake mixture. ››

4 Reduce the oven temperature to 170°C/150°C Fan/Gas Mark 3.

5 **To make the filling,** place the cream cheese, sugar and vanilla seeds in an electric mixer with the paddle attachment in place. Beat until smooth, then gradually add the eggs, beating all the time. Add the soured cream, lime zest and juice and continue to mix until combined. At this point the mixture will be quite runny, so remove the paddle attachment and finish whisking with a large hand whisk until completely smooth.

6 Sit the cake tin on top of a parchment-lined tray (to protect against any spillage from the base) and pour the cheesecake mix over the baked sponge: the batter will rise close to the top of the tin, but that's fine. Bake for 55 minutes: the centre will still be wobbly but, as long as the sides of the cheesecake are firm, this is how it should be. Don't worry if a crack has formed on the surface of the cake: this can often result from a long cooking time and will be hidden by the strawberries piled on top. Turn off the oven, but leave the cheesecake inside for an hour or so, with the oven door propped open with a wooden spoon. Remove from the oven and leave to cool to room temperature before transferring to the fridge for at least 4 hours, uncovered, until completely chilled. Don't be tempted to wrap the cake, as this will cause condensation.

7 On the day you plan to serve the cheesecake, preheat the oven to 250°C/230°C Fan/Gas Mark 9.

8 **To roast the strawberries,** sit the strawberries on a wire rack, tip end pointing up, and place the wire rack on a parchment-lined baking tray. Raising them above the tray allows the strawberries to roast rather than stew. Dust with the 20g of icing sugar and roast for 15 minutes, until the tips of the strawberries have slightly blackened: not all of the icing sugar needs to have melted. Remove from the oven and set aside to cool before placing in the centre of the cake, tip pointing up. Drizzle the cooking juices over the strawberries and dust with the remaining teaspoon of icing sugar. If not serving straight away, return the cake to the fridge: you want to serve this fridge-cold.

Tarts and pies

—

Tarts and pies have a real sense of occasion about them. Which occasion it is will determine which tart or pie is brought to the table. Homely weekend lunches need the Walnut and Black Treacle Tarts (see page 245), while more exotic feasts might require the Pineapple Tartlets with Pandan and Star Anise (see page 255), or those filled with fig and frangipane (see page 247). Classic chocolate tarts are for the smart and well-heeled event, while those baking for a more free-form, rustic occasion might prefer an open galette. The choice is entirely yours: as with all dress codes, guidance is there for those who want it rather than to be followed to the letter. Anything goes, really.

We use four different types of pastry in our tarts and pies: sweet shortcrust, flaky (pâte brisée), polenta and cream cheese.

SWEET SHORTCRUST PASTRY › Yotam first worked with this pastry during his time at Baker & Spice and it's been with us ever since. It's unusual in that it has both a delicate 'snap', yet is robust enough to contain all sorts of fillings. When blind-baked it becomes very light and crisp; when baked directly with the filling it becomes short and buttery. The pastry itself tastes so delicious – with a hint of lemon – that it could pass as a simple biscuit. As long as you chill and rest it properly, it's also very easy to work with.

Most of our recipes use only half a batch of sweet shortcrust pastry, the only exception being the Fig and Pistachio Frangipane Tartlets (see page 247) which uses about two-thirds. This is because one batch uses one egg yolk, so rather than mucking about with half an egg yolk, we find it preferable to make a full batch and freeze the half we do not use. If you find this annoying, you obviously haven't tried to split an egg yolk in two!

FLAKY PASTRY (PÂTE BRISÉE) › This crisp and light pastry comes from the Australian Bourke Street Bakery, always Yotam's first stop when he's visiting Sydney. The dough has a high proportion of water – 45ml – so shrinks (as the water evaporates) during baking. This makes it super light and crisp and is also, because of the flakiness, what leads to the slightly uneven or 'rustic' look of the baked shell. This is fine – we like rustic! – but take care not to over-work or stretch the dough when you're lining a tin: you don't want to encourage too much shrinkage.

CREAM CHEESE PASTRY › This is from *The Pie and Pastry Bible* by Rose Levy Beranbaum. In her introduction, Rose says of 'her favourite pie crust' that it took her several years and over fifty attempts to get right. Thank you, Rose, your hard work was not in vain! It's full of flavour, thanks to the cream cheese, turns a lovely golden brown when baked, and manages to be both tender and flaky at once. The flakiness of the pastry is attributed to the freezing of the butter and flour (for between 30 and 60 minutes), so don't be tempted to skimp on this stage. The cream cheese in the mix also makes it wonderfully pliable and a dream to roll. It makes for a very soft dough, though, so you might need to return it regularly to the fridge while rolling if the day is particularly warm. We have used regular plain flour in our version (rather than the pastry flour which – due to its lower protein content – Rose recommends), as this is the flour more widely available to us.

The consistency of cream cheese can vary hugely (according to its water content) from one brand or from one country to another (see pages 352-3). This can have a bearing on the making of the pastry. In America, for example, cream cheese is very firm, which means that the ingredients for the pastry won't come together in a food processor and the mix needs to be kneaded. In the UK, on the other hand, the cream cheese is more watery and soft, so the ingredients come together very quickly in the food processor. Our instructions are for the cream cheese we have worked with – the soft and spreadable kind – so this is something to be mindful of if your cream cheese is very firm.

POLENTA PASTRY › This was developed in the early days of Ottolenghi, when we needed a 'gritty' texture to stand against the creaminess of various curds and creams in some of our tarts or fruity galettes. We use it here in our Apricot and Thyme Galettes (see page 253).

Our tins, tips and tricks

If you really want to stock up and be able to bake all our tarts and pies, you'll need the following; don't worry if you don't have them all, however, as alternatives are suggested.

MINI-FLUTED TINS › A set of eight (or even twelve) mini-fluted tart tins, 8–9cm wide and 2–2.5cm deep, are needed to make the Walnut and Black Treacle Tarts (see page 245), the Mont Blanc Tarts (see page 235) and the Chai Brûlée Tarts (see page 239). The reality of our kitchen is that we have a selection of very-similar-but-slightly-different mini-tart tins: some are 8cm wide and 2.5cm deep; some are 9cm wide and 2cm deep; and some are 10cm wide and either 2 or 2.5cm deep. When writing *Sweet*, we spent some time obsessing about the difference between one tin and another, and an equal amount of time feeling very relaxed about the fact that whichever tin you use (even within our obsessive margins!), all will be fine: you might make one more or less tart than a recipe states, but worse things happen at sea. Whatever the exact dimensions of your tins, make sure they have removable bases.

LARGE FLUTED TART TINS › The Chocolate Tart with Hazelnut, Rosemary and Orange (see page 241) is made in a large (23 or 25cm) fluted tart tin with a removable base. In addition, if you don't have a set of mini-fluted tins, you can make the Walnut and Black Treacle Tarts (see page 245) and the Mont Blanc Tarts (see page 235) in a large fluted tin. The walnut tart will bake and slice as neatly large as it does in mini form; the Mont Blanc tart, on the other hand, is less neat and tidy when baked whole – it will still taste delicious, but will shatter when sliced. The Chai Brûlée Tarts (see page 239) only work in mini form.

REGULAR MUFFIN TINS › These have 12 moulds: 7cm wide at the top, 5cm wide at the bottom, and 3.5cm deep. A regular muffin tin is used for the Fig and Pistachio Frangipane Tartlets (see page 247) and Little Baked Chocolate Tarts (see page 232), and is also a suitable alternative to the traditional mince pie tin (see below).

TRADITIONAL MINCE PIE TINS › These have 12 moulds with curved bottoms: just under 6cm at the top and 1.5cm deep. They are used for the Pineapple Tartlets (see page 255).

COOKIE CUTTERS › You can't get an 11cm round cookie cutter, we know, so you can either use a 10cm round cutter or, as we do, improvise with whatever you can find that is round and 11cm wide: a lid or a bowl works well. Baking is a science, of course, but necessity can also be the mother of invention when you're trying to create the perfect round of pastry to fit the ideal muffin mould.

TRIMMING PASTRY › Whether you trim your pastry edges before or after baking (if they need trimming) is a matter of personal preference. If there's an overhang, some prefer to trim before baking, others like to trim after the tart is baked so that any shrinkage has been accounted for. We find the second option a bit too crumb-creating, so tend to trim things up before the tart goes in the oven. It's entirely up to you.

DOCKING THE PASTRY › Whether you dock the pastry – pricking it in a few places with the prongs of a fork once the tin has been lined and before it is baked – is something we also leave up to you. The reason for docking is to prevent the pastry rising and baking unevenly in the oven. It's not something we tend to do, regardless of whether the cases are being blind-baked or going straight in the oven with their filling, but if you were always taught to dock your pastry, there is no downside to doing so.

Working with pastry requires you to feel confident about assessing what you are creating and then making a call. If you've rolled your pastry a bit thinner than suggested, for example, it will need a minute or two less in the oven; thicker pastry will need a minute longer. The difference between the ideal 'slight wobble' of a filling and a filling which is so unset as to still be liquid is something you need to be able to recognize. As we've said before, the best way to become a really confident baker is to make the same thing more than once – bake and re-bake the same recipe until you can read it like an old friend. You'll soon know it better than it knows itself.

RHUBARB AND BLUEBERRY GALETTE

Rhubarb and blueberry galette

The rhubarb and blueberry are so good together here, but do play around with the fruits, if you like: figs and raspberries also pair nicely. If you'd prefer to use just one fruit, some thinly sliced peaches, apricots or apples work well. Serve this with some whipped cream or vanilla ice cream alongside.

The Amaretti biscuits are useful for soaking up the excess liquid from the fruits. You want the dry, crumbly variety, not the soft and chewy ones. They're not hard to get hold of, but if you find yourself without, crushed Savoiardi biscuits or ground almonds can be used instead. They won't provide the flavour hit of the Amaretti, but will be fine.

SERVES 8

CREAM CHEESE PASTRY

120g unsalted butter, fridge-cold,
   cut into 2cm cubes
185g plain flour, plus extra for dusting
¼ tsp salt
⅛ tsp baking powder
85g cream cheese
2–3 tbsp double cream
2 tsp cider vinegar

BASE

50g Amaretti biscuits
45g caster sugar
1 tbsp plain flour
1 tsp ground cinnamon

FILLING

220g rhubarb, trimmed and washed,
   halved lengthways, if thick,
   and cut into 5cm lengths
120g fresh blueberries
100g caster sugar
1 tbsp tapioca flour (or cornflour)
finely grated zest of 1 small orange
   (1 tsp)
⅛ tsp salt

GLAZE

1 large egg
2 tsp water
1 tbsp demerara sugar

The pastry can be made 2 days in advance (it will last longer, but the cream cheese will make it discolour) and kept in the fridge, wrapped in cling film. It can also be frozen, again wrapped in cling film, for up to 2 months.

Once baked, this will keep for 1 day at room temperature.

1   **To make the pastry,** wrap the cubes of butter in cling film and place in the freezer for about an hour for the butter to freeze solid. Place the flour, salt and baking powder in a re-sealable freezer bag and freeze for at least 30 minutes. See page 227 for more on freezing the butter and flour.

2   Tip the flour mix into the bowl of a food processor and process for about 30 seconds to combine. Add the cream cheese and process for another 20 seconds, or until the mixture has the consistency of coarse breadcrumbs. Add the frozen butter cubes and pulse to form crumbs: they'll be uneven in size – some the size of peas and some a bit larger – but that's fine.

3   Add 2 tablespoons of double cream and the vinegar and pulse until the dough starts to hold together: add the extra tablespoon of cream if the dough needs it. Tip on to a clean work surface and use your hands and knuckles to press the mixture until it holds together in one piece. Wrap the dough loosely in cling film (or put it in the bag you used to chill the flour) and press to flatten it into a disc. Place in the fridge for at least 45 minutes (or up to 2 days).

4   Preheat the oven to 210°C/190°C Fan/Gas Mark 6.

5   **For the base,** roughly crush the Amaretti biscuits into a small bowl. Add the sugar, flour and cinnamon and set aside.

6   **For the fruit filling,** place all the ingredients in a medium bowl, toss gently to combine and set aside.

7   Remove the disc of dough from the fridge 10 minutes before you want to roll it, so that it has some malleability. Place it on a large sheet of baking parchment which has been lightly dusted with flour. Roll the dough out evenly into a large circle, about 38–40cm wide and 2mm thick. Trim the edges to create a rough circle, then transfer it, along with the parchment paper (it is too soft to transfer alone), on to a large baking tray. Sprinkle the Amaretti biscuit crumb mix in a 25cm wide circle over the middle of the pastry. Spoon the fruit filling on top of the crumbs, then carefully draw the pastry border up and over the fruit, roughly pleating it as you go, and leaving a small area of the fruit-filled centre of the galette exposed. If the pastry has become too soft or warm during this process, place the galette in the fridge to chill for up to 1 hour before baking.

8   Beat the egg with the water in a bowl and brush all over the outside of the pastry. Sprinkle with the sugar, then bake for about 40 minutes, rotating the tray halfway through, or until the galette is golden. Remove from the oven and set aside on a wire rack to cool before serving, with whipped cream or vanilla ice cream alongside.

Little baked chocolate tarts with tahini and sesame brittle (or marmalade)

Rather than making one large chocolate tart to serve after a meal (see the Chocolate Tart with Hazelnut, Rosemary and Orange, page 241), it's sometimes fun to make lots of individual tarts. Chocolate mousse pairs so well with so many flavours that you can fill the base of these tarts with pretty much anything you like. We've given two options here – tahini and the marmalade – but you can play around with fillings: a teaspoon of crumbled halva, mint icing, some chopped nuts, a slice of banana, the brittle used in the large chocolate tart, a teaspoon of jam – they all work well. It's fun, if serving them as canapés, to have a mix of fillings, so that people have a pop of surprise. If you want to give a clue as to what's inside, you can do so with the garnish. A shard of Sesame Brittle, page 334, works well on top of the tahini tarts, as photographed, or a thin slice of candied orange peel on those with the marmalade filling.

Quantity wise, we've made enough of the marmalade filling to fill one whole batch of tarts. If you want to do half and half, you'll just need to reduce the amount of filling you make.

MAKES 12
—

SWEET SHORTCRUST PASTRY
(YOU WILL ONLY NEED ⅔ QUANTITY)
300g plain flour, plus extra for dusting
90g icing sugar
¼ tsp salt
200g unsalted butter, fridge-cold, cut into cubes, plus an extra 10g, melted, for brushing
finely grated zest of 1 lemon (1 tsp)
1 large egg yolk
20ml water

CHOCOLATE MOUSSE
200g chocolate (70% cocoa solids), roughly chopped
150g unsalted butter, roughly cut into 2cm dice
3 large eggs
50g caster sugar
Dutch-processed cocoa powder, for dusting
—

TAHINI FILLING
180g tahini paste
60g honey

MARMALADE FILLING
(HALVE THE QUANTITIES IF YOU ARE DOING HALF THE BATCH WITH MARMALADE AND HALF WITH TAHINI)
180g Seville marmalade, fine-cut or no-peel

MASCARPONE QUENELLES
120g mascarpone

The pastry will make more than you'll need. It will keep well in the fridge, wrapped in cling film, for up to 3 days. It also freezes well, wrapped first in cling film and then aluminium foil, for up to 2 months. If freezing the dough, do so in disc form or, if planning to make individual tarts, roll it out and cut it to size so that you're all set for your next bake.

Once baked, any uneaten tarts may be kept at room temperature or in the fridge for up to 2 days. If kept in the fridge, just bring them back to room temperature before serving.

1 **To make the pastry,** sift together the flour, icing sugar and salt and place in a food processor. Add the butter and lemon zest and pulse a few times, until the mixture has the consistency of fresh breadcrumbs. Lightly whisk together the egg yolk and water and add this to the mix: the dough will feel quite wet, but this is as it should be. Process once more, just until the dough comes together, then tip on to a clean, lightly floured work surface. Lightly knead the dough into a ball. Wrap loosely in cling film and press gently to form a flattish disc. The dough is very soft, so keep it in the fridge for at least 1 hour (or up to 3 days).

2 Lightly brush the moulds of a regular muffin tin with the melted butter and dust with flour, tapping away the excess.

3 When ready to roll out, allow the dough to rest at room temperature for 30 minutes (if it has been in the fridge for more than a few hours) and place on a lightly floured work surface. Tap all over with a rolling pin to soften slightly before rolling out until 2–3mm thick. Using a 10 or 11cm round cookie cutter (or alternative, see page 228), cut out twelve circles and gently ease these into the muffin moulds, pressing down to fill the moulds. Re-roll the pastry, if necessary, until you get twelve circles. Refrigerate for at least 1 hour before blind-baking the cases. The remaining third of the dough can be frozen for future use.

4 Preheat the oven to 180°C/160°C Fan/Gas Mark 4.

5 **To blind bake the tart cases,** line the pastry cases with squares of baking parchment or paper liners. Fill with a layer of rice or dried beans and bake for 20–25 minutes, or until the pastry shells are a light golden brown around the edges. Remove the parchment paper or liners and the rice or beans and return the pastry to the oven for another 3 minutes. Set the pastry cases aside (still in their tin) to cool down.

6 **To make the chocolate mousse,** place the chocolate and butter in a large heatproof bowl over a pan of simmering water, making sure the base of the bowl is not touching the water. Stir occasionally until melted, then remove from the heat and set aside to cool for about 10 minutes.

7 Place the eggs and sugar in the bowl of an electric mixer with the whisk attachment in place. Whisk on a high speed for at least 10 minutes, until the mixture is extremely pale, thick and foamy and has tripled in volume. Remove the bowl from the machine and, using a large slotted spoon or hand-held whisk, gently fold a third of the mix into the melted chocolate and butter. Gently but thoroughly fold in the rest of the egg-sugar mixture until well combined.

8 Increase the oven temperature to 200°C/180°C Fan/Gas Mark 6.

9 **If using the tahini filling,** place the tahini and honey in the bowl of an electric mixer with the whisk attachment in place and beat for approximately 3 minutes until thickened. Spoon 1 teaspoon of the tahini mixture into the base of each tart shell and set aside. **If going with the marmalade option,** spoon a teaspoon of marmalade into the base of each shell and set aside.

10 Pipe or spoon the chocolate mixture over the tahini or marmalade filling, right up to and over the rim. Be confident here: you want the mousse to rise up and form a dome shape. Once full, bake for 9–10 minutes, until a crust has formed on top but the centre is still gooey. Set aside to cool completely in the tin – the tarts are too molten to be served warm. When cool, use the tip of a small knife to prise the tarts out of their moulds. Dust lightly with cocoa powder and use two small teaspoons to form 'quenelles' of mascarpone to top each tart.

Mont Blanc tarts

Named after the snowy mountain they resemble, Mont Blanc tarts – with their white meringue, whipped cream and tan-coloured chestnut purée – can often taste more fabulous than they look, with all that beige and white. We wanted to see if we could improve their visual appeal – bring in some more contrast by playing around with the colours, for example – but after various experiments (dark chocolate pastry, a lighter-coloured purée) we were beginning to think that the tried-and-tested route up this particular mountain was the only winning one.

It was a moment of pure synchronicity, then, that at one of our weekly pastry meetings there were various things lying around which came together in a flash: some empty tart shells, candied pecans, an open can of chestnut spread. At the same time, Helen and Yotam both grabbed an empty shell, filled it with the chestnut spread, spooned over smooth whipped cream and added the element that had been missing – the candied pecans – which brought the crunch and the look needed. There's a metaphor in there, we're sure, about climbing mountains, and not giving up, and things tasting all the sweeter when you've had to work just that little bit harder to earn them.

MAKES 8

You will need eight mini-fluted tins, about 8–9cm wide and 2–3cm deep. Alternatively, you can make this in one large fluted tart tin, around 25cm wide and 3cm deep.

The pastry can be made up to 3 days ahead and kept in the fridge (wrapped in cling film) until ready to roll. It can also be frozen for up to 2 months. The candied pecans can be made up to 5 days in advance and kept in an airtight container.

Once assembled, the tarts are best eaten on the day they are baked.

FLAKY PASTRY
200g plain flour
120g unsalted butter, fridge-cold, cut into 1cm dice
30g caster sugar
¼ tsp salt
½ tsp white wine vinegar
3 tbsp ice-cold water

CANDIED PECANS
1 tbsp maple syrup
1 tbsp liquid glucose
1 tbsp caster sugar
120g pecan halves
⅛ tsp flaky sea salt

FILLING
60g dark cooking chocolate (70% cocoa solids)
320g sweetened chestnut spread (we use Clement Faugier; whichever brand you use, just make sure that it is not the unsweetened variety)

VANILLA WHIPPED CREAM
300ml double cream
1 tbsp icing sugar
1 tsp vanilla extract
½ tsp brandy

1   **For the pastry,** place the flour, butter, sugar and salt in the bowl of a food processor. Blitz a few times, until it is the consistency of fine breadcrumbs, then add the vinegar and water. Continue to work for a few seconds, then transfer to your work surface. Shape into a ball and flatten into a disc, wrap in cling film and set aside in the fridge for at least 1 hour (or up to 3 days).

2   Preheat the oven to 200°C/180°C Fan/Gas Mark 6.

3   **To line the tart cases,** allow the dough to rest at room temperature for 30 minutes (if it has been in the fridge for more than a few hours) and place on a lightly floured work surface. Roll out the dough to about 3mm thick and cut out eight circles, 14cm wide. Re-roll the dough, if necessary, to get eight circles. Transfer one circle at a time to the 8–9cm wide and 2–3cm deep fluted tins and gently press the pastry into the corners of the tart tin: you want it to fit snugly and for there to be a decent amount of pastry hanging over the edge of the tart case, as the pastry can shrink a little when baked. Place in the fridge for 30 minutes to rest. ››

4   **To blind bake the tart cases,** line the pastry bases with baking parchment or paper liners and fill with baking beans. Bake for 18 minutes, until the pastry is golden brown at the edges. Remove the beans and paper and cook for another 8 minutes, or until the base is golden brown. Remove from the oven and set aside to cool completely in the tray. Once cool, trim the pastry (so that it can be removed from the tray) and set aside until ready to fill.

5   Increase the oven temperature to 210°C/190°C Fan/Gas Mark 6. Line a baking tray (with a lipped edge) with baking parchment and set aside.

6   **To make the candied pecans,** put the maple syrup, glucose and sugar into a small saucepan and place over a low heat. Stir gently until the sugar has melted, then add the pecans and salt. Stir so that the nuts are coated in syrup, then tip the nuts on to the lined baking tray. Place in the oven for about 8 minutes, or until the syrup is bubbling around the nuts. Remove the tray from the oven and set aside until completely cooled. When the nuts are cooled, the glaze should be completely crisp; if not, return them to the oven for a few more minutes. Once cooled, break or roughly chop the nuts into 0.5cm pieces and set aside until ready to use.

7   **Make the filling** when you are ready to assemble. Place the chocolate in a heatproof bowl over a pan of simmering water, making sure that the base of the bowl is not touching the water. Stir occasionally until melted, then use a pastry brush to line the inside of each case with the chocolate. Set aside for about 30 minutes, to set, then fill with enough chestnut spread so that it rises about halfway up the sides of the tart cases.

8   **For the vanilla whipped cream,** pour the cream into the bowl of an electric mixer with the whisk attachment in place. Add the icing sugar, vanilla extract and brandy and whisk on a high speed for 1 minute, or until medium-soft peaks form.

9   Divide the whipped cream between the tarts, so that it is slightly domed on top of the chestnut spread. Sprinkle the candied pecans generously on top – you might have a tablespoon or two left over, but these can be saved to munch on, to sprinkle over your next bowl of breakfast granola or porridge, or to use in the Knickerbocker Glory (see page 293) – and serve.

Chai brûlée tarts

We've taken our inspiration for these from Sydney's Bourke Street Bakery, where Yotam had his first bite of their brûlée tarts. We've ramped up and chai-i-fied the spices, and we bake our custard in the oven (rather than on the stove top, as does Bourke Street), so it is set. A layer of skin can develop on the surface of the custard, but don't worry: once it's spooned into the tart cases and the tops are sugared and burnt, the skin won't be noticed, so don't be tempted to take it off. Hold your nerve when caramelizing the custard: the darker you can take it the better, in terms of flavour, contrast and looks.

MAKES 10–12

We use twelve fluted tart cases, 8.5cm wide and 2.5cm deep. If you have 10cm round tins, that's also fine: you'll just make eight tarts rather than twelve. You will also need a blowtorch to caramelize the custard (don't place them under a hot grill, as the pastry will burn). You don't need anything industrial or expensive: there are lots of smaller ones around which do the job well.

The dough can be made up to 3 days ahead and kept in the fridge (wrapped in cling film) until ready to roll. It can also be frozen for up to 2 months. You need to start preparing the custard a day ahead to allow the flavours to infuse.

Once assembled, the tartlets are best eaten on the day they are baked.

CUSTARD
560ml double cream
6cm piece of fresh ginger (45g), peeled and coarsely grated
7 cardamom pods, crushed, so that the seeds are released
3 large cinnamon sticks, broken in half
1 English breakfast teabag
3 bay leaves
½ tsp whole black peppercorns
1 whole nutmeg

65g caster sugar, plus an extra 80g for the caramelized topping
165g egg yolks (from 8 large eggs) (the whites can be frozen for future use)

FLAKY PASTRY
200g plain flour
120g unsalted butter, fridge-cold, cut into 1cm dice, plus extra, melted, for brushing
30g caster sugar
¼ tsp salt
½ tsp white wine vinegar
3 tbsp ice-cold water

1   To make the custard, place the cream in a large, heavy-based pan and add the ginger, cardamom (the green casing and inner seeds), cinnamon, teabag, bay leaves, peppercorns, nutmeg and 65g sugar. Bring slowly to the boil, then remove from the heat straight away. Set aside to cool, and leave in the fridge, covered, overnight.

2   The following day, preheat the oven to 180°C/160°C Fan/Gas Mark 4.

3   Gently warm the cream over a medium heat before straining through a fine sieve into a bowl and discarding the spices. Place the egg yolks in a large clean bowl and whisk to combine. Whisking the whole time so that the eggs don't curdle, slowly pour the cream over the eggs. Transfer the mixture to a 25 x 20cm glass or ceramic ovenproof dish and place this inside a larger baking tray. Place the baking tray in the oven before filling it with enough boiling water (poured straight from a just-boiled kettle) so that it rises halfway up the sides of the baking dish filled with the custard. Bake for 15–20 minutes, until just cooked: the middle will be a bit wobbly but the edges will have set completely. Lift the custard dish out of the water bath and set aside to cool before covering and chilling for about an hour, or until ready to use. Don't worry if a skin forms on top (see introduction).

4   For the pastry, place the flour, butter, sugar and salt in the bowl of a food processor. Blitz a few times, until the consistency of fine breadcrumbs, then add the vinegar and water. Continue to work for a few seconds, then transfer to your work surface. Shape into a ball and flatten into a disc, wrap in cling film and set aside in the fridge for about 1 hour (or up to 3 days). ››

5   Lightly brush twelve fluted tart cases, 8.5cm wide and 2.5cm deep, with melted butter. When ready to roll out, allow the dough to rest at room temperature for 30 minutes (if it has been in the fridge for more than a few hours) and place on a lightly floured work surface. Roll out the dough until it is just 2mm thick, then cut out twelve circles, 12cm wide, and line the tart cases. Re-roll the dough, if necessary, to get twelve circles. Gently press the dough into the corners of the tart cases so that it fits snugly; if there is any pastry hanging over the edges, trim this now. Place in the fridge for 30 minutes to allow the pastry to rest.

6   **To blind bake the tart cases,** preheat the oven to 200°C/180°C Fan/Gas Mark 6. Place the tart tins on a baking tray, then line the cases with squares of baking parchment or paper liners and fill with baking beans. Bake for 18 minutes, until the pastry is golden brown at the edges. Remove the beans and paper and cook for another 9–10 minutes, until the base is golden brown. Don't worry if your pastry shrinks a bit during cooking: you actually want a little bit of shrinkage to ensure the perfect ratio of custard to pastry. Don't worry, also, if the edges become a little uneven: once the tarts are filled with custard and the surface has been blowtorched, this will not be noticeable. Remove from the oven and set aside to cool.

7   Just before serving, remove the pastry cases from the tins. Carefully spoon the custard into the cases, filling them all the way to the top. Use a palette knife to even them off – not worrying, again, if the edges are uneven at this stage – then sprinkle the remaining sugar liberally on top of each one. Blowtorch the sugar to create a crisp, dark-golden caramel, and serve.

Chocolate tart with hazelnut, rosemary and orange

This rich and decadent tart is essentially a baked chocolate mousse. On its own it is smooth and rich and really rather good. Coupled with the hazelnut crunch on the base – which is similar to a brittle but easier, as you don't have to make a caramel – it's the high point on which to end a meal, alongside some lightly whipped cream to offset the richness.

MAKES 1 LARGE TART, SERVES 8–10

___

CRYSTALLIZED ROSEMARY GARNISH (OPTIONAL)
1–2 sprigs rosemary (5g)
½ large egg white, lightly whisked
20g caster sugar

FILLING
120ml double cream
90g unsalted butter, cubed
3 sprigs of rosemary (10g)
shaved peel of 1 orange (avoiding the bitter white pith)
270g dark cooking chocolate (70% cocoa solids), finely chopped
1 large egg, plus 3 large egg yolks
90g caster sugar
2 tbsp Dutch-processed cocoa powder, to serve

HAZELNUT 'BRITTLE'
2 tbsp golden syrup (or light corn syrup)
2 tbsp maple syrup (or clear honey)
2 tbsp caster sugar
⅛ tsp salt
100g chopped roasted hazelnuts

SWEET SHORTCRUST PASTRY (YOU WILL ONLY NEED ½ QUANTITY)
300g plain flour
90g icing sugar
¼ tsp salt
200g unsalted butter, fridge-cold, cut into cubes, plus extra for greasing
finely grated zest of 1 lemon (1 tsp)
1 large egg yolk
20ml water

___

1   **If crystallizing the rosemary sprigs for garnishing,** lay them flat on a chopping board and, one at a time, lightly brush each side with the egg white. Sprinkle the sugar evenly and lightly over both sides of the leaves, then set aside in a cool, dry place on a wire rack for about 8 hours, until crisp.

2   **To infuse the chocolate cream,** put the cream, butter, rosemary and orange peel into a small saucepan and place over a low heat. When the mixture is just coming to a simmer and the butter has melted, turn off the heat and set aside to infuse for an hour or two, or overnight in the fridge.

3   Preheat the oven to 220°C/200°C Fan/Gas Mark 7. **To make the 'brittle',** place the golden syrup, maple syrup, sugar and salt in a small saucepan over a low heat and stir until the sugar has dissolved. Add the hazelnuts and mix until the nuts are evenly coated, then transfer the mixture to a small parchment-lined baking tray and spread the nuts out with a spoon. Bake for 7–8 minutes, until the mixture is golden brown and bubbling, then remove from the oven and allow to cool completely before roughly chopping it into 0.5cm pieces. Set aside until ready to use and turn off the oven. ››

The pastry will make more than you'll need. It will keep well in the fridge, wrapped in cling film, for up to 3 days. It also freezes well, wrapped first in cling film and then aluminium foil, for up to 2 months. If freezing the dough, do so in disc form. The 'brittle' can be made up to 5 days in advance and kept in an airtight container at room temperature, or frozen for up to 1 month. Don't keep it in the fridge, where it will 'weep'. The infused cream can be prepared up to 1 day ahead and kept in the fridge. The crystallized rosemary sprigs can be made a day in advance and left at room temperature, uncovered, until ready to serve.

This can be made in a 23 or 25cm fluted tart tin with a removable base.

Once assembled, the tart is best eaten on the day it is baked but it will keep for up to 2 days, stored in an airtight container.

4   **For the pastry,** sift together the flour, icing sugar and salt and place in a food processor. Add the butter and lemon zest and pulse a few times, until the mixture has the consistency of fresh breadcrumbs. Lightly whisk together the egg yolk and water and add this to the mix: the dough will feel quite wet, but this is as it should be. Process once more, just until the dough comes together, then tip on to a clean, lightly floured work surface. Lightly knead the dough into the shape of a ball and divide into two equal halves. Wrap each half loosely in cling film and press gently to form two flattish discs. The dough is very soft, so you need to set it aside in the fridge for at least 1 hour (or up to 3 days).

5   **To line the tart case,** lightly grease your chosen tart tin, see Kit Note on page 241. When ready to roll out, allow the dough to rest at room temperature for 30 minutes (if it has been in the fridge for more than a few hours) and place on a lightly floured work surface. Tap all over with a rolling pin to soften slightly before rolling out, until it's about 33cm wide and 4mm thick. Drape the pastry over the tin and gently press it into place, filling any cracks that you have with a little extra pastry. Trim if desired, then place the pastry in the fridge for at least 30 minutes to rest and chill. The remaining pastry can be frozen for future use.

6   **To blind bake the tart case,** preheat the oven to 200°C/180°C Fan/Gas Mark 6. Line the tart case with a large piece of parchment paper, covering the base and sides. Fill with baking beans (uncooked rice or pulses also work well) and bake for 20 minutes. Scoop out the beans/rice/pulses, lift off the parchment paper and return the tart to the oven. Bake the pastry, uncovered, for another 6 or 7 minutes, or until lightly golden and dry. Remove from the oven and allow to cool for 10 minutes before sprinkling the chopped hazelnut 'brittle' all over the base. Set aside until needed.

7   **To make the chocolate filling,** place the chocolate in a heatproof bowl set over a pan of simmering water, making sure the base of the bowl isn't touching the water. Return the infused cream to a low heat and stir gently until hot. Strain the cream over the chocolate (the rosemary and orange peel can be discarded), then stir the chocolate (still over the pan of simmering water) until melted and smooth. Remove the bowl from the pan and set aside.

8   In the meantime, place the egg, yolks and sugar in the bowl of an electric mixer with the whisk attachment in place. Whisk on a medium-high speed for about 4 minutes, until light and thick. Fold a third of this sabayon mix through the melted chocolate, then gently transfer the lightened chocolate mix back into the sabayon. Fold through to fully combine, then scrape the chocolate filling into the tart case, over the hazelnut 'brittle'. Gently smooth out the top and bake for 12 minutes. Remove from the oven and set aside for 20 minutes or so to cool. Using a tea strainer or small sieve, sift the cocoa powder over the tart just before serving. If using, garnish with the crystallized rosemary sprigs and serve with some lightly whipped cream, if you like.

Walnut and black treacle tarts with crystallized sage

To say this is a very 'treacly' treacle tart might seem like tautology, but, in the world of treacle tarts, it's an especially soft and gooey offering. As well as being rich and sweet, though, it's got an edge of malty crispness from the addition of the bran flakes.

The crystallized sage leaves look great here and need to be prepared in advance so that they can dry. But they can be replaced with plain sage leaves, if you like. Alternatively, you can serve the tarts without any garnish at all, with a generous amount of crème fraîche or some vanilla ice cream.

SERVES 8

You will need eight mini-fluted tart tins, 9cm wide and 2cm deep. Alternatively, you can make this in one large fluted tart tin, 26 or 27cm wide and 3cm deep.

The pastry can be made up to 3 days ahead and kept in the fridge (wrapped in cling film) until ready to roll. It can also be frozen for up to 2 months. The sage leaves need to be made in advance in order to dry, and should be left at room temperature, uncovered, until ready to serve. They can be made a day in advance.

Once assembled, the tarts are best eaten on the day they are baked. They still taste great for 2 or 3 days afterwards: they'll just have lost their crispness.

CRYSTALLIZED SAGE GARNISH (OPTIONAL)
8 medium sage leaves
1 large egg white, lightly whisked
25g caster sugar

FLAKY PASTRY
200g plain flour
120g unsalted butter, fridge-cold, cut into 1cm dice, plus extra, melted, for brushing
30g caster sugar
¼ tsp salt
½ tsp white wine vinegar
3 tbsp ice-cold water

FILLING
180g walnut halves
110g wholemeal sourdough bread (crusts removed), roughly torn (80g net)
50g bran flakes
finely grated zest from 1 small orange (1tsp)
100g black treacle
220g golden syrup
30g unsalted butter
100ml double cream
2 large eggs, lightly whisked

1   **If crystallizing the sage leaves for garnishing,** lay them flat on a chopping board and, one at a time, brush each side lightly with the egg white. Sprinkle the sugar evenly and lightly over both sides and set on a wire rack in a cool, dry place for 8 hours, until crisp.

2   **For the pastry,** place the flour, butter, sugar and salt in the bowl of a food processor. Blitz a few times, until it is the consistency of fine breadcrumbs, then add the vinegar and water. Continue to work for a few seconds, then transfer to your work surface. Shape into a ball and flatten into a disc, wrap in cling film and set aside in the fridge for about 1 hour (or up to 3 days).

3   Lightly brush eight fluted tins, 9cm wide and 2cm deep (or one larger tin; see Kit Note), with melted butter. When ready to roll out, allow the dough to rest at room temperature for 30 minutes (if it has been in the fridge for more than a few hours) and place on a lightly floured work surface. Roll out the dough until just under 0.5cm thick, then cut out eight circles, 14cm wide, and transfer to the fluted tins. Re-roll the dough, if necessary, to get eight circles. If you are making one large tart, roll out the dough to form a 34cm wide circle. Gently press the pastry into the corners of the tart tins so that it fits snugly. There will be some pastry hanging over the sides of the tins, but don't trim it at this stage. Place in the fridge for 30 minutes to allow the pastry to rest. »

4   Preheat the oven to 180°C/160°C Fan/Gas Mark 4. Spread the walnuts out on a baking tray and cook in the oven for 10 minutes, until golden brown. Set aside to cool and increase the oven temperature to 200°C/180°C Fan/Gas Mark 6.

5   To blind bake the tart cases, line the cases with squares of baking parchment or paper liners and fill with baking beans. Bake for 18–20 minutes (or 25 minutes for the larger tart), until the pastry is golden brown at the edges. Remove the beans and paper and cook for another 10 minutes, or 12 minutes for the larger tart, until the base is golden brown. Remove from the oven and set aside to cool.

6   To make the filling, place the bread and bran flakes in the small bowl of a food processor and blitz to form fine crumbs. Transfer to a large bowl and then blitz 100g of the walnuts to a fine crumb in the food processor. Add these to the breadcrumb mix along with the orange zest. Roughly chop the remaining walnuts and add to the bowl. Mix to combine and set aside.

7   Put the black treacle, golden syrup and butter in a small saucepan and place over a high heat. Cook for 2–3 minutes, stirring frequently, until the butter has melted and the syrup is runny. Pour into the bowl with the breadcrumb mix, combine well and stir through the cream and eggs. Pour the treacle mixture into the tart shells and bake for 17 minutes (the larger tart will need a minute or two longer), until just set.

8   Remove from the oven and set aside to cool for about 20 minutes before trimming the pastry edges: this can be done by snapping off the overhanging edges with your fingers or by running a small knife around the outside of the tin. Remove from the tins and serve warm or at room temperature with a crispy sage leaf on top and some crème fraîche or ice cream alongside.

Fig and pistachio frangipane tartlets

These received an official online 'thumbs-up' when Yotam posted a picture of them from the display of our Belgravia shop. The stunningly Instagrammable picture – with the cut side of the figs facing up in the tarts – was flooded with thousands of 'likes'. They are lovely as they are, or served with a spoonful of vanilla ice cream, soured cream or crème fraîche alongside.

If you can't get large figs, use six smaller ones sliced in half (rather than quarters). Alternatively, raspberries work just as well: place three large raspberries in the centre of each tart and bake as usual.

As with many of our recipes which call for a nip of brandy, don't worry if you don't have an open bottle to hand. It's not there for its own flavour so much as to draw out the subtle flavour of the pistachios, but the tartlets work fine without it.

MAKES 12

The pastry will make more than you'll need. It will keep well in the fridge, wrapped in cling film, for up to 3 days. It also freezes well, wrapped first in cling film and then aluminium foil, for up to 2 months. If freezing the dough, do so in disc form or, if planning to make individual tarts, roll it out and cut it to size so that you're all set for your next bake. The frangipane can be made up to 2 days in advance and kept in the fridge until ready to use. It will set reasonably firm, so remove it from the fridge 30 minutes before you want to fill the tarts.

Once assembled, these are best eaten on the day they are baked. They will keep for up to 2 days, stored in an airtight container: you can eat them at room temperature or heat them through for 5 minutes before serving.

SWEET SHORTCRUST PASTRY
(YOU WILL ONLY NEED ⅔ QUANTITY)
300g plain flour, plus extra for dusting
90g icing sugar
¼ tsp salt
200g unsalted butter, fridge-cold, cut into cubes, plus an extra 10g, melted, for brushing
finely grated zest of 1 lemon (1 tsp)
1 large egg yolk
20ml water

PISTACHIO FRANGIPANE CREAM
90g shelled pistachios, plus extra, blitzed, to finish (optional)
35g ground almonds
35g plain flour
⅛ tsp salt
125g unsalted butter, at room temperature
125g caster sugar
finely grated zest of 1 lemon (1 tsp)
2 large eggs, lightly beaten
1 tbsp brandy (optional)
3 large ripe figs, quartered, or 6 smaller figs, halved (180g)

1   **To make the pastry,** sift together the flour, icing sugar and salt and place in a food processor. Add the butter and lemon zest and pulse a few times, until the mixture has the consistency of fresh breadcrumbs. Lightly whisk together the egg yolk and water and add this to the mix: the dough will feel quite wet, but this is as it should be. Process once more, just until the dough comes together, then tip on to a clean, lightly floured work surface. Lightly knead the dough into a ball, wrap loosely in cling film and press gently to form a flattish disc. The dough is very soft, so you need to keep it in the fridge for at least 1 hour (or up to 3 days).

2   Lightly brush the moulds of a regular muffin tin with the melted butter and dust with flour, tapping away the excess.

3   When ready to roll out, allow the dough to rest at room temperature for 30 minutes (if it has been in the fridge for more than a few hours) and place on a lightly floured work surface. Tap all over with a rolling pin to soften slightly before rolling out until 2–3mm thick. Using a 10 or 11cm round cookie cutter (or alternative, see page 228), cut out twelve circles and gently ease these into the muffin moulds, pressing down to fill the moulds. Re-roll the pastry, if necessary, until you get twelve circles. Refrigerate for at least 1 hour before blind-baking the cases. The remaining third of the dough can be frozen for future use. ››

4   Preheat the oven to 180°C/160°C Fan/Gas Mark 4.

5   **To blind bake the tart cases,** line the pastry cases with baking parchment or paper liners. Fill with a layer of rice or dried beans and bake for 25–30 minutes, or until the pastry shells are a light golden brown around the edges. Remove the parchment paper or liners and the rice or beans and set the shells aside to cool in the tin.

6   **To make the frangipane cream,** place the pistachios in the small bowl of a food processor and grind until fine but not oily. Transfer to a small bowl, mix in the ground almonds, flour and salt and set aside.

7   Place the butter, sugar and lemon zest in the bowl of an electric mixer with the paddle attachment in place. Cream on a medium speed for 1–2 minutes, until light but not too fluffy. Reduce the speed to low and gradually add the beaten eggs. Don't worry if the mixture curdles a bit at this stage: it will be brought back together later. Add the nut/flour mix, beat on a low speed until combined and, finally, add the brandy (if using).

8   Increase the oven temperature to 200°C/180°C Fan/Gas Mark 6.

9   When ready to bake, use a piping bag or two dessertspoons to fill the baked tart cases (still in the muffin tin) with the frangipane: it should rise about two-thirds of the way up the sides of the cases. Place a quarter (or half) of a fig in the middle of each tart, cut side facing up, pressing down very lightly so that it's slightly embedded in the mixture. Once they are all filled, bake the tarts for about 20 minutes, until the frangipane is starting to brown at the edges but the middle remains slightly soft. Set aside to cool in the tin for 10 minutes before easing the tarts out of the moulds and placing on a wire rack. The tarts can either be served warm or left to come to room temperature. Serve sprinkled with blitzed pistachios, if you like.

Schiacciata with grapes and fennel seeds

This is neither a tart nor a pie, we know. But in the absence of a bread or yeasted chapter, temporary lodgings have been found here for the schiacciata. It's a delicious alternative to bread at breakfast, but great as a snack or before a meal any time of the day. It's basically a very thin focaccia with – thanks to the oil – a nice crisp bottom. Making your own bread is always rewarding, but when the rewards are coupled with very little effort, as is the case here, it feels like a double win.

We use normal black grapes here, as they are easy to come by. If you can find Italian Strawberry grapes (Uva Fragola) or Muscat grapes, you'll get an extra layer of sweet flavour here.

SERVES 4–6

330g strong white bread flour,
　plus extra for dusting
¾ tsp active dried yeast
200ml lukewarm water (about 40°C)
about 100ml olive oil
1 large egg yolk
3½ tbsp dark muscovado sugar

2 tsp flaky sea salt
250g seedless black grapes,
　halved lengthways
1 tbsp fennel seeds, lightly crushed
　in a pestle and mortar
2 tsp polenta

You will need a large baking tray, around 40 x 30cm.

The bread is best eaten while still warm and crunchy, but any leftovers will keep for up to a day.

1   Place half the flour in the bowl of an electric mixer and add the yeast. Pour over the water and stir well to form a wet dough. Cover with cling film and set aside for 1 hour, in a warm and draught-free place, for the dough to rise slightly.

2   Transfer the dough to a food mixer with the dough hook attachment in place. Add the remaining flour, 1 tablespoon of oil, the egg yolk, 1½ teaspoons of sugar and 1 teaspoon of salt. Beat on a medium-low speed for 6 minutes, until the mixture comes together into a sticky ball. Transfer to a large bowl which has been brushed with 1 tablespoon of oil, cover with cling film and set aside for 1 hour until doubled in size.

3   Place the grapes in a small bowl with the fennel seeds and 2 tablespoons of sugar. Mix together and set aside in a warm place for at least 1 hour.

4   Preheat the oven to 250°C/230°C Fan/Gas Mark 9.

5   Tip the dough on to a lightly floured work surface and pull into a large 40 x 30cm rectangle – either stretch it by hand or use a rolling pin, if that helps. Brush a 40 x 30cm baking tray with 3 tablespoons of oil and sprinkle evenly with the polenta. Transfer the dough on to the baking tray, stretching out the edges to fit snugly. Brush with the remaining 2 tablespoons of oil, then spoon over the grape mixture, mashing some of the grapes with your fingers as you go. Sprinkle the final tablespoon of sugar, along with the remaining 1 teaspoon of salt, evenly over the dough and leave to rest for a further 10 minutes.

6   Place in the oven and bake for 12–14 minutes, rotating the tray halfway through, until the dough is crisp and a deep golden brown. Remove from the oven and let cool slightly for 10–15 minutes before serving warm.

Apricot and thyme galettes with polenta pastry

We're so used to using fresh fruit for the cakes and pastries in our shops that it's easy to become a bit snobby about tinned fruit. When a fruit has a very short season, such as apricots, however, tinned can often be a great option. It means that they are available year round and that the quality is consistently high. Tinned peaches also work well, if you want to play around. Mixing some polenta through the dough here is what gives the baked pastry its wonderful crunch.

MAKES 6

The pastry can be made up to a week in advance and kept in the fridge, or kept in the freezer for up to a month. The pastry cream can be made 2 days in advance and stored in the fridge.

Once assembled, these are best eaten on the day they are baked. They're still fine the following day, stored in the fridge overnight; either bring them back to room temperature before eating or, better still, warm them through gently in the oven.

POLENTA PASTRY
90g plain flour
45g quick-cook polenta
25g caster sugar
90g unsalted butter, fridge-cold, cut into 1cm pieces
⅛ tsp salt
1 tbsp cold water

TOPPING
2 x 400g tins of apricot halves, in syrup, or 9–12 fresh apricots (depending on size), halved
40g runny honey, slightly warm
60g apricot jam, to glaze
1½ tbsp water

PASTRY CREAM
100ml full-fat milk
scraped seeds of ¼ vanilla pod
1 tsp thyme leaves, finely chopped, plus an extra 1 tsp picked leaves, to garnish
10g unsalted butter
20g caster sugar
1 large egg yolk
1½ tsp cornflour
1 tsp plain flour

1   **For the pastry,** place all the ingredients except for the water in a food processor. Blitz together until the mixture has the consistency of breadcrumbs. Add the water and continue to blitz, just until the dough comes together. Tip the dough on to a clean work surface and knead gently: you just want to bring it together without over-working it. Wrap loosely in cling film, flatten into a rectangle and store in the fridge for about 1 hour.

2   **To make the cream,** place the milk, vanilla, thyme, butter and half the sugar in a small saucepan. Heat gently until the milk is just coming to a simmer and bubbles are beginning to form around the sides.

3   In the meantime, combine the egg yolk with the remaining sugar, cornflour and plain flour in a medium bowl and whisk together to form a paste. Just as the milk is coming to a simmer, slowly whisk half of it into the egg yolk mixture. It helps to have a damp cloth underneath the bowl to steady it while you whisk with one hand and pour with the other. Once combined, whisk this back into the remaining hot milk and cook over a medium-low heat for 3–5 minutes, until very thick and smooth. Check it is ready by lifting some of the mixture out of the pan on the whisk: it should slowly drop off. Transfer the custard to a clean bowl or jug, cover with cling film – you want it to be actually touching the surface of the custard to prevent it forming a skin – and set aside in the fridge until completely cool. ››

4   Remove the pastry from the fridge a few minutes before rolling it out, so that it becomes malleable. Line a baking tray (that will fit in your fridge) with baking parchment.

5   Roll out the dough on a lightly floured surface to form a 45 x 15cm rectangle, 0.5cm thick. Trim the edges so that it is approximately 42 x 13cm and cut this into six smaller rectangles, each about 7 x 13cm. Place on the lined baking tray and, one rectangle at a time, fold in all the sides by 1cm to form a second layer that will hold in the pastry cream and fruit: it will look quite rustic but this is as it should be. Place in the fridge to chill for about 30 minutes.

6   **To assemble and bake the tarts,** preheat the oven to 210°C/190°C Fan/Gas Mark 6. Spread the pastry cream evenly over the base of the galettes. For the topping, place the drained apricots in a medium bowl and pour the honey over the top. Mix well, then lay four or five apricots on top of the pastry cream in one long line, cut side up and tightly overlapping by 0.5cm. Place the baking tray in the oven and bake for about 35 minutes, or until the pastry is dark golden brown around the edges, golden brown underneath and the apricots are nicely coloured around the edges. Remove from the oven and set aside to cool for 15 minutes before transferring to a wire rack to cool.

7   **Make the glaze** while the galettes are still slightly warm. Place the apricot jam and water in a small saucepan over a medium-high heat. Stir until the apricot jam has dissolved, then allow the mixture to boil for about 1 minute, stirring continuously, until thick. Immediately brush the glaze over the top of the apricots and pastry and sprinkle over the extra teaspoon of thyme leaves. Set aside until ready to serve.

Pineapple tartlets with pandan and star anise

Around Chinese New Year, pineapple tarts are to Malaysia and Singapore what mince pies are to the UK and Australia around Christmas. People vote and argue about where to find the best one or who has the perfect recipe. Our version uses the sweet shortcrust pastry we use for a lot of pies and tarts: it's buttery and slightly crumbly in the mouth, but sturdy enough to hold the sticky pineapple jam. In other words, delicious. Speaking of mince pies, the jam can be replaced by store-bought mincemeat, if you like: the pastry case makes a very good mince pie base.

MAKES 18

We use traditional mince pie tins to bake these. Ideally you'd have two sets for this recipe, but don't worry if you only have one: you can just bake the tarts in two batches. They also work well in a regular muffin tin.

The pastry will make more than you'll need. It will keep well in the fridge, wrapped in cling film, for up to 3 days. It also freezes well, wrapped first in cling film and then aluminium foil, for up to 2 months. If freezing the dough, do so in disc form or, if planning to make individual tarts, roll it out and cut it to size so that you're all set for your next bake. The pineapple jam can be made up to 2 weeks in advance and kept in the fridge. Make double the quantity of jam, if you like, so that you always have a batch at the ready to spread on toast or pancakes, to swirl into yoghurt, or to use as part of a marinade for chicken or pork.

Once assembled, the tarts will keep for up to 3–4 days, stored in an airtight container: the jammy filling just means they will get a bit softer over time.

PINEAPPLE JAM
2 large pineapples (2.8kg), peeled, core removed and flesh roughly chopped into 4–5cm cubes (about 1.3kg)
360g caster sugar
6 pandan leaves, bruised with the back of a knife and tied together in a knot (or ¼ vanilla pod, sliced in half lengthways and seeds scraped)
6 whole star anise

SWEET SHORTCRUST PASTRY
(YOU WILL ONLY NEED ½ QUANTITY)
300g plain flour
90g icing sugar
¼ tsp salt
200g unsalted butter, fridge-cold, cut into cubes, plus an extra 10g, melted, for brushing
finely grated zest of 1 lemon or lime (1 tsp)
1 large egg yolk (plus an extra large egg, lightly whisked, to glaze)
20ml cold water
18 whole cloves, for studding the tarts

1   **To make the jam,** place the pineapple in a food processor (in batches) and pulse to form a coarse purée. Strain through a fine sieve into a bowl; don't actually press down on the purée: you just want to strain out the excess juice rather than extract any more from the pineapple flesh. The strained juice (about 250ml) can be used to make ice lollies or as a refreshing drink over ice.

2   Place the pineapple purée in a large saucepan. Add the sugar, pandan leaves (or vanilla pod and scraped seeds) and star anise. Place over a medium-low heat and stir just until the sugar has dissolved. Increase the heat to medium, bring to a boil and cook for about 1 hour, stirring with a wooden spoon every 5 or 10 minutes, until the mixture thickens. Take care as it may splutter and spit, and keep a close eye on it as it thickens: you might need to lower the heat halfway through the cooking time and stir more frequently, to prevent it catching on the bottom of the pan. You want to take it further than regular jam: it will be ready when it is a thick golden paste and holds its shape when spooned on to a plate. Remove from the heat and allow to cool in the pan for half an hour before transferring to a bowl (or an airtight container, if making in advance to store in the fridge). Set aside until completely cool before removing the pandan leaves (or vanilla pod) and star anise. Keep in the fridge until ready to assemble the tartlets. ››

3 **To make the pastry,** sift together the flour, icing sugar and salt and place in a food processor. Add the butter and lemon or lime zest and pulse a few times, until the mixture has the consistency of fresh breadcrumbs. Lightly whisk together the egg yolk and water and add this to the mix: the dough will feel quite wet, but this is as it should be. Process once more, just until the pastry comes together, then tip on to a clean, lightly floured work surface. Press or pat gently to form a ball, then divide the pastry in two. Wrap each half loosely in cling film and press gently to form two flattish discs. The pastry is very soft so you need to keep it in the fridge for at least 1 hour (or up to 3 days).

4 Brush the moulds of the mince pie or regular muffin tin with melted butter (see Kit Note, page 255) and set aside.

5 When ready to bake, allow the pastry to rest at room temperature for 30 minutes (if it has been in the fridge for more than a few hours) and place on a lightly floured work surface, working with one disc of pastry at a time. Tap all over with a rolling pin to soften slightly before rolling out until 2mm thick. Using a 7cm cookie cutter, stamp out eighteen circles and place one in each greased mould. Re-roll the pastry, if necessary, until you get eighteen circles. Set aside in the fridge to rest. The remaining pastry disc can be frozen for future use.

6 Press the pastry offcuts (from the used disc) together and roll into a rough rectangle, about 2mm thick. Cut the pastry into strips, about 6 x 0.5cm: these will form the lattice to decorate the tarts. Transfer to a baking tray and keep in the fridge until ready to use.

7 **To bake the tarts,** preheat the oven to 200°C/180°C Fan/Gas Mark 6. Spoon a heaped tablespoon of the pineapple jam – about 30g – into each pastry case (don't think you've missed a step here: the cases are not blind-baked) and level the surface with the back of a teaspoon. If the kitchen is warm and the pastry is softening, return the trays to the fridge for a few minutes. Place the strips of pastry on top of the tarts to form a lattice shape (the easiest way to do this is to first lay two or three strips parallel to each other and then lay another two or three on top) or any other pattern. Trim the ends with a paring knife to fit and press the ends into the edge of the pastry.

8 Brush the beaten egg over the pastry top, push a whole clove into the centre of each tartlet and bake for about 20 minutes, or until the pastry is golden brown all over. Remove from the oven and allow to cool in the tray for 10 minutes before transferring to a wire rack to cool completely. Remove the cloves before eating!

Desserts

—

You're sometimes unaware of a bias until the stats are laid out. With almost twenty 'desserts' here, there are no less than thirteen with fruit and five with a splash of booze. The evidence is clear: we like our fruit, we like our booze, and we *very* much like our desserts.

FRUIT › We like fruit in our desserts for all sorts of reasons. Not only does it lend a bright splash of colour to the end of a meal, it also has the ability to cut through and lighten an otherwise rich or creamy dessert. Orange Cape gooseberries, purple blackberries, dark pink raspberries – all have the colour you want and the tartness a dessert often needs. The citrus from the zest of a lime will lighten things up in a rich chocolate pudding; raspberries or blackberries will cut through the whipped cream in a pavlova; while fresh cubes of papaya are just what a rich little posset needs. Always feel free to play around with the fruit in a dessert, depending on what's in season. Just make sure that it's perfectly ripe and ready: comparing a ripe mango or papaya with an unripe mango or papaya is, well, like comparing apples and pears.

BOOZE › We like booze in our desserts for all sorts of reasons, too. One, of course, is that it's just a nice way to keep the party going. However, the presence of a nip of brandy in our desserts is often there not so much for the sake of celebration but because of the way it draws out the other flavours: soaking raisins or apples in brandy, for example, does more to heighten the inherent flavour of the raisins or apples than to showcase the flavour of the brandy. Don't open a bottle just for the sake of a couple of teaspoons or tablespoons, though. There are some recipes here which need the alcohol – the Campari and Grapefruit Sorbet (see page 304), for example – but a lot of the others – the sauce for the Chocolate, Rose and Walnut Ice Cream (see page 308) or the caramel sauce for the Frozen Espresso Parfait (see page 298), for example – still taste absolutely delicious without it. Some desserts are for all the kids, big and small; some are just reserved for the big kids amongst us.

A SMALL NOTE ON EPIC-NESS › 'Epic' feels like a word that, being over the age of twelve, we shouldn't really be using, but there's a handful of desserts here which are, well, just pretty epic. Epic as in you have to get a little bit organized to make them; epic as in you'll be high-fiving the air when you've made it for the first time; epic as in you're guaranteed a 'wow-eeeeee' when you bring it to the table. Not, however, epic as in 'don't try this one at home'.

One of the biggest secrets behind some of the most involved recipes is that they're often some of the easiest to make. This is because of how much can be prepared and achieved in advance. Some things *can* be made in advance – meringues can be baked, nuts can be caramelized, sponges can be cooked; some things *need* to be made in advance – the Ginger Crème Caramel (see page 279) and Kaffir Lime Leaf Posset (see page 283) both need to set overnight in the fridge, while others are a nice combination of most of the components being made in advance, leaving just the whipping of cream and the assembling of the dessert before serving. And that's the fun bit, really: making everything look pretty.

Whatever the reason and whatever the season, there's always a dessert to fit: epic or easy, boozy or not, comforting or hearty, zesty or light. But fruity, very nearly *always* fruity.

Kit

An ice cream maker is the obvious one here, if you are planning on making ice cream regularly. They are quite an investment, we know, but one that can bring a lot of pleasure over the years. Although some of the ice creams need an ice cream maker – the Saffron and Almond Ice Cream Sandwich (see page 301) and Chocolate, Rose and Walnut Ice Cream (see page 308) – others are semifreddos – the raspberry semifreddo for the Knickerbocker Glory (see page 293), for example – which means that whipped cream is folded in (rather than churned in an ice cream maker). If you want to make ice cream and don't have an ice cream maker, that's fine: you can churn it yourself, stirring the mix every few hours to break up the formation of ice crystals before returning it to the freezer. This process is stretched over a few hours, but the actual consumption of your time is very little.

Otherwise, the kit we recommend is useful, though not essential: a piping bag for the Cape Gooseberry Pavlova (see page 274) and Frozen Espresso Parfait (see page 298); a 20cm square loose-based tin for the Gingerbread (see page 266) and Frozen Espresso Parfait; a 23 or 25cm round fluted quiche dish for the Ginger Crème Caramel (see page 279); little glass ramekins or dariole moulds for the Hot Chocolate and Lime Pudding (see page 278); and a non-stick crêpe pan to make you look the part when preparing the Ricotta Crêpes with Figs, Honey and Pistachio (see page 268). We know that the ideal world is far removed from the reality of our drawers and cupboards, however, which do well to have matching Tupperware bases and lids, so feel free to either beg, borrow or improvise. And don't forget to make a note of the kit you'd like in that ideal kitchen of yours on your birthday wishlist. As ever, we've made alternative kit suggestions in the recipes where we can.

Rolled pavlova with peaches and blackberries

This is the showstopper to serve as part of a big summer meal – a real statement! – huge and divine. Don't be put off by its size, though: the larger pavlovas are actually easier to roll than the smaller ones. There's always a moment when rolling a pavlova when you think 'It's not going to come together!', but hold your nerve and trust in the recipe: it's actually very forgiving.

We pair late-summer peaches with the blackberries of early autumn, but meringue is so versatile that you can add whatever fruit filling you like, depending on what's in season: fresh berries – raspberries, strawberries, blueberries – slow-cooked quince or plums: they all work well. You can also play around with fillings. Try vanilla and chopped pistachios with strawberry (or mixed berries); or mango, lime and passionfruit works well with whipped cream flavoured with finely grated lime zest.

SERVES 10–12

The meringue base (unfilled) can be prepared up to a day ahead. Leave it in the tin and drape with a tea towel until needed. You are then ready to fill it with the fruit and cream up to 4 hours before (but ideally as close as possible to) serving.

This should be eaten on the day it is assembled and served, although leftovers can be stored in the fridge and eaten cold.

250g egg whites (from 6 large eggs, so you might want to buy egg whites in a carton), at room temperature (they whisk better if not fridge-cold)
375g caster sugar
2 tsp vanilla extract
2 tsp white wine vinegar
2 tsp cornflour

FILLING
400ml double cream
1 tsp vanilla extract
30g icing sugar, sifted, plus extra to dust
5 large, ripe peaches, washed but unpeeled, stone removed and cut into 0.5cm wide segments (600g)
300g fresh blackberries
60g toasted flaked almonds

1   Preheat the oven to 220°C/200°C Fan/Gas Mark 7. Line a 35 x 30cm shallow baking tray with baking parchment, so the paper rises 2cm over the sides of the tin.
2   **To make the meringue base,** place the egg whites in the bowl of an electric mixer with the whisk attachment in place and whisk on a medium-high speed for about 1 minute, until soft peaks form. Gradually add the sugar a tablespoon at a time, whisking all the time for at least 5 minutes, until the mixture turns into a thick and glossy meringue. Reduce the speed to low and add the vanilla extract, vinegar and cornflour. Increase the speed to medium and whisk for a minute, until fully combined.
3   Spoon the meringue mix into the lined tin and use a spatula to spread it out evenly in the tray. Place in the preheated oven and immediately lower the temperature to 200°C/180°C Fan/Gas Mark 6: the contrast in temperature helps create the crisp outside along with the gooey marshmallow-like inside. Bake for about 35 minutes, until the meringue is pale beige in colour and crusty on top. Remove from the oven and set aside until completely cool. The meringue will have puffed up in the oven but will deflate slightly when cooled. If keeping until the next day, the meringue can now be covered with a tea towel and set aside at room temperature. ››

4   **To make the filling,** beat the cream until very soft peaks form – this should take about 1 minute using an electric whisk on a medium-high speed, longer if whisking by hand. Add the vanilla and icing sugar and whisk to incorporate.

5   Place a clean tea towel flat on top of the meringue (or use the one that is already there, if you've made this the day before) and quickly but carefully invert it on to the work surface, so that the crisp top of the meringue is now facing down and sitting on top of the tea towel. Lift the tin off and carefully peel away the baking parchment before spreading the meringue evenly with two-thirds of the whipped cream. Cover generously with 500g sliced peaches and 200g blackberries, and sprinkle over 50g almonds.

6   To roll the meringue, start with the longest side closest to you and, using the tea towel to assist you, roll the meringue up and over, so that the edges come together to form a log. Gently pull away the tea towel as you roll, then slide the meringue on to a long tray or a platter, with the seam side facing down. Don't worry if the meringue loses its shape a bit or some of the fruit spills out: just hold your nerve and use your hands to pat it back into the shape of the log.

7   Pipe or spoon the remaining cream down the length of the roulade. Top with the remaining fruit, 10g almonds, a dusting of icing sugar and serve.

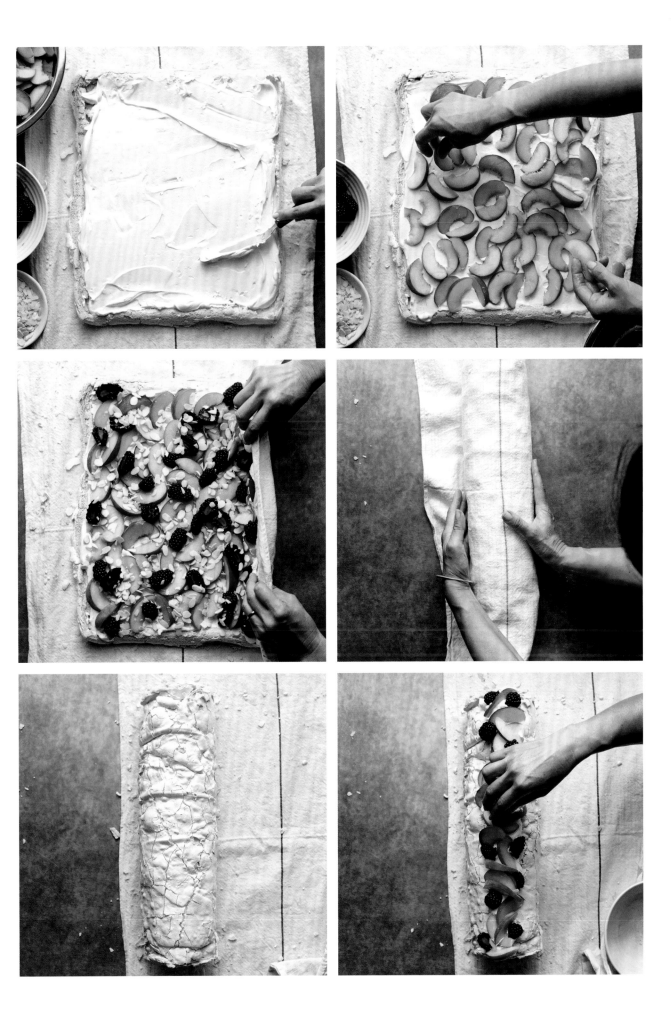

Gingerbread with brandy apples and crème fraîche

This can be served warm, as a dessert, with the sautéed apples and crème fraîche, or on its own at room temperature, with a cup of tea. We find that we can eat more of the cake when it's warm, which is why the same amount of cake serves a different number of people depending on whether it is eaten at room temperature or not. Paradoxically, it's the addition of the extras – the slightly tangy crème fraîche cutting through the sweetness of the treacle and the apples – that enables a bigger portion to be served!

SERVES 9 (WARM, AS A DESSERT) OR ABOUT 12 (AT ROOM TEMPERATURE)
—

300g black treacle (or blackstrap
    molasses)
100g soft light brown sugar
120g caster sugar
220g unsalted butter, melted
    and cooled slightly
3 large eggs
finely grated zest of 1 orange (1½ tsp)
400g plain flour
1 tbsp bicarbonate of soda
1 tbsp ground ginger
2 tsp ground cinnamon
½ tsp salt
300ml just-boiled water
100g stem ginger, roughly chopped
    into 0.5cm pieces
400g crème fraîche, if serving
    as a dessert (see introduction)

APPLES
5 Golden Delicious or Pink Lady apples
    (700g)
50g unsalted butter
120g caster sugar
½ vanilla pod, sliced open lengthways
strips of peel of 1 large lemon
50ml brandy
50ml lemon juice
⅛ tsp salt

This is best made in a high-sided (9–10cm high) 20cm square springform tin, but if you don't have one of these then use a high-sided 20cm round springform tin instead. If you go for the round option, you'll make eight large slices or twelve regular slices. It also looks great made in a 23cm bundt tin, as photographed.

The cake can be made up to 3 days in advance and kept at room temperature in an airtight container. If you're serving it as a dessert, just warm it through in the oven, covered with foil. The apples are best made on the day of serving.

1   Preheat the oven to 200°C/180°C Fan/Gas Mark 6. Grease a 20cm square (or round) springform tin and line with baking parchment, leaving an overhang at the sides to help you remove the cake from the tin later on.

2   Place the treacle, brown sugar, caster sugar, butter, eggs and orange zest in a medium bowl and whisk together by hand, or using a hand-held electric whisk, until combined.

3   Sift the flour, bicarbonate of soda, ginger, cinnamon and salt together into a separate larger bowl, then pour over the treacle mixture. Stir to combine and add the just-boiled water, whisking immediately to combine. Stir through the stem ginger, then pour the mixture into the cake tin. Bake for 50 minutes, or until a skewer inserted into the centre comes out clean. Remove from the oven and set aside on a wire rack to cool for 10 minutes before transferring to a serving platter.

4   While the cake is cooling, peel and core the apples and cut into 1–1.5cm slices. Place a large non-stick sauté pan over a high heat and, once hot, add about a third or half of the apples (depending on the size of your pan: you don't want them to be overcrowded as this will prevent them becoming golden). Sear for 2 minutes, turning regularly, until they are a nice golden colour. Remove from the pan, wipe clean and repeat with the remaining apples. Add these to the first batch and return the pan to a medium heat. Place the butter in the pan and, once melted, add the sugar, vanilla pod and lemon peel. Return the apples to the pan, stir well to coat and cook for 5 minutes, until the apples are soft but still holding their shape. Pour over the brandy, lemon juice and salt and reduce for 3 minutes over a medium-high heat, until the sauce is thick but not caramelized.

5   If serving warm, spoon some of the warmed apples on top of each portion of gingerbread and add a spoonful of crème fraîche alongside.

Ricotta crêpes with figs, honey and pistachio

These crêpes are a serious way to end a meal, but also work well for brunch, if you want to get the day off to a flying start. We've made a little bit more batter than you need for twelve crêpes; the tendency, we find, is that the first two or three crêpes don't work quite as well as those that follow, once the pan has warmed up and you know what's what, so we've built in this safety net. If you're very clever and manage to make them work from the start, you'll just have two or three extra to play around with. The crêpes are great just as they are, if you like, served with some lemon juice and sprinkled sugar.

Play around with the filling, as well, depending on what you have and what's in season. Strawberries are a good alternative to the figs, for example. Hull them, then macerate them with a little bit of orange juice, a tablespoon of brandy and a drop of orange blossom water. Walnuts also work well instead of the pistachios, if that's what you have.

MAKES 12 (PERFECT) CRÊPES

170g plain flour
⅓ tsp salt
3 large eggs
300ml full-fat milk
25g unsalted butter, melted,
    plus an extra 80g, melted,
    for cooking and brushing
finely grated zest of 1 large orange
    (1 tbsp)
6 fresh figs (Black Mission, if possible,
    or another ripe variety), halved,
    or quartered if large (250g)
20g shelled pistachio kernels,
    roughly chopped

FILLING
75g currants
30ml brandy
150g cream cheese
300g ricotta
60g caster sugar
scraped seeds of ¼ vanilla pod
1½ tsp orange blossom water
finely grated zest of 1 large orange
    (1 tbsp)
2 large egg yolks
⅛ tsp salt

HONEY SYRUP
60g honey
¼ tsp orange blossom water
1 tsp lemon juice

A proper non-stick crêpe pan, with shallow sides, is such a treat. It makes the cooking of crêpes easy and fun (and at the same time, crucially, allows you to look like a pro). Alternatively, use an 18cm sauté pan.

You can make the whole dish up to the point at which it's ready to go into the oven, then store in the fridge, covered, for up to 24 hours. Simply follow the cooking instructions below before serving.

1   **To make the filling,** place the currants and brandy in a small saucepan. Heat gently for a minute and set aside for the currants to plump up and cool.
2   Place the cream cheese in a medium bowl and beat with a wooden spoon or spatula until smooth. Add the ricotta, sugar, vanilla seeds, orange blossom water, orange zest, egg yolks and salt and beat to incorporate: the mix should be well combined but not completely smooth. Finally, drain the currants – there won't be much liquid left but it's still useful to do – and stir them through. Set aside in the fridge until ready to use.

3   **To make the crêpes,** sift the flour and salt into a medium bowl and make a well in the centre. Crack the eggs into the well and add the milk, whisking as you pour and gradually drawing in the flour mix until the batter is smooth. Finally, whisk in the melted butter until combined. Strain through a sieve – you need to do this to make sure there are no unwhisked eggs or lumps – into a clean container. Whisk in the orange zest and refrigerate, covered, for at least an hour or overnight.

4   Place an 18cm sauté pan (or crêpe pan, if you have one) over a medium heat and, once hot, brush lightly but thoroughly with melted butter. Add 3 tablespoons of batter and swirl the pan around to ensure that it spreads thinly and evenly over the surface. Cook for about 1 minute, or until the bottom is golden brown, then use a spatula (or your fingers, if you're careful) to turn it over. Cook for another 30 seconds or so, until golden brown. Repeat until you have used up all of the batter, brushing the pan with more butter between each crêpe: you should have twelve perfect crêpes. Stack them up on a plate and wrap in cling film or drape over a clean tea towel – this prevents them drying out and cracking at the edges – until ready to fill.

5   **When ready to assemble the crêpes,** spoon 2 tablespoons of the filling – about 30g – into the top quarter of one crêpe. Fold the bottom half of the crêpe up and over the filling (it looks like a semi-circle at this stage), then fold it in half again, left to right, over the filling, to form a quarter-circle.

6   Brush a 28 x 20cm ceramic or Pyrex baking dish with 10g of the remaining melted butter and place the crêpes in the dish in snug rows and slightly overlapping. Brush with another 10g butter and dot the figs on top. The crêpes can be kept in the fridge at this point until ready to cook (up to 24 hours).

7   Preheat the oven to 200°C/180°C Fan/Gas Mark 6. Place the crêpes in the oven and bake for 30 minutes.

8   **Make the honey syrup** 2 minutes before the crêpes are ready. Warm the honey in a saucepan over a medium heat. Remove from the heat, stir in the orange blossom water and lemon juice and brush this over the crêpes and figs as soon as they come out of the oven. Place two crêpes on each plate and spoon two fig halves alongside. Drizzle over any remaining syrup, sprinkle with the pistachios and serve.

Rice pudding with roasted rhubarb and tarragon

This is as sweet and comforting as you want a rice pudding to be, but with a welcome savoury note too, from the tarragon and bay leaves. This is as delicious for breakfast as it is after lunch or supper.

SERVES 6

100g pudding rice
700ml full-fat milk
shaved peel of 1 medium orange
3 large fresh bay leaves, torn in half
1 large cinnamon stick
⅛ tsp salt
530g rhubarb (about 9 thin sticks),
    cut into 5cm long pieces
75g caster sugar

10g tarragon (about 6 sprigs),
    half the sprigs left whole,
    the remaining leaves removed
    and roughly chopped
1 vanilla pod, sliced in half lengthways
    and seeds scraped
1 tbsp water
100ml double cream
30g icing sugar, sifted
100g Greek yoghurt

You can make the rice pudding (up to the stage before the cream is folded through) and roasted fruit the day before serving. You can then either serve it straight from the fridge (folding the cream through will bring it to room temperature) or warm it through in the oven, adding the cream just before serving, if you prefer.

1   Preheat the oven to 170°C/150°C Fan/Gas Mark 3.
2   Place the rice, milk, orange peel, bay leaves, cinnamon and salt in a high-sided 30 x 20cm baking tray and bake for 70 minutes, uncovered, stirring halfway through, until the rice is cooked through but still holds its shape and most of the milk is absorbed. Remove from the oven and set aside to cool before removing the orange peel, bay leaves and cinnamon stick. Transfer to a medium bowl, let cool completely then cover and keep in the fridge until required.
3   **To cook the rhubarb,** increase the oven temperature to 250°C/230°C Fan/Gas Mark 9. Place the rhubarb in a clean high-sided 30 x 20cm baking dish along with the sugar, the whole tarragon sprigs, vanilla pod and seeds. Add the water, toss together and roast for 15–20 minutes, until the rhubarb has completely softened. Remove from the oven and set aside to cool. Remove the tarragon sprigs and vanilla pod: the tarragon can be discarded, but the pod is worth saving to flavour caster sugar (see page 356).
4   While the rhubarb is cooking, place the cream in a bowl and add the icing sugar. Whisk until the cream thickens and holds its shape. Fold the cream into the cold rice, followed by the yoghurt, and return to the fridge.
5   When ready to serve, divide the rice pudding between six bowls and spoon a generous amount of rhubarb on top, along with some of the juices. Serve with a final sprinkle of the tarragon leaves.

Cape gooseberry pavlova

Cape gooseberries are so lovely to look at – with their glossy yellow skin and papery husks – that they can often be used as just an exotic garnish rather than as an ingredient in their own right. They're not to be underrated, though, with their distinct taste: slightly citrusy with tones of strawberry and honey. They pair really well with the honey-spiked yoghurt cream here.

SERVES 8

MERINGUES
125g egg whites (from 3 large eggs)
⅛ tsp salt
¼ tsp cream of tartar
250g caster sugar
400g Cape gooseberries (set 8 aside for the toffee Cape gooseberries; remove the husks from the remainder and slice them in half)

TOFFEE CAPE GOOSEBERRIES
8 Cape gooseberries (see left), papery husks intact
60g caster sugar

YOGHURT CREAM
200g full-fat Greek yoghurt
200ml double cream
scraped seeds of ¼ vanilla pod
35g runny honey
25g icing sugar, plus extra for dusting

A piping bag with a 1cm wide nozzle is useful for piping out the meringues, but is not essential.

The meringue can be made up to 3 days ahead and stored in an airtight container, layered between sheets of baking parchment. The yoghurt cream and toffee Cape gooseberries are best prepared no more than a couple of hours before serving: the toffee tends to become sticky and will 'weep' if made too far in advance.

---

1   Preheat the oven to 140°C/120°C Fan/Gas Mark 1 and line two baking trays with baking parchment. Trace or draw eight circles – each about 8.5cm wide – on each of the paper sheets so that you have sixteen circles in total. Turn the paper over so the drawn-on side is facing down but still visible.

2   **For the meringues,** place the egg whites and salt in the bowl of an electric mixer with the whisk attachment in place. Beat on a medium-high speed until frothy, then add the cream of tartar. Continue to beat until soft peaks form before adding the sugar, one tablespoon at a time. Keep beating until the mixture is thick and glossy.

3   Spoon the mixture into a piping bag (if you have one) with a 1cm wide nozzle in place. Using the circles you have traced as your guide, pipe a layer of meringue on to each of the circles: they should be just under 1cm thick. Use a small spatula or the back of a spoon to smooth over the tops. If you don't have a piping bag, simply dollop a large spoonful of the meringue mixture on to each circle and smooth it out with a small metal spatula: again, they should be just under 1cm thick.

4   Place the trays in the oven and bake for 2 hours, or until the meringues are dry. Switch off the oven but leave the meringues inside until they are completely cool. Once cool, remove from the oven and set aside.

5   **To make the toffee Cape gooseberries,** peel back the papery husk from the eight fruit but leave it attached and set aside. Put the sugar into a small saucepan and place over a medium-high heat. Cook the sugar, without stirring, until it melts and begins to brown around the edges of the pan. Tilt and swirl the pan so that the sugar melts evenly and turns amber. Remove from the heat and, moving quickly but carefully, tilt the pan so that the toffee pools in one corner. Pick up a Cape gooseberry by the husk and carefully dip the entire fruit (not the husk) in the toffee. Hold for a few seconds over the pan for any excess to drip away, then place on a parchment-lined tray or plate. Continue with the remaining fruit and toffee and set the dipped fruit aside.

6   **To make the yoghurt cream,** whisk together all the ingredients by hand, or using a hand-held electric whisk, until soft peaks form. Keep in the fridge until needed.

7   **To assemble the pavlovas,** place a small dollop of the yoghurt cream on to each serving plate (this will hold the meringues in place) and place a meringue disc on top of the cream, flat side down. Dollop a few tablespoons of the yoghurt cream (about 40g) in the centre of each meringue and use the back of a spoon to smooth out the entire surface. Spoon about 50g of the halved Cape gooseberries over the cream – it will seem like a lot, but they can handle it! – then spread the flat base of the remaining meringue discs with the remaining yoghurt cream. Sit them on top of the fruit, cream side down. Dust the tops of the meringues lightly with icing sugar and place a toffee-coated Cape gooseberry in the centre of each. Serve as close to assembling as you can – within about 1 hour – as the thin discs of meringue will soften from the fruit and the cream.

CAPE GOOSEBERRY PAVLOVA

Hot chocolate and lime puddings

These puddings, gently baked in a bain-marie, deliver the lightness of a soufflé without any of the anxiety often associated with baking them. A portion of pudding baked in a 10cm wide ramekin dish might sound like rather a lot (particularly when you see them rise in the oven), but don't be intimidated: they are as light as they are large and, anyway, they soon deflate to a far more reasonable size.

There is just a suggestion of lime from the zest of the fruit, but feel free to substitute with orange zest if the combination of chocolate and orange appeals more.

SERVES 6

15g unsalted butter, softened,
    for greasing
200g dark cooking chocolate
    (70% cocoa solids), roughly chopped
100g milk cooking chocolate
    (37% cocoa solids), roughly chopped

finely grated zest of 3 limes (1 tbsp)
4 large eggs, at room temperature
60g caster sugar, plus an extra 30g
    for preparing the moulds
110ml double cream
200g crème fraîche, to serve

1 Preheat the oven to 200°C/180°C Fan/Gas Mark 6. Brush the ramekins or dariole moulds (see Kit Note) with the softened butter, then sprinkle over a little caster sugar to evenly coat, tapping away the excess, and set aside.

2 Place the chocolate in a medium heatproof bowl set over a pan of simmering water, making sure the base of the bowl isn't touching the water. Stir gently with a spatula from time to time to ensure that the chocolate melts evenly. Once melted, remove the bowl from the heat, stir in the lime zest and set aside to cool for 10 minutes, until tepid.

3 Place the eggs and sugar in the bowl of an electric mixer with the whisk attachment in place and beat on a high speed for about 6 minutes, until the mixture is very light and fluffy and has trebled in volume. Meanwhile, place the cream in a separate medium bowl and whisk by hand or with a hand-held electric whisk until very soft peaks form.

4 Remove the egg and sugar bowl from the electric mixer and add the melted chocolate in two batches, gently folding through by hand. When almost combined – there will still be some streaks – fold in the whipped cream until thoroughly combined. It will lose a little volume, but be careful not to over-mix.

5 Spoon the mixture into the prepared ramekins or moulds, filling them three-quarters of the way up the sides. Place the ramekins or moulds in a large, deep baking dish, transfer to the oven and pour boiling water into the tray, around the ramekins, so that it rises a third of the way up the sides. Bake for 20–22 minutes, or until the puddings are softly set in the middle: check they are ready by gently tapping the centre of the puddings with your finger. Carefully remove the baking dish from the oven and, using oven gloves, transfer the ramekins on to serving plates and serve immediately. Alternatively, you could unmould the puddings by setting aside for 10 minutes before inverting on to a plate. Serve with a little of the crème fraîche spooned alongside.

These can be made in ceramic or glass 200ml ramekins (ours are 10cm wide). Alternatively, use 200ml dariole moulds.

These are best served warm, but will keep for a day or two at room temperature (don't keep them in the fridge or the soft inside will set). Their texture will be a little denser, but they will still taste great as they are, or warm them through in the oven or microwave.

Ginger crème caramel

Crème caramel can often be a rather heavy end to a meal, but ours is unexpectedly light, which we prefer. This is due to a higher ratio of milk to cream than is traditional, and also because the milk and cream are not heated before being whisked into the eggs. Helen, who cooks a lot of Chinese food, says that this is one of the few Western desserts which does not taste out of place after a Chinese meal. It's particularly perfect after a main of steamed fish.

Thanks to Suzy Zail for sharing this recipe.

SERVES 8–10

We like to make this in a 23 or 25cm round ceramic or glass dish with a fluted edge – like a quiche plate. A metal dish (so long as it is watertight and does not have a removable base) will also be fine. You could also make small individual flans, but the sense of turning out a whole flan on to your serving platter, with the caramel glistening on top, is great.

The fresh ginger in the custard is wonderful, but you can skip this stage if you are looking for a shortcut and don't want to infuse the custard the day before baking it. You will still need to bake the dish at least a day before serving as, once out of the oven, the whole thing needs to be chilled in the fridge overnight, or for up to 3 days.

Once made, this will keep in the fridge for up to 3 days.

780ml full-fat milk
120ml double cream
7cm piece of fresh ginger (60g), peeled and coarsely grated

½ vanilla pod, sliced in half lengthways and seeds scraped
400g caster sugar
6 large eggs
1 tsp vanilla extract

1   If infusing the custard with the ginger, you will need to start 2 days before you want to serve the dish. Place the milk, cream, ginger, vanilla pod and seeds in a medium bowl or jug and whisk to combine. Cover with cling film and keep in the fridge for at least 6 hours, or ideally up to 24 hours, to infuse.

2   When you are ready to make the crème caramel, preheat the oven to 170°C/150°C Fan/Gas Mark 3. Place the flan dish (or whichever dish you are using, see Kit Note) in the oven to keep warm until required: heating the dish will make it easier to coat it with the hot caramel.

3   **To make the caramel,** add 200g of sugar to a large sauté pan or skillet and place over a medium heat. Cook for about 5 minutes, resisting the urge to stir but tilting and swirling the pan instead, until the sugar has melted and begins to brown around the edges. You will need to do this slowly and continually until the sugar has turned a dark amber colour. Remove the hot flan dish from the oven, and immediately pour in the caramel, using a tea towel to protect your hands. Tilt the dish around so that the caramel coats the entire base and rises halfway up the sides of the dish. Place the dish in a high-sided baking tray and set aside for 15 minutes: the caramel does not need to set rock hard, but it should be firm enough that pouring the custard over the top will not disturb it in any way.

4   **For the custard,** place the eggs in a large bowl with the remaining 200g sugar and the vanilla extract. Whisk until smooth, then strain the milk/cream mixture into the eggs through a fine-mesh sieve – it's okay that it's fridge-cold – pressing the ginger against the mesh to extract as much flavour as you can. Discard the ginger and whisk the milk and egg mixture until thoroughly combined, but not too frothy. ››

5   Pour the mixture into the caramel-coated flan dish and place the baking tray (with the flan dish inside) in the oven. Pour some recently boiled water into the baking tray so that it comes about halfway up the sides of the flan dish. Bake for approximately 90 minutes: the crème caramel should still have a wobble in the middle but a skewer inserted into the centre should come out clean. The wobble is as it should be – it will firm up in the fridge – but cooking time can vary, depending on the size of your pan and what it is made from (glass, metal, etc): it can take up to 2 hours.

6   Remove the baking tray from the oven and carefully transfer the crème caramel to a rack to cool. Set aside until completely cool, then cover with cling film and keep in the fridge overnight (or for up to 3 days) to allow the caramel to melt and the custard to firm up.

7   After refrigerating, if the custard part of the crème caramel is stuck to the sides of the flan dish or tin, carefully run a small knife along the edge to release it. Then place a large plate (larger than your flan dish, and with a 'lip' to catch the liquid caramel) on top of the flan dish. Grasping the dish and the plate together, quickly flip the whole thing over. Gently lift off the flan dish to reveal the set crème caramel. Slice with a large kitchen knife, and serve – you'll be amazed at how easily and perfectly it slices as well.

Yoghurt panna cotta with basil and crushed strawberries

Panna cotta is usually made with cream – the name itself means 'cooked cream'. Our version, however, is made with milk and yoghurt, with a texture more like that of a set milk pudding. It's not set very firmly, though, so you'll still get the reassuring wobble you want. If you want to turn your panna cottas out well before they're served, that's fine: just keep them in the fridge so that they stay set. Alternatively, you can make and serve these in individual glasses, in which case they won't need turning out at all.

MAKES 6 (USING 200ML MOULDS) OR 8 (USING 150ML MOULDS)

---

4 gelatine leaves (platinum strength), or 1 tbsp (9g) powdered gelatine
650ml full-fat milk
160g caster sugar
shaved peel of 2 lemons, avoiding the bitter white pith
30g basil leaves, plus an extra 10 leaves for the strawberries

sunflower oil (or another flavourless oil), for greasing
350g Greek yoghurt
60ml lemon juice
300g strawberries
2 tbsp icing sugar

---

1   Place the gelatine leaves in a bowl, cover generously with cold water, and set aside to soak. (If using powdered gelatine, place 50ml of cold water in a small bowl and sprinkle the gelatine powder over it. Stand the bowl in a pan of hot water and stir until the gelatine dissolves. Set aside until needed.)

2   Combine the milk, sugar and lemon peel in a medium saucepan and place over a low heat. Stir until the sugar has dissolved, then increase the heat to medium-high. As soon as it comes up to a boil, remove the pan from the heat. Roughly tear the basil leaves and drop them into the hot milk.

3   Remove the gelatine leaves from the water, squeeze out any excess liquid and drop them into the milk. If you are using powdered gelatine, add it to the milk now. Whisk gently, until the gelatine dissolves, then set aside to cool until tepid. Prepare the six 200ml or eight 150ml dariole moulds by brushing very lightly with the oil.

4   When the milk is ready, place the yoghurt in a large bowl or jug and whisk lightly. Strain the milk into the yoghurt through a fine-mesh sieve, pressing on the basil and lemon peel to extract as much of their essence as possible. Whisk to just combine – you don't want to whisk so vigorously that air bubbles are created – then add the lemon juice. Stir, pour into the moulds and place on a baking tray that will fit in the fridge. Cover with cling film and place in the fridge for at least 6 hours (or up to 2 days).

5   An hour or so before serving, hull the strawberries and roughly chop them. Place the strawberries in a small bowl, sprinkle over the icing sugar and stir. Julienne the remaining ten basil leaves by rolling them up as a bunch into a tight cigar shape and slicing them finely. Add to the strawberries and set aside to infuse.

6   To turn out the panna cottas, gently press all around the edges, then turn them upside down over individual plates. Hold down the mould with one hand, grab the plate with the other and give it a shake to release the panna cotta. Spoon the strawberries and basil over the top and serve at once.

We use six 200ml dariole moulds here; you could use 150ml moulds instead – you'll just end up with a couple extra.

These can be made up to 2 days in advance and kept in the fridge until serving. The strawberries must be prepared just before serving.

Kaffir lime leaf posset with fresh papaya

Possets have been enjoyed for centuries. Traditionally served as a warm drink to the wealthy – and said to help people if they were feeling ill, much as a cup of cocoa would be offered today – they are now chilled until set and served as a custard-like pudding.

The dominance of the cream explains why it is so often paired with clean citrus flavours to cut through all the heavenly richness. Other tropical fruit can be used instead of (or alongside) the papaya – slices of mango or banana, chunks of pineapple, passionfruit pulp – just make sure the fruit you choose is nice and ripe.

Use fresh kaffir lime leaves for this: the dried variety just won't be the same. You can buy them frozen in large bags from Asian grocers, and they'll continue to freeze well at home, so you won't have to worry about racing through a whole bag.

SERVES 6

We make these in six 150ml ramekins or bowls, but any similar-sized dishes will work just as well.

These should be made the day before serving, if you can. They need at least 6 hours in the fridge to set, so it's best to just leave them overnight.

Once made, they can be kept in the fridge for 2 days.

600ml double cream
12 fresh kaffir lime leaves, bruised
   with a rolling pin or pestle
   and mortar
4 strips of shaved lime zest, plus ¾ tsp
   finely grated zest, to serve

140g caster sugar
⅛ tsp salt
3 tbsp lime juice
½ small ripe papaya, peeled,
   de-seeded and cut into long,
   thin slices (150g)

1 Place the cream in a medium saucepan, add the kaffir lime leaves and shaved lime zest and bring to a very gentle simmer over a medium-high heat, then remove from the heat. Set aside for 30 minutes to infuse.

2 Add the sugar to the cream with the salt and return to a medium-high heat. Bring to the boil, stirring frequently, and cook for 1–2 minutes, continuing to stir, until the cream rises to the top of the pan: watch it carefully so it doesn't boil over. Strain through a fine sieve into a large measuring jug, stir in 1 tablespoon of lime juice – the cream will thicken quickly at this stage – then pour into six ramekins (or bowls): the mixture should rise three-quarters of the way up the sides. Keep in the fridge for at least 6 hours, or overnight, to set.

3 When ready to serve, spoon the papaya on top of the possets and sprinkle with grated lime zest. Finish with a teaspoon of lime juice, per portion, and serve.

YOGHURT PANNA COTTA WITH BASIL
AND CRUSHED STRAWBERRIES

KAFFIR LIME LEAF POSSET
WITH FRESH PAPAYA

Sticky fig pudding with salted caramel and coconut topping

A variation of this cake, using dates instead of figs, was all the rage in cafés throughout Australia and New Zealand when Helen was working and baking there. It's hardly ever seen these days, which is a mystery, really, as it's so delicious: moist and fruity with a crunchy caramelized topping. We serve this warm, with some thick double cream.

MAKES 8
—

We make these in eight 7.5 or 8cm bottomless round rings, 4cm high. You can also make them in a regular muffin tin: the result is not quite as elegant, but they still work very well.

These will keep for up to 2 days at room temperature (or in the fridge, if it's particularly warm) in an airtight container. Serve them as they are, or warm them through for 5 minutes in an oven set to 200°C/180°C Fan/ Gas Mark 6.

2 medium Granny Smith apples
200g soft dried figs, tough stalk removed, roughly chopped
1 tsp bicarbonate of soda
250ml water
200g plain flour
2 tsp baking powder
¼ tsp salt
125g unsalted butter, at room temperature, plus extra for greasing

200g caster sugar
1 large egg
1 tsp vanilla extract

SALTED CARAMEL COCONUT TOPPING
75g unsalted butter
95g soft light brown sugar
60ml double cream
95g unsweetened coconut flakes, or desiccated coconut
¼ tsp salt

—

1   Peel and core the apples and cut into 1cm pieces (you should have about 200g). Place the apples, figs, bicarbonate of soda and water in a saucepan. Bring to a boil, then simmer over a medium heat for about 5 minutes, stirring from time to time, until the figs are starting to break down. Remove from the heat and set aside until cool.

2   Preheat the oven to 200°C/180°C Fan/Gas Mark 6. If using the bottomless cake rings (see Kit Note), line a baking tray with baking parchment, lightly butter the rings and place them on the tray. Cut strips of baking parchment, large enough to rise 3cm above the cake rings, and place them around the inside of each ring; the base of the ring should be exposed when it's placed on the tray. If using the muffin tin, line eight moulds with paper tulip liners – or any muffin liners – which rise about 7cm high.

3   Sift the flour, baking powder and salt together into a bowl and set aside. Place the butter and sugar in the bowl of an electric mixer with the paddle attachment in place and beat on a medium-high speed for about 2 minutes, until light and fluffy. Add the egg and vanilla and beat until combined. Reduce the speed to low and, in alternate batches, fold in the fig-apple mix and the sifted dry ingredients.

4   Divide the mix between the rings (or muffin liners) and bake for about 25 minutes, or until a skewer inserted into the centre comes out clean.

5   **Make the topping while the cake is baking.** Place all the ingredients for the topping in a saucepan and stir over a low heat until the butter is melted and the ingredients are combined. Once the cakes are cooked, remove from the oven (keep the oven on) and spoon about 1½ tablespoons of the topping mixture over the surface of each pudding: it should rise up about 1cm. Return to the oven for another 12 minutes, or until the topping is golden brown.

6   Remove from the oven and leave to cool for 10 minutes, or until they come to room temperature, before removing the rings and paper and serving: use a knife if you need to here, to help release the cake. If making them in the muffin tin, let them cool in the tray for 10 minutes before transferring to a wire rack to cool before serving.

Pot barley pudding with roasted apples and date syrup

Think of this as a Middle Eastern rice pudding. This is either a hearty end to an autumnal Sunday lunch, or wonderful eaten at breakfast to fuel you for the day ahead. The two options are not mutually exclusive, though: just make it first for lunch and then eat the leftovers the following day.

Use pearl barley in place of pot barley, if necessary. It won't have quite the bite of the pot barley because the hull and bran layers have been removed, but it will still work well.

SERVES 6
—

1.5 litres water
200g pot barley, rinsed
3 tbsp date syrup, plus an extra 4 tbsp to drizzle
3 small cinnamon sticks
shaved peel of 1 lemon, plus 1 tbsp lemon juice
1 tsp ground nutmeg
¼ tsp salt

2 large Pink Lady apples
2 large Bramley apples (use Granny Smiths, as an alternative)
50g demerara sugar
50g unsalted butter, melted
1 vanilla pod, sliced in half lengthways and seeds scraped out
200g plain yoghurt

—

You can make this a day in advance, if you like: just keep it in the fridge until ready to serve, then warm through on the stove, adding a couple of tablespoons of water to the pot to loosen it up. The roasted apples can also be made a day or two in advance and stored in the fridge; again, just warm them through before serving.

1   Pour the water into a medium saucepan and place over a high heat with the barley, 3 tablespoons of date syrup, cinnamon, lemon peel, nutmeg and salt. Once boiling, reduce the heat to medium and simmer for 1 hour, or about 30–35 minutes if using pearl barley. Stir from time to time, until the consistency is that of rice pudding but the barley still retains a bite. If using the pearl barley, keep an eye on water levels towards the end of cooking: you might need to add another 100ml or so to make sure it doesn't boil dry before cooking through. Remove and discard the lemon peel and cinnamon sticks and keep the barley somewhere warm until ready to serve.

2   Halfway through cooking the pot barley, or at the start of the pearl barley cooking time, preheat the oven to 200°C/180°C Fan/Gas Mark 6. Line a baking tray with baking parchment.

3   Peel and core the apples and cut into 2–3cm slices (you should have about 650g), then place the slices in a medium bowl with the lemon juice, sugar, butter, vanilla seeds and pod. Mix well and spread out on the lined baking tray. Place in the oven for 30–45 minutes, until the apples are cooked, soft and nicely coloured. Remove from the oven, discard the pod, stir the apples gently to combine – the Bramley apples and Granny Smiths will be completely soft, but the Pink Lady apples will retain their shape – and set aside somewhere warm.

4   If the barley has set, add a couple of tablespoons of water to the pan and gently warm over a medium heat. Divide the warm barley between six bowls and spoon the apples on top. Top with about 2 tablespoons of yoghurt per portion, drizzle with the date syrup and serve.

Cinnamon pavlova, praline cream and fresh figs

This is a stunning dessert for a special occasion. It also has a nice element of surprise, as the meringue base is not quite what you might expect: gooey – almost toffee-like – rather than dry and crispy. This is due to the brown sugar in the mix. Combined with the praline cream and fresh figs, it's absolutely delicious. Pavlova is the dessert to make when you have a bit of time and are feeding people you adore.

The recipe calls for flaked almonds but you can easily substitute those with chopped pistachios, as photographed.

SERVES 10–12 (IT'S QUITE RICH, SO THE SLICES ARE NOT TOO BIG)

The praline (after blitzing but before it's mixed with the cream) can be made up to 3 days in advance and stored in an airtight container. The meringues need to be made in advance – they take 3 hours to cook, 2 hours to cool in the oven, and another 2 hours to set, so you're forced to get ahead by at least this much – but they will also keep for up to 3 days loosely wrapped in foil.

Once assembled, the pavlova should be eaten as soon as possible. It will hold for a couple of hours, but it won't look as good after that.

20g flaked almonds
50g dark cooking chocolate
(70% cocoa solids), finely chopped
600g fresh figs, cut into 1cm discs
3 tbsp honey

MERINGUE
125g egg whites (from 3 large eggs)
125g caster sugar
100g dark muscovado sugar
1½ tsp ground cinnamon

PRALINE CREAM
50g flaked almonds
80g caster sugar
2 tbsp water
200ml double cream
400g mascarpone

1   Preheat the oven to 170°C/150°C Fan/Gas Mark 3.

2   Spread out all the almonds (for both the pavlova and the praline, 70g) on a baking tray and toast for 7–8 minutes, until golden brown. Remove from the oven, divide into two piles (20g for the pavlova, 50g for the praline) and set aside to cool.

3   Reduce the oven temperature to 120°C/100°C Fan/Gas Mark ½. Cover a large baking tray with baking parchment and trace a circle, about 23cm in diameter, on to the paper. Turn the paper over so the drawn-on side is facing down but still visible.

4   **First make the meringue.** Pour enough water into a medium saucepan so that it rises a quarter of the way up the sides: you want the bowl from your electric mixer to be able to sit over the saucepan without touching the water. Bring the water to a boil. Place the egg whites and sugars in the bowl of an electric mixer and whisk by hand to combine. Reduce the heat under the saucepan so that the water is just simmering, then set the mixer bowl over the pan, making sure the water doesn't touch the base of the bowl. Whisk the egg whites continuously by hand until they are warm, frothy and the sugar is melted, about 4 minutes, then transfer back to the electric mixer with the whisk attachment in place and whisk on a high speed for about 5 minutes, until the meringue is cool, stiff and glossy. Add the cinnamon and whisk to combine.

5   Spread the meringue inside the drawn circle, creating a nest by making the sides a little higher than the centre. Place in the oven and bake for 3 hours, then switch off the oven but leave the meringues inside until they are completely cool: this will take about 2 hours. Once cool, remove from the oven and set aside. ››

6   Place the chocolate into a small heatproof bowl and set it over a small saucepan of simmering water, making sure the base of the bowl is not touching the water. Stir occasionally until melted. Cool slightly, then brush the chocolate inside the meringue nest, leaving the top and sides bare. Do this gently, as the meringue is fairly delicate. Leave to set for about 2 hours.

7   **Make the praline.** Place the 50g toasted almonds on a parchment-lined baking tray (with a lipped edge) and set aside. Put the sugar and water into a small saucepan and place over a medium-low heat, stirring until the sugar has melted. Cook, swirling the pan occasionally, until it turns a dark golden brown. Pour the caramel over the nuts (don't worry if they're not all covered) and leave until completely cool and set. Once cool, transfer the praline to the small bowl of a food processor and blitz until fine.

8   Place the cream, mascarpone and blitzed praline in a large bowl and whisk for about 1 minute, until stiff peaks form. Be careful not to over-whisk here – it doesn't take much to thicken up – or it will split. If this begins to happen, use a spatula to fold a little more cream into the mix to bring it back together. Refrigerate until needed.

9   **To assemble,** spoon the cream into the centre of the meringue and top with the figs. Warm the honey in a small saucepan and stir through the 20g almonds (or pistachios, as pictured). Drizzle these over the figs, and serve.

Knickerbocker glory

This is our go-to happy-making dessert: the colour, the connotations, the conical glasses, the distinctive long-handled spoons you eat it with – it's just the definition of good old-fashioned fun. Happiness should not be dependent upon props, however, so don't worry if you don't have the traditional sundae glasses or long-handled spoons. Any other tall glass (or indeed spoon) will work fine. We like to pop our glasses in the freezer until ready to use, as this gives them a frosted look and also helps to keep the ice cream chilled after serving.

The ice cream here is a semifreddo, which does not need churning: good news for those who don't have an ice cream maker. The candied pecans are the same as those used in the Mont Blanc Tarts (see page 235).

Fresh raspberries are lovely, of course, but frozen also work really well in the semifreddo. In fact, the liquid exuded when frozen raspberries defrost gives the purée a lovely consistency.

SERVES 6

The candied pecans can be made up to 5 days ahead and kept in an airtight container. The semifreddo needs to be made at least 12 hours in advance. You'll have about a third of the semifreddo left over, and this will keep in the freezer for 1 month.

SEMIFREDDO
600g raspberries, fresh, or frozen
   and defrosted
2 tbsp icing sugar
200ml double cream
1 large egg, plus 2 large egg yolks
1 tsp lemon juice
180g caster sugar
⅛ tsp salt

CANDIED PECANS
1 tbsp maple syrup
1 tbsp liquid glucose
1 tbsp caster sugar
120g pecan halves
⅛ tsp flaky sea salt

CHANTILLY CREAM
300ml double cream
2 tbsp icing sugar, sifted
1 tsp vanilla extract

PLUMS
about 5 red plums, stones removed,
   chopped into 3cm chunks (300g)

1   **To make the semifreddo,** place the raspberries in a food processer and blitz to a purée, then pass them through a fine sieve set over a bowl to remove the seeds. You may need to do this in batches, using a large spoon to scrape the purée through the sieve. Measure out 260ml of the purée and set aside. Sift the icing sugar into the remaining purée – you should have about 100ml – and decant it into a jug. Set aside in the fridge until ready to use.

2   Place 200ml double cream in the bowl of an electric mixer with the whisk attachment in place. Whip until soft peaks form, then scrape into a bowl. Set aside in the fridge until ready to use.

3   Pour enough water into a medium saucepan so that it rises 2cm up the sides: you want the bowl from your electric mixer to be able to sit over the saucepan without touching the water. Bring the water to the boil, then reduce to a low simmer. ››

4   In the meantime, whisk together the egg, egg yolks, lemon juice, sugar and salt in a clean bowl of an electric mixer. Place the bowl over the simmering water and whisk continuously for about 5 minutes, until the sugar has dissolved and the mixture is very warm. Transfer the bowl back to the electric mixer with the whisk attachment in place and beat on a medium-high speed until the mixture is thick and cool: it will thicken quite quickly but takes about 10 minutes or more to cool. Add the 260ml of purée and whisk on a low speed until combined. Scrape down the sides of the bowl and continue to mix until thoroughly combined. Remove the whipped cream from the fridge and fold through until incorporated. Scrape the mixture into a large freezer container, cover the top with cling film and freeze for at least 12 hours.

5   **To make the pecans,** preheat the oven to 210°C/190°C Fan/Gas Mark 6. Line a baking tray (with a lipped edge) with baking parchment and set aside. Place the maple syrup, glucose and sugar in a small saucepan and place over a low heat. Stir gently until the sugar has melted, then add the pecans and salt. Stir so that the nuts are coated in the syrup, then tip the nuts on to the lined baking tray. Place in the oven for about 8 minutes, or until the syrup is bubbling around the nuts. Remove the tray from the oven and set aside until cool. When the nuts are cool, the glaze should be completely crisp; if not, return the tray to the oven for a few more minutes. Once cooled, break or roughly chop the nuts into 0.5cm pieces and set aside until ready to use.

6   **For the Chantilly cream,** place the double cream in a clean bowl of an electric mixer with the whisk attachment in place. Add the icing sugar and vanilla and whip until soft peaks form. Transfer to a bowl or container and keep in the fridge until ready to assemble.

7   **To assemble,** remove the semifreddo from the freezer 10 minutes before serving so that it is soft enough to scoop. Remove the glasses from the freezer and divide the chopped plums between them. Drizzle over half a tablespoon of the reserved sweetened raspberry purée, add a tablespoon of pecans, then spoon a large scoop of the semifreddo on top. Drizzle over the remaining sauce – ½ tablespoon per glass – followed by a small tablespoon of nuts and a couple of large dollops of the whipped cream. Finish with a final sprinkle of the chopped nuts and serve at once.

Frozen espresso parfait for a crowd

This is, in effect, an over-sized ice cream sandwich: what Helen would have called an 'Eskimo Pie', growing up in Australia. There are various components to this crowd-pleasing dessert, but the whole thing can be made well in advance and kept in the freezer to prevent any on-the-day meltdowns. However much work is involved, it is worth it: people cry with joy when they have this!

If you want to lose one element, you can do without the caramel sauce (which would also make the whole thing booze-free). We love it, but the parfait still works well without this sweet and final 'ta da'.

SERVES 12–16 (IT IS RICH, SO SLICES NEED NOT BE LARGE)

—

MERINGUE BASES
75g chopped hazelnuts (or 75g
    whole blanched hazelnuts)
80g icing sugar
20g Dutch-processed cocoa powder
125g egg whites (from 3 large eggs –
    the yolks are used in the parfait)
⅛ tsp salt
⅛ tsp cream of tartar
100g caster sugar
200g dark cooking chocolate
    (70% cocoa solids), roughly chopped
    into 1cm pieces

COFFEE PRALINE
125g caster sugar
2 tbsp water
1½ tsp finely ground espresso coffee
    (such as Lavazza)

ESPRESSO PARFAIT
350ml double cream
6 large egg yolks (you will have
    3 from the meringues)
250ml espresso coffee
200g caster sugar
2 tsp coffee extract (we use
    Trablit Liquid Coffee Extract,
    but any brand is fine)

CARAMEL SAUCE
330g caster sugar
80ml water
160ml double cream
75ml whisky

—

We like to make this in a 20cm square cake tin with a removable base. The removable base makes things easier, but it's not strictly necessary. So long as it's lined, you'll be fine to use any similar-sized tin or tray. You will also need a sugar thermometer for the parfait.

The caramel sauce can be made up to a week ahead and stored in the fridge, ready to be drizzled over just before serving. The coffee praline can be made up to 2 weeks in advance and stored in an airtight container in the freezer (not in the fridge, where the sugar will 'weep') until ready to use. You can also make the meringue bases in advance (before spreading with the melted chocolate and praline): they keep well in an airtight container for 3 days. However much you decide to get ahead, the parfait needs freezing for at least 12 hours once assembled, so you are forced to get ahead this much at least!

1   **For the coffee praline,** put the sugar and water into a small saucepan and place over a low heat. Stir to combine until the sugar has melted. Increase the heat to medium and simmer for about 5 minutes, until the sugar begins to brown at the edges. Gently swirl the pan so that the sugar cooks evenly, resisting the urge to stir. When the caramel has turned a clear amber – after about 1 minute – remove from the heat and pour on to a small parchment-lined tray (with a lipped edge). Tilt the tray as it sets to get a thin layer of caramel. Sprinkle all over with the ground coffee and set aside until completely cool and hard. Once cool, transfer to a food processor and blitz until roughly ground: pieces will range in size from powdery to about 0.5cm wide. Set aside until ready to use.

2   **To make the meringue bases,** preheat the oven to 180°C/160°C Fan/Gas Mark 4 and position two shelves in the oven: one in the middle and one at the bottom. Cut two sheets of baking parchment to fit two large baking trays. Using the base of the tin in which you are going to freeze the parfait (we use a 20cm square tin, but other tins work: see Kit Note), trace around the base on to each of the sheets of parchment. Turn the paper over and place on the baking trays so that the side you have drawn on is facing down but still visible. Set aside: this will be the template for the meringue bases.

3   If starting with whole hazelnuts, spread them out on a baking tray and roast for about 15 minutes, or until the nuts are lightly brown. Remove from the oven and, once cool enough to handle, chop them finely into 0.5cm pieces. If starting with chopped nuts, just spread them out on a baking tray and roast for 7–8 minutes. Set aside until completely cool.

4   Sift the icing sugar and cocoa powder together into a bowl and set aside. Place the egg whites in the bowl of an electric mixer with the whisk attachment in place. Add the salt and cream of tartar and beat on a medium-high speed for about 2 minutes, until soft peaks form. Gradually add the caster sugar – a tablespoon at a time – and continue to beat for 2–3 minutes, until very stiff. Gently fold in the sifted icing sugar and cocoa powder and the hazelnuts.

5   Divide the meringue mixture in two and dollop on to the two traced sheets, smoothing it out with a small metal spatula to fit the traced shapes. It will spread slightly, but you can trim it back so that it fits the tin snugly later.

6   Place the meringue sheets on to the middle and bottom shelves of the oven and bake for about 1 hour, or until the meringues are crisp and dry (the inside will still be a little bit soft). Check the meringues halfway through the cooking time, rotating the trays and swapping them between the shelves if one is taking on more colour than the other. Remove from the oven and set aside to cool. Once the meringues are cool, trim the edges so that they fit neatly into the tin in which the parfait will be frozen. If the pan has a removable base, use this to help you trim the meringue bases.

7   Place the chocolate in a small heatproof bowl and set it over a small saucepan of simmering water, making sure the base of the bowl is not touching the water. Stir occasionally until melted, then set aside to cool slightly. Brush the flat side of each of the meringue bases with the melted chocolate and immediately sprinkle the coffee praline all over the chocolate so that it has time to adhere to the chocolate before it sets. Set aside to dry while you make the parfait.

8   **To make the espresso parfait,** place the cream in the bowl of an electric mixer with the whisk attachment in place. Beat until soft peaks form, then transfer to a container and store in the fridge until ready to use. »

The parfait can be assembled and stored in the freezer for up to 1 week, ideally, but it will keep well in the freezer for up to 1 month.

If making the meringue bases the day before the parfait, reserve the egg yolks for the parfait. Store the yolks in a small bowl, add a teaspoon of water directly on top, wrap the bowl in cling film and place in the fridge.

9   Place the egg yolks in a clean bowl of an electric mixer with the whisk attachment in place, in preparation for the next stage. Put the espresso coffee and sugar into a medium saucepan and place over a low heat, stirring until the sugar has dissolved. Increase the heat to medium-high and simmer the coffee syrup. In the meantime, begin whisking the egg yolks on a medium-high speed. Keep checking the coffee syrup with a sugar thermometer and when it has reached 118°C ('soft ball' stage), pour the hot coffee syrup slowly down the rim of the bowl on to the beating yolks, which should be thick and creamy by now. Continue to whisk at medium-high speed until the bowl is no longer warm to touch – 10–15 minutes – then add the coffee extract. Whisk to combine, then turn off the mixer.

10   **Prepare the tin;** while the yolks are whipping and cooling, line the sides and base of your chosen tin with baking parchment, making sure there is an overhang on all sides. Place one of the meringue bases on the bottom, chocolate side down. It should fit neatly, with no large gaps around the sides.

11   When the yolk mixture is cool, remove the bowl from the mixer and use a large rubber spatula to fold in the whipped cream in three batches. Do not over-mix as you want to keep the parfait light and airy, but do make sure that there are no big lumps of cream. Pour the parfait over the meringue base and use a small spatula to smooth and even it out. Carefully place the second meringue sheet over the top of the parfait, chocolate side up. Press gently to ensure the meringue is completely in contact with the parfait. Cover with cling film and place in the freezer for at least 12 hours, or until completely firm.

12   **To make the caramel sauce,** combine the sugar and water in a medium saucepan and place over a low heat. Heat until the sugar has dissolved, stirring occasionally, then increase the heat to high. Do not stir beyond this point. Cook until the caramel is a deep amber colour, then remove from the heat. Carefully add the cream – stand back here, as the mixture will bubble and splutter – and return the pan to a low heat. Stir until the caramel is smooth, add the whisky and decant into a jug. If making the sauce ahead of time, store it in the fridge, then reheat in a pan over a low heat when ready to serve.

13   When ready to serve, remove the frozen parfait from the freezer and, using the overhanging paper, gently pull the whole thing out. If your tin or tray has a removable base, push the parfait up from underneath. Slice into small blocks or rectangles with a warm knife, pour over the caramel sauce, and serve.

Saffron and almond ice cream sandwich

This is an ice cream sandwich for grown-ups. The appeal is timeless – Ice cream! In a sandwich! Made with biscuits! – but the flavour of the saffron makes this one a treat for the big kids. Don't be put off by all the different stages here: it looks like a lot of work, but the joy of an ice cream maker is that a lot of the work is done for you.

MAKES 12

Ideally, an ice cream maker is needed to churn the ice cream. If you don't have one, you can churn it yourself, stirring the mix every few hours to break up the formation of ice crystals before returning it to the freezer.

Both the biscuits and nuts can be made 3 or 4 days ahead and kept, separately, in airtight containers.

Once assembled, the sandwiches will keep in the freezer for up to 1 month.

120g whole almonds, skin on
200g plain flour, plus extra for dusting
55g Dutch-processed cocoa powder
½ tsp baking powder
½ tsp salt
100g unsalted butter, at room temperature
160g soft light brown sugar
½ tsp vanilla extract
60ml full-fat milk

ICE CREAM
4 large egg yolks
100g caster sugar
320ml full-fat milk
300ml double cream
½ vanilla pod, sliced in half lengthways and seeds scraped
¼ tsp saffron threads

1   Preheat the oven to 180°C/160°C Fan/Gas Mark 4.

2   **To make the biscuits,** start by spreading the almonds out on a tray and bake for 8 minutes. Set aside to cool, then blitz in a food processor to roughly 0.5cm pieces. Store in an airtight container until needed.

3   Increase the oven temperature to 200°C/180°C Fan/Gas Mark 6. Line two baking trays with baking parchment.

4   Sift the flour, cocoa, baking powder and salt together into a bowl and set aside.

5   Add the butter and sugar to the bowl of an electric mixer with the paddle attachment in place. Beat on a high speed for about 3 minutes, until pale, then add the vanilla. Mix to incorporate, reduce the speed to low and add a third of the flour mix. Continue to incorporate, then add half the milk. Mix to combine, then repeat with another third of the flour, the remaining milk, and finishing with the flour. Mix until just combined: the dough will be soft but not sticky.

6   Transfer the dough to a lightly floured work surface and knead until smooth. Divide in two and set one half aside. Roll the dough to 3mm thick and use an 8cm round cookie cutter to cut out discs. Arrange the discs on a tray, separating the layers with baking parchment so they don't stick to each other, then repeat the process with the second piece of dough. Re-roll any offcuts to make twenty-four biscuits in total. Place in the freezer for at least 15 minutes.

7   When ready to bake, arrange the discs on the lined baking trays and bake for about 6–8 minutes, until firm on the outside but still a little soft in the centre. Remove from the oven and set aside to cool for 5 minutes before transferring to a wire rack to cool completely. Place the biscuits in an airtight container until ready to use. ››

8   **To make the ice cream,** place the yolks and sugar in a medium bowl, whisk to combine and set aside. Put the milk, cream, vanilla seeds and pod, and saffron into a medium saucepan and place over a medium heat. Warm through for 3–4 minutes, until little bubbles start forming. Slowly pour half the hot milk into the yolk mixture, whisking constantly until smooth, then pour all the mixture back into the saucepan with the remaining milk. Return to a medium-low heat and cook for 8–10 minutes, stirring constantly, until the mixture coats the back of a spoon. Remove from the heat, discard the vanilla pod, transfer to a bowl and set aside to cool completely: the best way to do this is to chill the mixture over an ice bath or in the fridge before churning. When cold, place in an ice cream maker and churn until firm waves appear.

9   Before assembling, place a baking tray (or any other tray) in your freezer. This is to put the ice cream sandwiches on as soon as they are assembled.

10   When assembling the sandwiches, keep the ice cream churning (to prevent it melting). Spoon about 50g of ice cream on the underside of one biscuit and place another biscuit on top, smooth side up. Gently squeeze the biscuits together so that the ice cream just comes to the edge of the biscuits. Run the tip of a teaspoon between the two biscuits to remove any excess ice cream and to create a smooth finish. Give the biscuits one final gentle squeeze together so that the ice cream sits evenly with the biscuits. Place each one on the tray in the freezer as soon as they are assembled, before starting on the next. Once they are all together, freeze for at least 6 hours before serving.

11   Just before serving, remove the biscuits from the freezer to allow the edges of the ice cream to soften slightly. Spread the blitzed almonds out on a flat plate, roll the exposed ice cream in the nuts, and serve.

Campari and grapefruit sorbet

This is so refreshing and party-like that it can be served at pretty much any point during a meal. Before you start eating, for example, with a splash of Prosecco on top; as a palate-cleanser between courses; or for dessert in frosted Martini glasses with one of the Cats' Tongues (see page 27) alongside and possibly also a naughty extra glug of Campari.

Don't be tempted to use pale yellow grapefruit here: you really want the ruby red variety, as it provides both the shock of colour and the sweetness you want to bring to the party.

Once you've made the sorbet, you're all set to make the Chocolate-coated Ruby Red Grapefruit Peel (see page 326), if you like, as you'll have the peel all ready to go. If you don't want to do this straight away, collect the peel in a zip-lock bag and store it in the fridge for up to 3 days.

SERVES 6 (AT THE END OF A MEAL), **12** (IN THE MIDDLE) **OR MORE** (AT THE START OF A MEAL)

500ml fresh ruby red grapefruit juice
  (from 2–5 grapefruit, depending on
  their size and juiciness)
60ml lemon juice

100ml orange juice
200g caster sugar
80ml Campari

---

1   If you are going to make the Chocolate-coated Ruby Red Grapefruit Peel, follow the slicing instructions on page 326, retaining the flesh for use here, and storing the peel until ready to use. Otherwise, cut each grapefruit in half and remove the flesh. Make sure there are no pips in the flesh, then place it in a blender or food processor and blend until the grapefruit is crushed. Strain it into a bowl through a fine-mesh sieve: you need 500ml of juice, so feel free to drink any excess (or make a cocktail with it).

2   Add the lemon and orange juice to the grapefruit juice and mix together. Pour 250ml of this into a small saucepan with the sugar, and set the remaining juice aside. Heat the pan over a low heat, stirring until the sugar is dissolved, then set aside for 10 minutes to cool. Pour this into the remaining juice, add the Campari, and chill completely by setting it over an ice bath or placing it in the fridge.

3   Once chilled, transfer to an ice cream maker and churn until soft waves form. Transfer the sorbet to a container, cover with cling film – so that the cling film is actually touching the surface of the sorbet, to prevent ice particles forming – and seal the container. Freeze until firm enough to scoop into a glass, and serve.

Ideally, an ice cream maker is needed to churn the sorbet. If you don't have one, you can churn it yourself, stirring the mix every few hours to break up the formation of ice crystals before returning it to the freezer.

Once churned, the sorbet will keep in the freezer for about 1 week.

Prickly pear sorbet

Prickly pears are really idiosyncratic: they're the fruit form of the desert cactus, with a flavour so distinct that it's hard to recommend a substitute. They are reminiscent of watermelon and quince: almost strawberry-like, but then not at all! Common in the Middle East and South America, they can be hard to get hold of elsewhere. They freeze really well, though, so keep an eye out from late summer to early winter, when they're more likely to be around and will certainly be at their best. If you want to keep the South American connection, a dash of mezcal is lovely poured over just before serving.

These days, prickly pears are usually sold with their thorns removed (or burnt off), but it's still a good idea to wear rubber gloves when you're peeling them, just in case. You don't want one of their fine spines lodged in your skin: the sting is surprisingly uncomfortable.

This is lovely either by itself or served with a little light biscuit. The Cats' Tongues (see page 27) or Brown Butter Almond Tuiles (see page 30) work really well.

SERVES 6–8

200g caster sugar
250ml water
10–12 prickly pears, peeled (700g): their colour can vary from pale yellow to deep magenta, with every shade in between

60ml lime juice
⅛ tsp salt

---

1   **To make the syrup,** put the sugar and water into a small saucepan and place over a low heat. Swirl the pan every once in a while, until the sugar has dissolved, then increase the heat to medium-high. Simmer for about 8 minutes, swirling the pan frequently until you have about 250ml of thick syrup. Remove from the heat, set aside to cool, then store in the fridge until ready to use (up to 2 weeks).

2   **To prepare the pears,** put on some rubber gloves (washing-up gloves are fine) and use a small paring knife or vegetable peeler to peel off and discard the skin. Slice the flesh roughly into quarters, transfer to a food processor and blitz to form a fine purée. Transfer to a sieve set over a medium bowl and, using a spatula, press as much of the liquid as you can through the sieve, discarding the seeds: you should have about 650ml of purée. The seeds are edible, but we prefer to strain them out so as not to detract from the delicate soft fruit. Stir through the sugar syrup, lime juice and salt, then either plunge the bowl into an ice bath or place it in the fridge for an hour until very cold: this really helps it along in the machine.

3   Transfer to an ice cream maker and churn for about 35 minutes (this can vary, depending on your machine and how cold the mixture is when it goes in), until soft waves form. Transfer to a sealed container and freeze, covered, until solid: this should take about 6 hours. About 10 minutes before you are ready for dessert, remove it from the freezer to soften slightly, and serve.

Ideally, an ice cream maker is needed to churn the sorbet. If you don't have one, you can churn it yourself, stirring the mix every few hours to break up the formation of ice crystals before returning it to the freezer.

The syrup can be made up to 2 weeks in advance and stored in the fridge until needed.

Once churned, the sorbet will keep in the freezer for up to a month.

Lemon, yoghurt and juniper berry ice cream

The spark of inspiration for this dish was struck over a gin and tonic. The recipe went off-piste to become something else entirely, but the gin link remained with the presence of the juniper berries (from which gin is made). It's a link which can be reinforced by serving the ice cream in an ice-cold glass and adding a splash of gin at the table, if you like.

This egg-free ice cream has such a distinctive taste – a pronounced lemon flavour, along with spicy tones from the juniper berries – that it really doesn't need any accompaniment. If you do want a little extra something, though, one of the Cats' Tongues (see page 27) or Brown Butter Almond Tuiles (see page 30) work well.

SERVES 6

200g caster sugar
250ml water
shaved peel of ½ lemon, avoiding
   the bitter pith, plus 60ml lemon juice
1 small fresh bay leaf

250g Greek yoghurt
1 tsp dried juniper berries, finely
   crushed in a mortar and pestle
   or using a rolling pin
60ml double cream

1   **To make the syrup,** put the sugar and water into a small saucepan, place over a medium heat and stir to dissolve. Add the lemon peel and bay leaf and simmer for 12 minutes, until you have about 300ml left in the pan. Remove from the heat, set aside to cool, then strain the syrup and discard the lemon peel and bay leaf before using. Store in the fridge until ready to use (up to 2 weeks).

2   Place the yoghurt in a large bowl and gently whisk in the strained sugar syrup and lemon juice, followed by the juniper berries. Store in the fridge, covered, until ready to churn (up to 2 days).

3   Just before you are ready to churn, pour the cream into a bowl and whisk until soft peaks form, by hand or using a hand-held electric whisk. While continuing to whisk, pour in the yoghurt sugar syrup, whisking until combined. Place in an ice cream maker and churn for about 30 minutes, until soft waves form. Transfer to a container and freeze, covered, until solid: this should take about 6 hours. Remove it from the freezer 15 minutes before serving – 3 small scoops look nice, or 2 larger scoops – in glasses which have also been placed in the freezer for an hour beforehand.

Ideally, an ice cream maker is needed to churn the ice cream. If you don't have one, you can churn it yourself, stirring the mix every few hours to break up the formation of ice crystals before returning it to the freezer.

The syrup can be made up to 2 weeks in advance and stored in the fridge until needed. The ice cream mixture can be made up to 2 days ahead of churning and stored in the fridge, covered.

Once churned, the ice cream will keep in the freezer for 2 weeks. It will still be fine after that, though it might form ice crystals.

Chocolate, rose and walnut ice cream

There's something a little bit Arabian nights about the combination of ingredients here, with the Turkish delight and rose water. The rose is key, but make sure you start with some good-quality rose water, preferably Lebanese.

Thanks to Caroline Liddell and Robin Weir's *Ices: The Definitive Guide* for the technique of 'cooking out' the cocoa powder in the recipe for the chocolate base, in the same way that you 'cook out' the flour when making a béchamel.

SERVES 6–8

65g walnut halves
350ml full-fat milk
300ml double cream
20g Dutch-processed cocoa powder
3 large egg yolks
100g caster sugar
100g dark cooking chocolate
   (70% cocoa solids), chopped
1 tsp instant coffee granules
1 tbsp rose water

3 digestive biscuits, broken into
   1cm pieces
120g rose-flavoured Turkish delight,
   cut into 1cm cubes
1 tsp dried rose petals (optional)

CHOCOLATE SAUCE
50g dark cooking chocolate
   (70% cocoa solids), finely chopped
100ml double cream
¼ tsp brandy (optional)

Ideally, an ice cream maker is needed to churn the ice cream. If you don't have one, you can churn it yourself, stirring the mix every few hours to break up the formation of ice crystals before returning it to the freezer.

The ice cream can be churned a day in advance and stored in the freezer: remove from the freezer 20 minutes before serving.

1   Preheat the oven to 180°C/160°C Fan/Gas Mark 4.

2   Spread the walnuts out on a baking tray and roast for 7 minutes. Remove from the oven and, once cool enough to handle, chop roughly into 1cm pieces. Set aside.

3   Pour the milk and cream into a medium saucepan and place over a medium heat. Cook for 3–4 minutes, until it starts to simmer. Pour about 80ml into a small bowl, add the cocoa and whisk together until combined. Return the mixture to the pan, stir through, reduce the heat to medium-low and cook gently for another 6–7 minutes, stirring often, to 'cook out' the cocoa. Remove from the heat and set aside.

4   Place the yolks and sugar in a medium bowl and whisk until pale. Slowly pour over about 100ml of the hot chocolate cream and continue to whisk. Return everything to the saucepan, along with the chocolate and coffee, stir through to melt, then cook gently over a medium heat for another 10 minutes, stirring regularly, for the custard to thicken slightly. Set aside to cool completely: you can do this by either setting it over an ice bath or chilling it in the fridge (for a few hours or overnight). Starting off with properly chilled custard is important, as it won't over-work the ice cream machine. Once chilled, gradually add the rose water (don't add it all at once: taste to make sure the rose flavour doesn't take over).

5   Transfer to an ice cream maker and churn until soft waves form, then spoon into a plastic container with a lid. Stir in the walnuts and digestives and freeze, covered, for at least 1 hour (or overnight).

6   **Make the chocolate sauce** just before serving. Put the chocolate in a bowl and set aside. Place the cream in a saucepan over a medium heat. As soon as it starts to boil, pour it over the chocolate and stir until melted. Stir in the brandy, if using, and spoon over the ice cream. Sprinkle with the Turkish delight and rose petals and serve.

Confectionery

—

People love to be baked for and people love to receive gifts. Combine the two and all your Christmases have, quite literally, come at once.

Christmas is a big time for confectionery in our shops: our displays are piled high with festive treats. Some things taste like Christmas – the Chocolate Panforte with Oranges and Figs (see page 332), for example, with all those winter spices. Some things look like Christmas – the little log-shaped Pecan and Prosecco Truffles (see page 324) – while others manage to both taste and look like Christmas, in the case of the over-sized Spiced Praline Meringues (see page 323), which can be hung from your tree before being eaten.

The long shelf life, general robustness and generous yield of many of the recipes in this chapter allows you to be very generous. A batch of the Almond and Aniseed Nougat (see page 328) or the Chocolate Panforte with Oranges and Figs (see page 332) will enable you to cross off all the cousins on your Christmas list in one go, should you so choose. Cut, slice and wrap as you like, depending on who you are making them for and how big you want your slices to be. The Pecan and Prosecco Truffles (see page 324) and the Chocolate-coated Ruby Red Grapefruit Peel (see page 326) make well over twenty pieces each. Arrange a handful of these in individual parchment-lined boxes, and happiness is guaranteed. The bright-red Raspberry Lollipops (see page 318) look great packaged in individual see-through bags, as do the Woodland Meringues (see page 319) in packs of about ten.

Confectionery is for life, though, not just for Christmas. Valentine's day, Mother's day, Father's day, Hanukkah, Chinese New Year, a friend's birthday, Easter, Thanksgiving, Eid . . . whatever the occasion, there's nothing more satisfying than turning up at a friend's house with a little bag, box or stick of something, and being able to slip in the fact that you made them. 'You made them?!' It's a real 'ta da!' moment: the celebration of small and sweet things.

The satisfaction of giving is second only, perhaps, to the satisfaction you get when you crack the making of a confectionery recipe for the first time. Quite literally in the case of the Raspberry Lollipops (see page 318), as it does take practice to get them to their perfectly brittle state. Working with sugar – making nougat, making caramel – also takes practice. It's not that it's particularly complicated, it just requires you to be on top of timings and to know sugar well enough to gauge what's going on in the pan. A sugar thermometer will be your best friend at this stage, taking the guesswork out of the equation and allowing you to relax in the knowledge that, so long as you do exactly as you are told in terms of timings and temperatures, Willy Wonka will be proud.

Kit

As we say, a sugar thermometer is a big must: you won't be able to make many of the recipes in this chapter successfully without one. A piping bag is also needed for a couple of recipes: you can either invest in a piping bag which comes with a range of nozzles, or you can buy disposable piping bags and cut holes in the ends. Of course, if you don't have either of these things but would like to have them, you're all set with your answer to the inevitable question 'But what would you like for Christmas?' from all those who are so grateful for the confectionery gifts you have just given them.

A note on the weather

Although the confectionery in this chapter should be enough to cheer everyone up whatever the weather, the weather is actually something you need to be mindful of when working with sugar. If it's particularly humid or muggy, it can cause problems with the setting of the caramels or lollipops, for example. The former can end up 'weeping' and the latter can end up bendy. This is not to put you off making either of these if it is warm, but to explain why things may not be going to plan. Even the patience of Sarah Joseph – known to be neither weepy nor flaky – was tested through the re-creation of both of these recipes during a particularly humid July. Sarah worked closely with us on the making of *Sweet*, testing every recipe to make sure that what works in our shops and bakery also works at home. When you crack your first lollipop – 'It works! It cracks! It's not bendy!' – spare a smile for Sarah: things cracking when they're meant to and not cracking when they shouldn't is in no small part due to all her hard work.

Saffron and pistachio brittle

Helen was inspired to create this after her first visit, with her good friend Goli, to the annual Persian market held in the run up to Nowruz – Persian New Year – in the heart of London's Marylebone. Crowded with savvy and purposeful Iranian women getting hold of the goods they needed for their New Year preparations, Helen – not entirely sure what she was preparing for – returned home with a cashmere scarf, a ceramic replica of a pomegranate, a box of chickpea halva, two goldfish (real ones), jars of carrot jam and vegetable pickles, a dozen hyacinth bulbs and, crucially, some wonderful saffron nut brittle.

Our version departs from the Sohan Asali she bought, but mention needs to be made of how strongly the lady who sold it to Helen felt about her using Persian saffron in the first instance. 'Anything else,' said Mimi, 'is inferior.' The same could also be said of Iranian pistachios – they are long and elegant and a vibrant green – but regular pistachios are also fine.

MAKES 12 PIECES (OR MORE OR LESS, DEPENDING ON SIZE)

150g flaked almonds
270g soft light brown sugar
120g unsalted butter
2 tbsp boiling water
½ tsp saffron threads, steeped in
    2 tsp boiling water
¼ tsp flaky sea salt

½ tsp bicarbonate of soda
20g shelled pistachio kernels,
    roughly chopped (or, if you can
    find them, the green Iranian variety
    are even better and do not need
    to be chopped)

1   Preheat the oven to 180°C/160°C Fan/Gas Mark 4. Spread the almonds out on a baking tray and roast for about 7 minutes, or until light golden brown. Turn off the oven but leave the nuts inside so that they stay warm (so that the brittle won't harden so quickly when the nuts are added).

2   Line a 30 x 23cm baking tray (with a lipped edge) with baking parchment and set aside.

3   Put the sugar, butter and water into a medium saucepan and place over a low heat. Stir until the sugar has melted. Increase the heat to medium and stop stirring. Simmer until the temperature reaches between 140°C and 143°C on a sugar thermometer ('soft crack' stage). Turn off the heat but leave the pan on the stove top. Carefully add the saffron threads with the steeping water and flaky sea salt: it will bubble up a bit, so be careful. Stir very gently to combine, then add the bicarbonate of soda and warm almonds. Stir again until the mixture froths up and is evenly mixed.

4   Working quickly, pour the mix all over the lined tray and carefully tilt the tray until it is evenly spread. Do not use any utensils to do this, as the consistency of the caramel will be changed. Sprinkle the chopped pistachios all over the top and press lightly with a spatula or the back of a spoon so they stick to the caramel. Set aside to cool completely – this will take about 45 minutes – before breaking into smaller pieces to serve.

If the brittle sticks to the saucepan so much that it's hard to clean, add some boiling water to the pan and return it to the heat for a minute: the brittle will quickly loosen.

A sugar thermometer is a must here.

The brittle will keep for about 10 days in an airtight container. Don't be tempted to store it in the fridge, as it will 'weep'.

(GF)

Raspberry lollipops

We make these in heart shapes around Valentine's day, but they're a wonderful way to make loved ones smile all year round – in a round shape! You can either shape them by hand or – if you're after perfection – use bottomless cake rings as your mould: 7 or 8cm rings are good for regular round lollipops, but there are all sorts of shapes you can play with – hearts, stars, and so forth.

Whether you are shaping them by hand or using a cake ring, don't make these on a rainy or humid day: the caramel will 'weep' and you'll end up with bendy lollipops (which will not be so smile-inducing).

MAKES 12

60g fresh raspberries
250g caster sugar
250g liquid glucose

40ml water
20g freeze-dried raspberries,
    half left whole and half
    lightly crushed

---

1   Line three baking trays with baking parchment, then lay twelve lollipop sticks out flat on the lined trays – the lollipops are large so they require some space – and set aside.

2   **To make the raspberry purée,** blitz the fresh raspberries in the small bowl of a food processor, then strain through a fine-mesh sieve placed over a bowl: you should end up with 1½–2 tablespoons of seedless purée. Set aside.

3   Put the sugar and glucose into a medium saucepan and stir in the water. Place over a medium heat and cook for about 3 minutes, stirring, until the sugar melts. Increase the heat to medium-high and boil for about 10 minutes, until it reaches 147°C on a sugar thermometer. Precision is key here, but it is better to be 1 degree hotter than 1 degree below. Remove from the heat and add the raspberry purée: take care here, as the sugar will be bubbling. Stir slowly and gently with a metal spoon until combined, taking care not to mix too quickly, as this will create large air bubbles which will stay in the lollipops. Once fully combined, lightly stir through the whole and lightly crushed dried raspberries, again taking care as you do so. The caramel should have stopped bubbling by this time.

4   **Immediately shape the lollipops;** spoon 2–3 dessertspoons of the mixture on to the top one-third of the lollipop sticks. Use the spoon to create a circle if shaping by hand. You'll need to work fast here, as the sugar mixture will thicken quickly. Divide the freeze-dried raspberries equally between the lollipops.

5   If you are using cake rings (see introduction), place them over the top third of the lollipop sticks and pour in 2–3 tablespoons of the caramel.

6   Loosely lay a sheet of baking parchment over the top of the lollipops to stop them sweating. Set aside until completely cool and set: this should take about half an hour. Once cool and set, remove the rings from the lollipops (if using) and serve.

A sugar thermometer is a must here, along with twelve lollipop sticks. The metal cake rings are optional.

These will keep for up to 1 week in an airtight tin, stored between layers of baking parchment.

Woodland meringues

Helen was inspired to create these after a walk around Kew Gardens with her young sons. It was autumn and the ground was covered in conkers. Delighting in her boys' delight at the little fallen treats, Helen then had to be the one to inform them that, no, eating conkers was really not such a good idea. Their look of collective bafflement was so great that Helen's imagination set out to create something that both looks like it has fallen from a tree and, crucially, is eminently edible. These 'woodland meringues' are the result.

We've made two versions here – dark chocolate with hazelnuts and white chocolate with freeze-dried strawberries. You can make one or the other or a combination of both. The dark chocolate versions are pictured. We sell them in the shops in little see-through bags, for people to take home or to buy as a gift. They're a lovely bite-sized way to end a meal or party.

MAKES ABOUT 70

When melted and used as a coating, dark chocolate can develop white streaks after a day or so. This won't affect the taste but can be avoided by tempering the chocolate (see page 345). Tempering the chocolate is optional here, however, as the chocolate is covered by the chopped hazelnuts so any white streaks won't really be seen.

You will need a piping bag with a 1.5cm wide nozzle. You can also buy disposable piping bags, if you prefer.

These will keep for up to 10 days, stored in an airtight container.

MERINGUE
120g egg whites (from 3 large eggs)
½ tsp cream of tartar
240g caster sugar
¾ tsp cornflour
⅛ tsp baking powder
½ tsp vanilla extract

WHITE CHOCOLATE COATING
(HALVE THE QUANTITIES IF YOU ARE DOING A MIX OF DARK AND WHITE CHOCOLATE)
140g white chocolate, chopped
    into 1–2cm pieces
50g freeze-dried strawberries,
    finely chopped

DARK CHOCOLATE COATING
(HALVE THE QUANTITIES IF YOU ARE DOING A MIX OF DARK AND WHITE CHOCOLATE)
200g hazelnuts
100g dark cooking chocolate
    (70% cocoa solids), chopped
    into 1–2cm pieces
40g milk chocolate, chopped into
    1–2cm pieces

1   Preheat the oven to 180°C/160°C Fan/Gas Mark 4.

2   If making the dark chocolate coating, spread the hazelnuts out on a small baking tray and roast for 10 minutes. Transfer to a clean tea towel, draw in the sides, then rub together to remove some of the skins. Chop the nuts very finely – it's better to do this by hand, rather than in a food processor, where the nuts will become 'dusty' – then set aside in a bowl.

3   **To make the meringue,** reduce the oven temperature to 140°C/120°C Fan/Gas Mark 1. Put the egg whites into the bowl of an electric mixer with the whisk attachment in place. Beat on a medium-high speed for about 2 minutes, until they appear foamy. Add the cream of tartar and continue to beat until they are stiff but not dry or crumbly: about 30 seconds. Place the sugar in a bowl, add the cornflour and baking powder (adding both ensures a completely dry and crisp meringue), and gradually – one tablespoon at a time – add the sugar to the egg whites. Continue to beat for about 3 minutes, until the mixture is thick and glossy. Beat in the vanilla, then spoon into a piping bag with a 1.5cm wide nozzle in place. ››

4   Line two large baking trays with baking parchment (sticking each sheet firmly to the tray with a bit of the meringue mix). Pipe small droplets – or 'kisses' – on to each lined tray: the base of each droplet should be about 3cm wide. Raise the piping bag as you pipe, so that they are 4–5cm high and you create a fine tip at the top. Once all the meringues have been piped, place both trays in the oven at once. Immediately reduce the oven temperature to 120°C/100°C Fan/Gas Mark ½ – you want it to be slightly hotter when they go in, to give the meringues a crunch – and bake for 2½ hours. The meringues are done when they look dry and sound hollow when tapped gently underneath. Turn off the oven but leave the meringues inside until they are cool, propping the door open with a wooden spoon.

5   **For the dark chocolate topping,** place the dark and milk chocolate in a medium heatproof bowl over a pan of simmering water, making sure the base of the bowl is not touching the water. Stir occasionally until melted. One at a time, dip the base of the meringues into the melted chocolate, followed by the chopped hazelnuts, then place on a parchment-lined tray.

6   **For the white chocolate topping,** follow the instructions for the dark chocolate above, dipping the base into the dried strawberries instead.

Spiced praline meringues

Yotam first made these around Christmas time for his weekly column in the *Guardian*. They are intentionally over-sized – just as good hung from the tree as a decoration as they are to eat – and last for ten days, so, fortunately, their use as both decoration and edible treat are not mutually exclusive options.

If you want to make them just for the table, use the same amount of mix to produce twelve meringues. These are great served with cream and stewed cranberries as a seasonal dessert.

MAKES 6 (EXTRA-LARGE) OR 12 (REGULAR-SIZED)

These will keep for 10 days. If hanging the meringues, use a strip of ribbon to gently wrap each one, as you would a present, creating a bow and leaving a long piece of ribbon to hang them with. If you are not hanging them on the tree, wrap them loosely in aluminium foil and keep at room temperature.

(GF)

50g blanched almonds
300g caster sugar
25ml water
½ tsp ground cinnamon
⅛ tsp ground cloves

finely grated zest of 1 large orange (1 tbsp)
¼ tsp flaky sea salt
150g egg whites (from 4 large eggs)

1   Preheat the oven to 190°C/170°C Fan/Gas Mark 5.

2   Spread the almonds out on a small baking tray and roast in the oven for 5–7 minutes, until lightly browned. Set aside to cool. Line two large baking trays with baking parchment and set aside.

3   Place 50g of sugar in a small saucepan with the water and stir to combine. Cook over a high heat for about 4 minutes, until it has turned a light golden brown; do not stir, just gently shake the pan to help the sugar dissolve. Add the almonds and cook for 1 minute, so the nuts are coated and the caramel turns dark, without burning. Pour the mixture on to one of the lined baking trays and set aside until cool.

4   Once cool, break the praline into smaller pieces, place in a food processor and blitz to form a rough powder. Remove from the machine and place in a shallow bowl with the spices, orange zest and salt. Mix, then set aside until ready to use.

5   Spread the remaining sugar out on the second lined baking tray and place in the oven for 7 minutes, until the sugar is hot. Remove from the oven and reduce the temperature to 130°C/110°C Fan/Gas Mark ¾. As soon as the sugar is out of the oven, place the egg whites in the bowl of an electric mixer with the whisk attachment in place, and whisk on a high speed until they begin to froth up. Carefully add the hot sugar to the whisking egg whites, 1 tablespoon at a time, and continue beating for 7–8 minutes until the mixture is completely cold. At this point it should be silky and thick and keep its shape when you lift a little bit from the bowl.

6   Line the two large baking trays once again with baking parchment. Use an extra-large serving spoon to scoop up some meringue, and use another large spoon to help shape it into a rough ball the size of a large apple. Sprinkle some praline over half the meringue ball, then place on the baking tray. Repeat with the rest of the mixture, spacing the balls about 10cm apart to allow room for increase in size.

7   Place the meringues in the oven for 2–2½ hours. Check that they are done by lifting them from the tray and gently tapping to make sure the outside is completely firm and the centre is only a little soft. Remove from the oven and leave on the tray to cool completely.

Pecan and Prosecco truffles

These were made for the Christmas menu at Ottolenghi, hence their shape as little Yule logs, but you can just roll them into balls, if you prefer. Coating the truffles in a thin layer of chocolate is messy, we know, but it's worth it for the satisfaction of biting into the thin shell to reveal the rich, smooth truffle underneath.

MAKES ABOUT 35

___

45g pecan halves
55g milk chocolate, blitzed in a
    food processor until fine
170g dark chocolate (70% cocoa
    solids), blitzed in a food processor
    until fine, plus an extra 80g, melted,
    for coating

50ml double cream
30g unsalted butter
50ml Prosecco
1½ tsp brandy
30g Dutch-processed cocoa powder,
    for dusting

___

1   Preheat the oven to 180°C/160°C Fan/Gas Mark 4.

2   Spread the pecans out on a baking tray and roast for 10 minutes. Remove from the oven, set aside for 5 minutes, then chop into very small (roughly 2mm) pieces. Set aside.

3   Place the chocolate in a large heatproof bowl and set aside. Put the cream and butter into a small saucepan and place over a medium-high heat. As soon as they come to the boil, pour the cream and butter over the chocolate. Leave for a minute, then stir gently to melt. If there is any solid chocolate remaining, place the bowl over a pan of gently simmering water to help things along. Add the Prosecco, brandy and pecans and fold gently to combine until a smooth ganache is formed. Set aside for the mix to come to room temperature so that it is firm enough to pipe. It takes a long time to set at room temperature, but this is essential for the perfectly smooth and even texture needed. Give it a gentle stir from time to time so that it is malleable enough to pipe. Don't be tempted to speed up the cooling process in the fridge, as this will result in an uneven and lumpy set.

4   Transfer the mix to a piping bag fitted with a 1cm wide plain nozzle and pipe seven 30cm long logs on to a large parchment-lined baking tray. Place in the fridge for at least 30 minutes to set, then cut the logs into five smaller logs, each about 6cm long: using a warm, dry knife will help you cut them cleanly.

5   Have the extra melted chocolate in one bowl at the ready and the cocoa powder in a separate shallow bowl or tray alongside. Dip one log at a time into the chocolate to lightly coat, then roll it in the palm of your hand to remove the excess and ensure that the chocolate coating is nice and thin and sets evenly. Drop the truffle into the cocoa powder and roll gently to lightly coat. You'll need to work fast here, as the chocolate will set quickly. Get someone to help, if you can, so that one person is on the melted chocolate and the other is on the cocoa dusting; this means you won't have to keep washing your hands between coating and rolling. Once set, after about 30 minutes, lightly shake to remove any excess cocoa, and serve.

A piping bag with a 1cm wide nozzle is needed if you want to make these into log shapes.

The truffles will keep for up to 10 days in an airtight container in the fridge.

Chocolate-coated ruby red grapefruit peel

Other citrus fruits can be used instead of the grapefruit, if you prefer, so long as they have a thick skin and can be peeled with the fingers: oranges work well. Fruits with a thinner skin – lemons and limes, for example – aren't really suitable. When peeling your fruit, keep the white pith attached. Don't worry about the bitterness, most of this is removed through blanching.

We like to make these at the same time as the Campari and Grapefruit Sorbet (see page 304), as you will have the peel from two large grapefruit left over from making the sorbet.

MAKES 32 PIECES

2 large ruby red grapefruit (670g)
180g chocolate (70% cocoa solids),
   roughly chopped

SUGAR SYRUP
1 litre water
500g caster sugar
1 cinnamon stick
1 bay leaf

1   Slice each grapefruit into quarters and then each quarter in half lengthways, so you have eight segments per grapefruit (sixteen in total). Carefully separate the fruit from the thick peel (eat or use the flesh for the sorbet on page 304): take a small paring knife and halve each of the sixteen segments of peel lengthways so that you have thirty-two pieces altogether.

2   Fill a large saucepan with plenty of water and bring to the boil over a high heat. Once boiling, add the pieces of grapefruit peel. Press them down lightly into the water with a large spoon and blanch for about 30 seconds, just until the water comes back to the boil. Drain the peel over a colander into the sink. Rinse well under cold running water, then repeat the whole process once more, starting with fresh water – this removes some of the bitterness from the peel. Tip the grapefruit peel on to a clean tea towel and leave to dry. It is important to allow the skins to dry to prevent the sugar syrup from crystallizing later.

3   **To make the sugar syrup,** place all the ingredients in a medium saucepan over a medium-high heat. Cook for about 2 minutes, stirring a few times, until the sugar has dissolved. Bring to a boil, then add the grapefruit peel. Cover the liquid with a cartouche – a round of baking parchment – and place a plate on top to ensure that the peel is fully submerged. Keep the pan on a lively simmer for 60–90 minutes, until the skins are translucent and you are left with about 100ml of syrupy liquid. This can take up to 1½ hours.

4   Drain the grapefruit peel and, using tongs or a slotted spoon, transfer them to a wire rack. The cinnamon, bay leaf and remaining syrup can be discarded. Set the grapefruit peel aside at room temperature, uncovered, until dry, this may take up to 12 hours or more depending on the humidity of the room.

When melted and used as a coating, dark chocolate can develop white streaks after a day or so. This won't affect the taste, but can be avoided by tempering the chocolate (see page 345).

Peel the fruit up to 3 days in advance and store in a zip-lock bag or airtight container in the fridge.

Once coated, the peel keeps for around 10 days in an airtight container at room temperature.

5   Once dry, **coat the peel;** place the chocolate in a heatproof bowl set over a pan of simmering water, making sure the base of the bowl is not touching the water. Stir occasionally until melted, then remove the pan from the heat but keep the bowl over the hot water so that it does not cool too quickly and thicken (if it does, simply return the pan to the heat for a while). Taking one piece of candied peel at a time – lifting them by hand here is the best option, rather than using tongs – dip half into the melted chocolate and shake gently to remove any excess. Transfer to a wire rack to set, and serve.

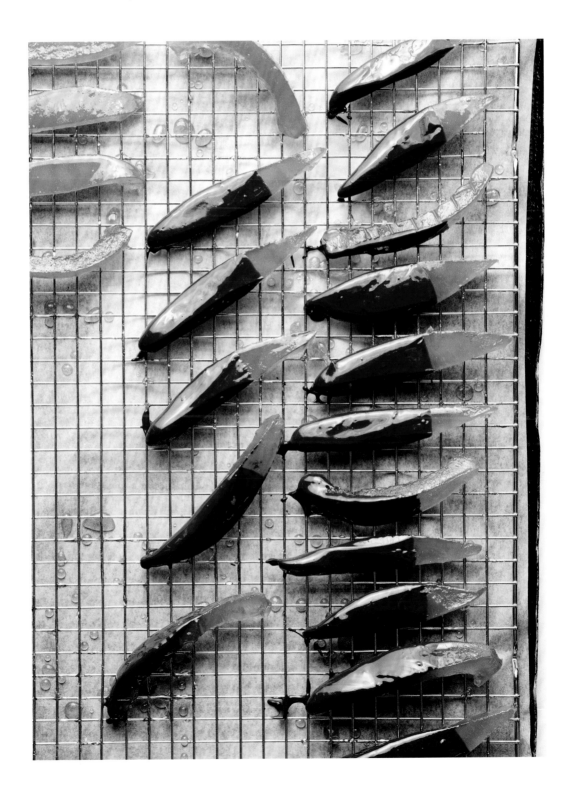

Almond and aniseed nougat

Helen learned how to make nougat from a VHS cassette she found in the 1990s! It showed the Italian mother of an Australian chef called Marco Lori making her family's famous torrone. Essentially the same thing as nougat, it's known as torrone in Italy and nougat in France. It can range in texture from soft to firm, depending on how high you take the temperature of the sugar syrup: the higher the temperature, the harder the nougat. Ours falls into the soft-but-chewy camp: it's still a little firm, but won't break your teeth. You'll know you've been on the right track when, 24 hours after it's made, your nougat has a small amount of movement when pressed. It shouldn't be too sticky and should hold its shape when cut.

Making your own nougat might seem a bit intimidating, but don't be put off: the results are hugely rewarding and (as is always the case when cooking with sugar) it's just about being organized and staying on top of temperatures and timings. The syrup needs to be at the correct temperature just as the egg whites reach soft peaks, and you'll need to work fast, as the nougat firms up quickly once it's been made.

MAKES 6 BARS OR 36 SMALLER PIECES

———

2 sheets (31 x 23cm) edible rice paper (or wafer paper, made from potato starch; or baking parchment)
400g whole raw almonds, skin on
260g whole blanched hazelnuts
2 tbsp whole aniseed (optional)
300g caster sugar
200ml water

270g liquid glucose
60g orange blossom honey (or another floral variety)
25ml Pernod or ouzo (or another aniseed liqueur)
scraped seeds of 1 vanilla pod
⅛ tsp salt
95g egg whites (from 3 medium eggs)

———

A sugar thermometer is a must here. We use a 24 x 23cm baking tin, 4cm deep; alternatively, you could use two 18 x 18cm square tins.

Wrapped tightly in baking parchment and cling film, the nougat will keep for up to a month in an airtight container at room temperature or in the fridge.

1 Line the base of a 23 x 24cm baking tin with baking parchment and grease the edges of the tin. Lay one sheet of rice paper, smooth side down, on top of the parchment paper – the edges of the paper will rise up the shorter sides of the tin – then set the tin aside.

2 Preheat the oven to 170°C/150°C Fan/Gas Mark 3. Spread all the nuts out on a baking tray and roast for 18 minutes, until they are fragrant and golden brown. Reduce the oven temperature to 90°C/70°C Fan/Gas Mark ¼ and leave the nuts in the oven until ready to fold into the nougat: the mix will seize up if the nuts are added cold.

3 Place the aniseed, if using, in a medium heavy-based saucepan and toast over a medium heat for 2 minutes, until fragrant. Transfer to a pestle and mortar, lightly crush and set aside.

4   In a medium saucepan, combine the sugar, water, glucose, honey, Pernod or ouzo, vanilla seeds and salt, and whisk to combine. Place over a medium heat and simmer gently until the sugar has dissolved, then increase the heat to medium-high. Resisting the urge to stir, continue to cook for about 15–20 minutes, until the temperature on a sugar thermometer is close to reaching 118°C. At this stage, place the egg whites in the bowl of an electric mixer with the whisk attachment in place and whisk on medium speed to form soft peaks. Keep an eye on the boiling syrup and, when the temperature on the thermometer registers exactly 121°C, pour half of the hot syrup into the soft peaks in a steady stream. Continue to whisk on a medium speed and return the remaining half of the syrup to the heat.

5   Continue to simmer the remaining syrup until the temperature reaches exactly 145°C, taking care that it does not go over 148°C. Once the temperature is reached, pour the hot syrup – it will be light golden at this stage – over the egg whites in a steady stream, whisking all the time. Continue to whisk for another 6–8 minutes, until you have a thick ribbon-like consistency. To check if it is ready, take a little of the mixture between your fingers and press together then pull apart: the mix should stick together like chewing gum. Using a plastic spatula or large metal spoon, fold through the aniseed and warm nuts. You need to be careful here, as the bowl of the machine will still be hot. Scrape the mixture into the lined baking tin and even out with an offset or regular spatula or palette knife.

6   Cover the surface with some more rice paper, smooth side up, and press down firmly to remove any air bubbles. Set aside to cool overnight, uncovered or with a clean, dry tea towel draped over the top, then slide a hot knife around the edges to remove it from the tin. Cut into 6 long bars (23 x 4cm), if giving as gifts, or into smaller squares.

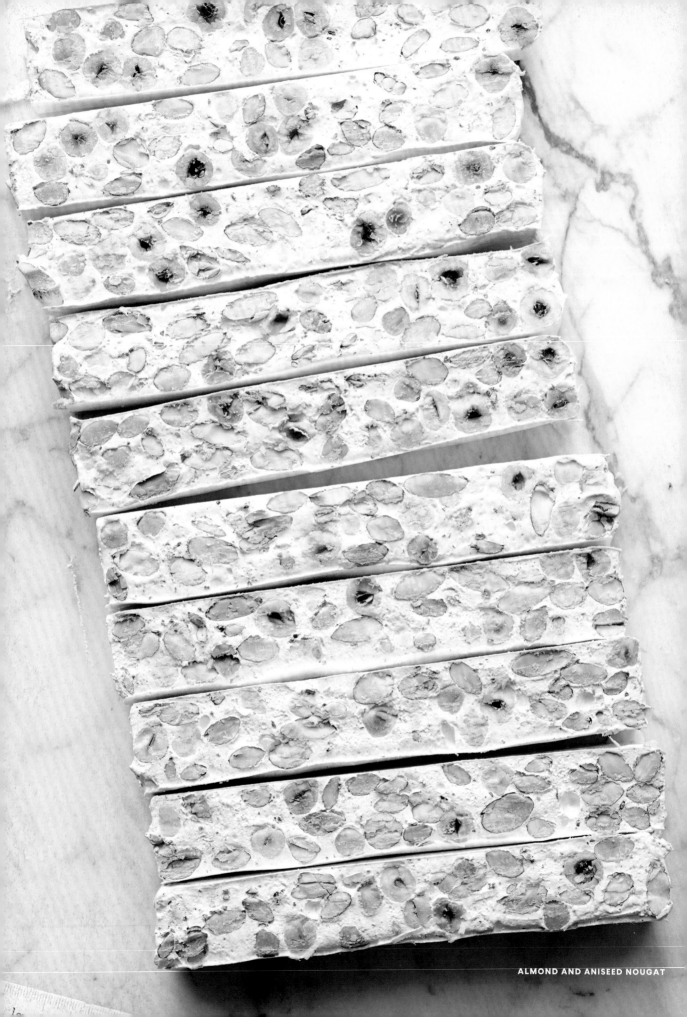

ALMOND AND ANISEED NOUGAT

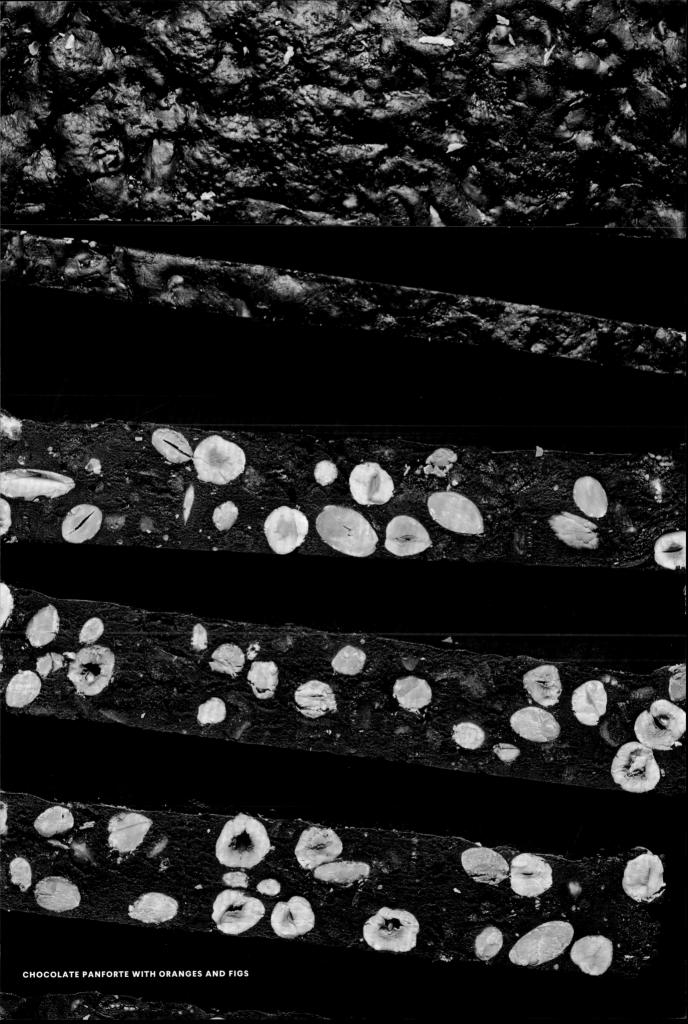

CHOCOLATE PANFORTE WITH ORANGES AND FIGS

Chocolate panforte with oranges and figs

We always love to have a wheel of panforte around. A little slice is perfect mid-morning with coffee, or throughout the day whenever there is a tangy cheese on the table, looking for something sweet to complement it. It also makes for a really lovely gift, given whole or as individually wrapped segments, when you're going out to supper. The thrill of saying, 'Something for the table – I made it for you!' never fails to satisfy.

Start with the best-quality dried fruit and nuts you can find, and with really fresh spices. It will make all the difference.

MAKES 10 SEGMENTS (USING A 23CM ROUND TIN) **OR BARS** (USING A 20CM SQUARE TIN)

150g whole blanched hazelnuts
150g whole blanched almonds
200g candied whole (or sliced) oranges or clementines, cut into 1cm pieces (or mixed peel, as an alternative)
100g dried figs, tough stems removed, cut into 1cm pieces
finely grated zest of 1 orange (1½ tsp)
240g plain flour
100g Dutch-processed cocoa powder
2 tsp ground cinnamon
1 tsp ground ginger

¼ tsp ground cardamom (see pages 351–2; increase to ½ tsp if starting with shop-bought, pre-ground)
½ tsp ground cloves
½ tsp freshly grated nutmeg
½ tsp salt
½ tsp freshly ground black pepper
150g dark cooking chocolate (70% cocoa solids), roughly chopped
175g caster sugar
250g honey (use whatever honey you like the taste of: orange blossom will bring a floral note; chestnut will bring an 'earthiness')

A sugar thermometer is a must here. If you want to create a wheel shape, use a 23cm round cake tin; alternatively, use a 20cm square tin.

This keeps very well – for at least 2 months – wrapped in baking parchment and cling film and stored in a cool, dry place. You can eat it as soon as it's set, but it's actually much better left for a week so that it's had some time to sit.

1   Preheat the oven to 180°C/160°C Fan/Gas Mark 4. Grease a 23cm round or 20cm square tin and line with baking parchment, then set aside.

2   **To roast the nuts,** spread the hazelnuts and almonds out on a baking tray and roast for about 10 minutes, until they are light brown and fragrant. Reduce the oven temperature to 120°C/100°C Fan/Gas Mark ½ and leave in the oven until ready to use: this will make them easier to fold through the mix, which will seize up if the nuts are added cold.

3   Place the chopped oranges or clementines in a large bowl with the figs and orange zest. Combine the flour, cocoa powder, the spices, salt and pepper in a small bowl and sift directly over the chopped fruit and zest. Combine with a wooden spoon or, better still, use your hands to get a more even distribution. Set aside.

4   Place the chocolate in a small heatproof bowl set over a pan of barely simmering water, making sure the base of the bowl is not touching the water. When it has nearly all melted, stir gently with a small spatula and turn off the heat, leaving the bowl over the hot water to keep the chocolate warm.

5   **Make the syrup** by placing the sugar and honey in a small saucepan over a low heat, stirring from time to time. As soon as the sugar has dissolved, stop stirring and increase the heat to high. Allow the mixture to simmer until the syrup has reached 114°C on a sugar thermometer (the 'soft boil' stage). Keep a close eye on the syrup here, as it will come to temperature very quickly. Don't panic if your batch goes over 114°C: the recipe will still work, it just means the set will be firmer.

6   Carefully pour the hot syrup over the chopped fruit and flour, then add the warm nuts straight from the oven (increasing the oven temperature to 180°C/160°C Fan/Gas Mark 4 as soon as the nuts are out). Pour the warm melted chocolate over the fruit and nuts and stir everything together with a large wooden spoon until well combined. The mixture will be very thick and will take a bit of effort to combine, but don't worry, this is normal. Use a spatula to press the mix into the prepared tin. When just cool enough to touch, wet your hands and pat the mix down so that it is even. Use a small piece of baking parchment to help flatten it, if you find it useful.

7   Bake for 18 minutes, until the panforte is set but not too hard. Remove from the oven and leave to cool completely in the tin (preferably for a few days, see note opposite) before slicing into ten segments or bars (around 10 x 4cm).

Sesame brittle

We make large sheets of this in the Ottolenghi bakery, which are then broken into shards. Large shards are great as a garnish for all sorts of desserts – a chocolate mousse, for example, while smaller shards look great on the large or mini chocolate tarts (see pages 241 and 232). Have a play around with shapes and sizes and with all sorts of desserts. They're also lovely to snack on just as they are.

You can make this with white sesame seeds only, if you like, but do try and get hold of the black as well: the contrast looks fantastic.

MAKES 20 SHARDS (OR MORE OR LESS, DEPENDING ON SIZE)

35g black sesame seeds
90g white sesame seeds
100g caster sugar
100g liquid glucose

50g unsalted butter, at room
   temperature
⅛ tsp salt

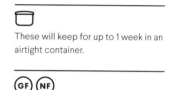

These will keep for up to 1 week in an airtight container.

1   Preheat the oven to 190°C/170°C Fan/Gas Mark 5.

2   Spread all the sesame seeds out on a baking tray and toast for 10–15 minutes, stirring halfway through, until golden brown. Keep the seeds warm in a low oven while you make the syrup.

3   Cut four pieces of baking parchment to fit on two large baking trays. Set aside.

4   Place the sugar, glucose, butter and salt in a small saucepan over a high heat and stir continuously until the mixture is combined and coming to the boil. Remove from the heat, add the warm sesame seeds and stir through.

5   Place two of the pieces of baking parchment on a heatproof surface and pour half of the sesame caramel on to each sheet. Cover with the other pieces of parchment paper and use a rolling pin to spread the caramel until 2mm thick.

6   Slide the paper and caramel on to the baking trays, then remove the top layer of parchment; if any caramel sticks to the top layer of paper, just scrape it back down. Place the trays in the oven and bake for 20 minutes, until golden. Remove from the oven and set aside to cool before breaking into shards.

Coconut meringue brittle

These are somewhere between a meringue and an old-fashioned coconut macaroon: as sweet as you'd want and expect, but with more of a crunch. They're informal, rustic and exceptionally moreish.

We've offered both dark and white chocolate versions here, so either choose between the coatings or cover half the batch in one and half in the other. We've kept the dark chocolate version plain but, as with the white chocolate version, a sprinkle of freeze-dried cherries or raspberries also works well.

MAKES 12
—

75g slivered almonds (or whole
   blanched almonds)
100g icing sugar
50g desiccated coconut
75g egg whites (from 2 large eggs)
⅛ tsp salt
75g caster sugar
½ tsp almond extract

DARK CHOCOLATE COATING
**(HALVE THE QUANTITIES IF YOU ARE DOING
A MIX OF DARK AND WHITE CHOCOLATE)**
120g dark cooking chocolate
   (70% cocoa solids), roughly chopped
   into 1cm pieces, to coat

WHITE CHOCOLATE COATING
**(HALVE THE QUANTITIES IF YOU ARE DOING
A MIX OF DARK AND WHITE CHOCOLATE)**
120g white chocolate, roughly chopped
   into 1cm pieces
25g freeze-dried cherries or
   raspberries, roughly blitzed
   in a food processor

When melted and used as a coating, dark chocolate can develop white streaks after a day or so. This won't affect the taste, but can be avoided by tempering the chocolate (see page 345).

These will keep for up to 1 week in an airtight container, with pieces of baking parchment between the layers of meringue.

1   Preheat the oven to 170°C/150°C Fan/Gas Mark 3. Spread the slivered almonds out on a baking tray and roast for about 5 minutes, or 10 minutes if starting with whole almonds, until the nuts are starting to turn light brown. Remove from the oven and set aside to cool before chopping roughly. Keep the oven turned on.

2   Sift the icing sugar into a small bowl, add the coconut and the chopped almonds and set aside until ready to use. Line two large baking trays with baking parchment and set aside.

3   **To make the meringue,** place the egg whites and salt in the bowl of an electric mixer with the whisk attachment in place. Beat on a medium-high speed until soft peaks form. Gradually add the caster sugar, one tablespoon at a time, continuing to whisk for about 5 minutes, until the mixture is thick and glossy and stiff peaks form. Stir through the almond extract, then remove the bowl from the mixer. Use a large rubber spatula to gently but thoroughly fold in the icing sugar mixture.

4   Spoon twelve large spoonfuls of the mixture on to the parchment-lined trays. Using a small spatula, roughly spread them out to form shapes about 8cm wide and 1–1.5cm thick. Don't try for uniform shapes and sizes here: rustic is good! Place the trays in the oven and immediately lower the temperature to 140°C/120°C/Gas Mark 1. Bake for 1 hour, until the meringues are dry throughout but have not taken on too much colour. Turn off the oven but leave the meringues inside for about 30 minutes, propping the door open with a wooden spoon, to continue to cool and dry out. Remove from the oven and set aside to cool completely.

5   **To coat the meringues:** if making the dark chocolate coating, place the chocolate in a heatproof bowl set over a pan of simmering water, making sure the base of the bowl is not touching the water. Stir occasionally until melted, then use a small metal spatula to spread the chocolate all over the base (flat side) of the meringues. Set aside for about 1 hour until the chocolate has set, then pile high on a plate and serve.

6   If making the white chocolate coating, follow the instructions for the dark chocolate above, sprinkling some of the blitzed cherries or raspberries on top of the chocolate after it's been brushed over the meringues.

Honey, macadamia and coconut caramels

These caramels started life as the filling to a sweet tart. Time and again, though, there was never quite enough to fill the tart shell. This had less to do with an issue of ratios in the recipe, however, and more to do with how hard it was to stop eating the caramel by the spoonful in the first place. The tart shell was soon dispensed with altogether so that we could concentrate on the filling alone! The resulting caramels look lovely as little bonbons. They also keep well, so make for terrific gifts, individually wrapped in baking parchment. We like them on the long side – around 9cm – but you can make them shorter, if you like, in which case you'll make more. Making caramel is not difficult, but it takes practice, so don't give up if you don't perfect it first time round.

MAKES 18 (OR MORE, IF CUT INTO SMALLER PIECES)

A sugar thermometer is a must here.

The caramels will keep for 2 weeks at room temperature, out of direct sunlight, and for up to 1 month stored in the fridge. Store together in an airtight container, or wrapped individually in cellophane sheets or baking parchment and cling film.

160g macadamia nuts
70g unsweetened coconut flakes
100g unsalted butter
250ml double cream
100g runny honey

100g liquid glucose
160g soft light brown sugar
scraped seeds of ½ vanilla pod
¼ tsp flaky sea salt

1   Preheat the oven to 170°C/150°C Fan/Gas Mark 3. Line a 20cm square tin (at least 3cm deep) with baking parchment, making sure that the paper rises 3–4cm over the edges of the tin, and set aside.

2   **Toast the nuts** by spreading them out on a baking tray and roast for 7 minutes, until a light golden brown. Spread the coconut out on a separate baking tray and toast for just 2 minutes, until beginning to turn golden brown. Remove both trays from the oven, lightly crushing the coconut with your fingers or a rolling pin. Place the nuts and coconut in a medium heatproof bowl and set aside.

3   **To make the caramel,** melt the butter in a medium saucepan over a low heat, then add the cream, honey, glucose, sugar, vanilla seeds and salt. Stir until combined, then increase the heat to medium. Bring to a boil, resisting the urge to stir, and continue to boil until the temperature on a sugar thermometer reaches 123–124°C (the top end of 'firm ball' stage, but certainly not 'hard ball' stage, which would lead to the caramels being brittle). This can take anywhere between 12 and 20 minutes. Remove from the heat immediately – move fast here, as the temperature of the caramel will continue to rise – and pour over the nuts and coconut. Mix together, then pour into the lined tin, flattening the surface with a small spatula or the back of a spoon, and set aside at room temperature for an hour to firm up.

4   Cut the slab in half and then each half into nine 9 x 2cm rectangles (or 6 x 2cm rectangles if you want them to be more bite-sized). If not eating the same day, set aside to cool, then cover with baking parchment and cling film.

Middle Eastern millionaire's shortbread

A three-layered bar with a shortbread bottom, halva in the middle, and a glossy tahini caramel on top. This was a winning combination just waiting to happen. And happen it did, thanks to Paulina Bembel, our head pastry chef. Paulina, who comes from Poland, skilfully uses our Middle Eastern favourites – tahini and halva – to transform the famously cloying millionaire's shortbread into something so much better, with a slight bitterness and a touch of salt to offset all that sweetness.

MAKES 16

The shortbread layer can be made up to 4 days in advance and stored in an airtight container. It also freezes well.

These will keep for up to 1 week in an airtight container in the fridge. Remove them from the fridge 20 minutes before serving, to take off the chill.

SHORTBREAD
40g icing sugar
35g cornflour
40g caster sugar
175g unsalted butter, melted, and set aside to cool slightly
½ tsp vanilla extract
250g plain flour
⅛ tsp salt

HALVA
200g halva, roughly crumbled into small pieces
80g tahini

TAHINI CARAMEL
200g caster sugar
120ml water
100g unsalted butter, at room temperature, cubed
80ml double cream
150g tahini paste
¼ tsp flaky sea salt

1   Preheat the oven to 200°C/180°C Fan/Gas Mark 6. Line a 20cm square tin with baking parchment, making sure that the paper rises up over the edges of the tin.

2   **For the shortbread,** sift the icing sugar and cornflour into the bowl of an electric mixer with the paddle attachment in place, then add the caster sugar and mix on a medium speed. With the machine still running, slowly pour in the melted-but-cooled butter and beat until combined. Add the vanilla and reduce the speed to low, then sift in the flour and salt and continue to beat until the dough comes together. Tip the mixture into the tin and use your hands to pat and even out the surface. Bake for 25 minutes or until golden brown. Remove from the oven and set aside until completely cool: this will take an hour or so, so don't start making the caramel too soon or it will have set by the time the shortbread is cool.

3   **For the halva layer,** place the halva and tahini in a small bowl and mix with a wooden spoon to combine. Spread the mix over the cooled shortbread and use the back of a spoon to smooth it out to an even layer.

4   **To make the caramel,** place the sugar and water into a small saucepan and place over a medium-low heat. Stir occasionally, until the sugar has dissolved, then increase the heat to medium-high. Bring to a boil and cook – still at a boil – for about 12 minutes, until the sugar is a deep golden brown. Remove from the heat and add the butter and cream: take care here, as the mixture will splutter. Whisk to combine and, once the butter has melted, add the tahini and salt. Whisk to combine again, then pour evenly over the halva layer in the tin, so that all of the halva is covered.

5   Place in the fridge for at least 4 hours until set, before cutting into bars, about 10 x 2.5cm. Sprinkle a pinch of sea salt over the middle of each bar and serve.

Throughout the book there are lots of tips and notes alongside the recipes. Most are also here, for general ease of reference. It's not a comprehensive 'baker's bible': it's the things we think are useful and interesting to know, or which need more explanation than a recipe has the space to give.

Bain-marie

We use a bain-marie – a water bath – when baking our Hot Chocolate Pudding (see page 278), Ginger Crème Caramel (see page 279), and also for the custard in the Chai Brulée Tarts (see page 239). Although a lot of people bake their cheesecakes inside a water bath placed in the oven – the rationale being that because the temperature of the water cannot rise above 100°C, the cheesecake will cook evenly – we are not fans. For the recipes in which we do use the technique, take care when filling your tray with hot water. Place the tray in the oven before pouring the water in, rather than trying to lift and move a tray full of water across the kitchen, which can be both messy and dangerous.

Butter

BURNING › Burnt butter – or beurre noisette – is the process by which butter is heated on the stove for so long that it starts to foam, turn a light brown colour and smell nutty. Small brown specks of sediment will form on the side of the pan, which are then removed when the butter is strained through a fine sieve. The strained butter – the 'burnt' butter – brings a nutty caramel note (as well as a golden brown colour) to your baking. We use it in our Brown Butter Tuiles (see page 30), Blackberry Friands (see page 103) and Coffee Financiers (see page 105).

TEMPERATURE OF › The temperature of butter when you start baking is always important. Sometimes it needs to be fridge-cold (if you are

rubbing it into flour to form a crumb-like consistency for a dough, for example). Sometimes it needs to be at room temperature (if you want it to be malleable enough to be mixed with other ingredients until smooth, or if you want a batter to drop nicely and evenly into a cupcake mould). Sometimes you want it to be what we call 'soft but not oily'. This is where it is softer than room temperature but not so soft as to be sitting in an oily puddle (as it would be if you'd melted it for a few seconds in the microwave, for example), which would result in a dense cake. We get our butter to this point by sitting it in a bowl close to the stove top while we are getting on with other bits and bobs in the kitchen. Cutting the butter into roughly 3cm cubes and spreading them out over the wrapper or a plate will speed up the process further. Either way, keep an eye on it: if it's no longer solid then you've taken it too far.

When melting butter, we also cut it into cubes, so that it melts faster and more evenly: you don't want it to boil away and reduce.

Sometimes we say that butter should be melted and then returned to room temperature before, say, being added to a mix with lots of eggs in it. This is to prevent the eggs being 'cooked' by the heat of the butter.

All the butter we start with is unsalted. This then allows us to control the amount of salt used in a recipe.

Chocolate

CALLETS/CHIPS VS BLOCK › In the shops and bakery we use chocolate callets (or chips) in our baking. They come in a range of cocoa percentages and have the great advantage of melting evenly, which makes the chocolate less temperamental to work with. Callets or chips are available online, in specialist chocolate shops and more generally in supermarkets, but for the ease of the home cook, we have started with blocks of chocolate which are then chopped by hand. How precise you need to be when breaking up or chopping the chocolate is indicated in each recipe. Precision will matter more in some cases than others. There are some instances where callets or chips are needed: in our Chocolate Chip Pecan Cookies (see page 26), for example: if you started with a whole block of chocolate and cut it into uneven chunks, this would lead to an uneven bake.

MELTING › When melting chocolate, avoid the temptation to stir it too often or too vigorously, as this will cause it to seize up. It will always stiffen up a bit if another hot liquid is added to it – hot water or coffee, for example, in the Flourless Chocolate Layer Cake (see page 170) – but it will smooth out again with just a little bit of gentle stirring. If folding melted chocolate into another mixture – whisked egg yolks and sugar, for example – your melted chocolate should be slightly cooled (rather than completely cooled, which will make it too firm).

Sometimes we melt chocolate by pouring scalding milk or cream over chopped chunks of chocolate and only stirring it through once it's been left to sit. To scald milk or cream you heat it just up to the point before it starts boiling. Once there are one or two bubbles on the surface, remove it from the heat; if it actually comes to a proper boil, you've taken it too far and the chocolate will scorch or split.

TEMPERING › When chocolate is melted and used as a coating or spread, it sometimes develops white streaks. These occur as a result of the chocolate melting then cooling, and the cocoa butter – the fat naturally present in cocoa beans, which gives chocolate its irresistible mouth-feel – solidifying into fat crystals which all have different shapes and melting points. These white streaks – known as 'fat bloom' – can give the chocolate a slightly dull appearance or gritty texture. The chocolate is perfectly edible, but it doesn't look great. If you want to prevent the formation of white streaks, you need to temper the chocolate. This is the process of carefully melting and cooling chocolate to ensure that the cocoa butter crystallizes properly.

There are several ways to temper chocolate, from elaborate mixing techniques with finely controlled temperatures, to tempering machines which do all the work for you. The simplest way is to chop or shave the chocolate into small, even-sized pieces, then remove about a quarter of the chocolate and set these pieces aside. Melt the remaining three-quarters of the chocolate in a bowl set over a pan of barely simmering water, making sure the base of the bowl is not touching the surface of the water. Remove the bowl from the simmering water and, when it's off the heat, add the reserved pieces of chocolate. Stir through until melted and cooled.

You don't need to temper chocolate every time you work with it. We only temper it when the chocolate is going to be used and seen as a coating: in the Coconut Brittle (see page 336) and Grapefruit Peel (see page 326). You could do it for the chocolate-coated meringue in the Frozen Espresso Parfait (see page 298), if you like, but this again is optional, as the whole thing is covered in praline before being frozen.

This might all seem like a lot of information for a process you only use one or twice, but we hope it's interesting and useful, nevertheless!

CHOCOLATE (WHITE) › White chocolate can be more temperamental than other chocolate when it's being melted. If it's heated too quickly, it will seize up. To prevent this, either start with callets (or chips), or shave your block of chocolate into flakes, or simply make sure you chop your block of chocolate into even-sized pieces. If uneven, the pieces will melt at different times and will seize up when stirred. When melting, do so over a low heat, either in a heatproof bowl over a pan of gently simmering water or on a low temperature in a microwave.

Citrus fruit (peeling)

When shaving peel off citrus fruit – lemons, limes, oranges – always avoid the white pith. This is bitter and can carry its bitterness through your baking (unless you are blanching the whole peel, as for the Grapefruit Peel, page 326).

Eggs

NUMBER OF › The more eggs you have in a cake batter, the closer eye you need to keep on it towards the end of baking: a relatively large number of eggs means that a cake can go from being a little bit liquid in the middle to being cooked in just a few minutes. As ever, a skewer inserted into the centre of the cake will give you a good indication as to what's going on inside.

SIZE AND TEMPERATURE OF › Unless otherwise stated, we assume that eggs are large and at room temperature when you start baking. This is what our baking times are based on. For some recipes, though, the temperature of the eggs is not just important, it's crucial. In the Hot Chocolate Pudding (see page 278) or the Coffee Pound Cake (see page 181), which contain a lot of eggs, if you start with fridge-cold eggs then the mix won't just split: it will lead to a cold, heavy batter that has to work harder to rise in the oven. If your eggs are in the fridge and you want to start baking straight away, bring them to room temperature by placing them in a small bowl and covering with hot tap water (not boiling water) for 5 minutes before using.

Egg whites also whisk more effectively when they are not fridge-cold, so bring these out of the fridge an hour or so before you are going to make a meringue.

FREEZING EGG WHITES › Egg whites freeze well, so always save those not used if a recipe calls for egg yolk only.

Genoise sponge (making)

For all the ambitious and involved things one can do while baking, there's almost nothing more satisfying than making the perfect genoise: one that's rich and buttery, but light at the same time. There's just something a little bit magic about it! Behind the magic, there is quite a lot of method – none of it complicated, but all of it important.

› Get organized before you start. Have everything weighed out and ready for when it's needed. The sponge mixture is delicate and you don't want to lose the precious air bubbles you've worked so hard to achieve by making them wait around while you weigh things out.

› Start with eggs at room temperature (see left). Speed is important and they will whip quicker (with lighter results) than fridge-cold.

› Don't be tempted to skimp on the number of times the flour needs to be sifted. For the cake to be as light and fluffy as can be, three really is the magic number.

› Do not grease your cake rings. In order to get an even rise, you want the mixture to stick to the sides as it rises.

› Make sure the butter is fully melted but not hot. It needs to be poured into the cake mix by gently dribbling it down the sides of the bowl and folded in swiftly but gently. If the butter is too hot, or poured in too quickly, it will sink to the bottom and create a dense, oily texture.

› Make sure your oven is at the correct temperature when the cakes are ready to go in. We would say this is the case for all recipes, but some cake batters are more robust than others and can afford to wait around for an oven to come to temperature if needs be. The sponge is too delicate and light to sit around: it needs to go into the oven as soon as it is ready, otherwise it will deflate. Close the oven door gently and do not be tempted to open it for the first 10 minutes.

› You'll know when the cake is cooked as it will be lightly browned, the edges will have shrunk slightly away from the sides of the rings, and the centre should spring back when pressed lightly.

› Once baked, the sponge is fragile, so take care when slicing it (particularly if you've made one large cake rather than several mini-ones, which will be easier to slice). When slicing in half horizontally, we insert toothpicks around the cake to mark where to cut it, to ensure a straight line. When cutting, insert your knife, then move the cake around (rather than jigging your knife around the cake). When lifting the top off, ready to ice, use a cake lifter or jumbo cookie spatula – or even the base of a springform tin – to help. It might crumble if you lift it with your hands.

Ice bath

An ice bath is simply a bowl filled with ice and water. It is used to quickly bring down the temperature of whatever is plunged into it (in a separate and smaller bowl). We often use ice baths when making custards for ice cream or sugar syrups for sorbets. Starting off with very cool custard or sugar syrup helps things along greatly when it is then transferred to a machine to be churned.

Meringues

There are three types of meringue: Swiss, French and Italian. They're all made in a different way and produce slightly different results.

SWISS MERINGUE › The egg whites and sugar are heat-treated together before they are whipped. This happens when the meringue is not going to get any further cooking (when it's piped on to a cheesecake, for example). Heat-treating it in the first instance gives it the 'cooking' it needs to be safe to eat (it must be heated to 71°C) and makes it stable enough to hold its shape when piped on to a cake. Swiss meringue is denser than either French or Italian meringue, with a texture that's smooth, silky and marshmallow-like.

FRENCH MERINGUE › The sugar is drizzled on to the egg whites as they are being beaten, creating a light and crisp meringue. French meringue always needs to be baked, to prevent the egg whites in the mix breaking down. This is the meringue we use for our Rolled Pavlova (see page 263) and Woodland Meringues (see page 319). The reason the meringue goes into a hot oven and the temperature is turned down straight away is to give it a nice crisp exterior and a soft and marshmallow-like interior.

ITALIAN MERINGUE › Probably the most stable of all the methods. This is the result of a very hot sugar syrup being poured over the egg whites as they are beaten. This method requires a bit more attention and patience than the other two, as the temperature of the sugar syrup needs to reach 118°C on a sugar thermometer before it is poured into the egg whites. In turn, the egg whites must be whisked to a good volume without becoming grainy (over-whisked) before the sugar syrup is dribbled in. Timing is

everything, as we so often say when cooking with sugar. But with all your ingredients at-the-ready, and with one eye on the thermometer and the other on the whipping egg whites, you will have shiny, fluffy fabulous meringues. 'I felt like I grew a metre taller,' Helen says, remembering the day she mastered Italian meringue.

Moisture in a cake (oil vs butter)

Using oil rather than butter in cakes tends to keep them moist for longer. This is because oil remains liquid at cooler temperatures, whereas butter solidifies to make cakes firm over time. The lack of butter can sometimes translate to diminished flavour, however, so this needs to be compensated for by turning up the volume on the other ingredients. In our Pineapple Chiffon Cake (see page 179), for example, the fresh pineapple, star anise and orange zest are there to make sure the cake delivers in all areas.

Nuts

ROASTING › Even if you start with pre-roasted nuts, always give your batch a quick re-roast in a warm oven for 5 minutes. The success of a biscuit or cake often relies on the nuts being fragrant: just 5 minutes in an oven set to 200°C/180°C Fan/Gas Mark 6 will help release their oils. For our recipes, we have assumed that all nuts will be in need of roasting. Timings and temperatures are given in each recipe.

When a recipe calls for toasted flaked almonds, we prefer to start with untoasted flaked almonds and toast them ourselves, as we have more control over how long they are cooked for, and a fresh toasting is always good to draw out the oils. You can start with ready-toasted flaked almonds, if you prefer, however.

BLITZING › Always wait for nuts to come to room temperature before you blitz them: they'll turn to an oily paste if blitzed when warm.

REMOVING THE SKIN › If roasting nuts so as to remove their skins (as with hazelnuts, for example), transfer the nuts to a clean tea towel after roasting, fold in the sides of the cloth and give a vigorous rub to release them from the skin.

TASTING › For notes on the importance of tasting your nuts before adding to your bake (to make sure they are not rancid), see page 354.

Oven temperature and tray positioning

Oven temperature is key to success in baking. At the same time as following our guidelines, you have to be mindful of the fact that all ovens are slightly different, so you need to use your initiative if you think something needs a few minutes more or less in the oven. As well as a cooking time, visual guides are also given so that you know what to look for. The best way to get it right is to get to know your oven – you'll soon know if you consistently need to be giving things, say, 3 minutes longer than suggested – and to get to know a particular recipe really well; it's in being able to gauge for yourself whether something is ready that you'll become a really confident cook.

Unless otherwise stated, always position your cake or tray in the middle of your oven to get an even bake (or create an even distance between your trays, if you're baking with more than one). Rotating your tray halfway through baking will also ensure an even bake.

If a bake starts with an initially high oven temperature which is then reduced as soon as it goes in the oven, this is often done to bring about a contrast between a brown crisp crust and a gooey, soft inside. This is a technique we employ in our Blackberry Friands (see page 103).

Pastry

Tips and notes on the various pastries used in the book can be found at the beginning of the Tarts and pies chapter (see page 226).

Pineapple purée (cooking of)

We always heat through our pineapple purée before adding it to a cake mix. This works to intensify the flavour of the pineapple (rather than just adding more pineapple, which would make the batter too runny and prevent the cake from rising) and to destroy the enzyme bromelain, which can break down the gluten in the flour, resulting in a dense cake.

Proving dough

The rate at which your dough will prove depends hugely on the temperature of your kitchen. You'll need to use the visual guides given in a recipe to gauge whether your dough needs more or less time to rise. The reason we keep the dough for Roma's Doughnuts (see page 113) in the fridge overnight after the first prove is to much decrease the amount of time spent waiting for the dough to prove for a second time on the day you want to fry and eat them. In the case of the doughnuts, the benefits of proving the dough on individual squares of baking parchment is a baker's tip we were very happy to learn and which we're very happy to share (see page 113).

Resting (the importance of)

Don't be tempted to miss out on the resting stage before a cake is baked, if it's recommended. If there are lots of ground almonds in a mix, for example (as with the Flourless Chocolate 'Teacakes', page 108), it's really important to allow them to fully absorb the liquids: this will make the cake as moist as can be.

Roulade 'training'

In order to prepare our roulade before it's rolled, we like to 'train' it. This is done by rolling it in a clean, dry tea towel after it's been baked so that it rolls seamlessly (and without breaking) once the cream filling is in place. It's a neat trick. Once you've cracked it (or not, in the case of your sponge!) you'll feel like a roulade-making pro. This also applies to the sponge in the Blackcurrant Stripe Cake (see page 145).

Sifting

DRY INGREDIENTS › The key to pillow-y lightness is often in sifting together the dry ingredients. Not once, not twice, but sometimes (in the case of the Powder Puff recipes on page 82) three times! It might sound a bit much, we know, but it makes all the difference, ridding the mix of any impurities at the same time as getting all that aeration into the mix.

Where we have more than one dry ingredient – flour, salt, spices, icing sugar, etc – we like to sift these all together into the mixing bowl (rather than separately or in advance): this ensures that everything is evenly distributed throughout the batter or dough.

CASTER SUGAR › When the sugar is part of the dry ingredients (as opposed to being creamed with the butter, for example), we also tend to sift that with the flour. However, in cakes where there is a high level of liquid – in the Take-home Chocolate Cake (see page 152) or the Chocolate Guinness Cakes (see page 117) – the sugar is added early on, while the liquid is still warm, so that it melts into the cake batter and produces a more even texture. Since it's added at the same time as the cocoa powder, we've sifted them at the same time as it makes it easier to incorporate into the liquid. This also prevents the cocoa powder from clumping, which it can do when dumped into the liquid by itself.

ICING SUGAR › With icing sugar, whether or not we sift it depends on what it's used for. If it is going into a meringue, for example, it is always sifted. If mixing icing sugar with water or another liquid, there is no need to sift it. If creaming with butter, whether or not we sift depends on how old the icing sugar is: the older it is the lumpier it can become, from moisture in the air. Icing sugar in the UK usually contains cornflour to reduce the lumpiness, but in places where 'pure' icing sugar is sold, it's often lumpy and must be sifted before using.

This might seem like a lot of information on the nature of sifting, but it does make a smoother batter: a sift in good time saves nine, and all that.

Storage

The way in which things are stored will really affect how long they last. Notes are always given as to whether things should be kept in an airtight container or wrapped loosely in foil. Again, whether they are kept at room temperature, in the fridge or in the freezer will also make a difference to whether something dries out, goes soggy or starts to 'weep'. Do try to follow the guidelines given: it will make such a difference.

Sugar

CARAMELIZING › There are two ways to caramelize sugar: a 'dry' method and a 'wet' method. In the 'dry' method the sugar is cooked, without water, in a large shallow frying pan or skillet. In the 'wet' method, water is added to the sugar to begin the caramelizing process and the caramel is cooked in a saucepan. 'Wet' caramel starts off as a thick sugar syrup, which begins to

caramelize as the water evaporates. If there is no water, the sugar begins to caramelize faster.

The 'dry' method produces a darker, more complex-flavoured caramel in a shorter time. It's the method we use when we want a small amount of caramel, as with the caramelized pineapple on our Passionfruit Cheesecake (see page 207), for example. You need to be vigilant when making it and keep a very close eye on the pan: don't be tempted to move away until the caramel is all done. The 'wet' method is useful when you need to make a large batch of caramel for a sauce, perhaps, or for the coffee praline in the Frozen Espresso Parfait (see page 298).

CARAMEL (THE DIFFERENT STAGES OF COOKED SUGAR) › When making caramel, the cooked sugar will go through stages, from 'thread stage' to 'hard crack'. The stages are reached at different temperatures and each results in a caramel with a very different consistency and purpose.

THREAD STAGE › The first stage of caramel, when the sugar and water have melted together and the consistency is that of sugar syrup. This stage is reached when the temperature is 110–112°C.

SOFT BALL › The texture here is that of a soft, sticky ball, like buttercream, fudge or fondant. This is reached when the temperature is 113–116°C.

FIRM BALL › This is when the caramel is firm but pliable. It is the stage you want to reach when making certain caramels or toffees. The temperature for this stage is 118–120°C.

HARD BALL › The consistency here is that of a harder ball, one that holds its shape. It's the stage reached by caramels, toffees and nougats with a slightly firmer texture. The temperature here should be 121–130°C.

SOFT CRACK › This is when the caramel has developed firm yet pliable strands: it is what you want for the making of butterscotch or firm nougat. The temperature should be 132–143°C.

HARD CRACK › This is the firmest stage of the caramel, almost brittle-like, where the stiff threads break easily. It is the stage you want to reach when making hard candy and spun sugar. The temperature should be 149–154°C.

Cooking with sugar requires a sugar thermometer, to take any guesswork out of the equation. It also requires the baker to be in control of timings, as the sugar syrup often needs to be at a certain stage at the exact same time as something else needs to be happening.

Temperature (of ingredients)

We have talked about the importance of eggs and butter being at the correct temperature when baking (see pages 344 and 346). In addition, the temperature of other dairy ingredients needs to be noted. In the White Chocolate Cheesecake (see page 203), for example, both the cream cheese and soured cream need to be fridge-cold. This allows the mix to remain cool enough for the chocolate not to melt when added. In the Coffee Pound Cake (see page 181), the milk and the eggs need to be at room temperature, to minimize the risk of the mix splitting.

Tins

GREASING › We like to grease our baking trays and tins with (barely) melted butter. We prefer this to cooking sprays (vegetable oils), which can affect the taste of the cake. If the moulds of a tray are lined with paper liners – when making cupcakes, for example – then we are happy to use this spray, as the batter will not come into direct contact with it. In the case of muffin tins (or other tins in which the cake mixture is going to rise up and over the top rim of the mould), it's always useful to spray or grease the surface of the tray, as well as the moulds, to prevent the cooked cake from sticking to the tin and crumbling when you try to remove it.

The more nooks and crannies a tin has, the more care you need to take when greasing it, to prevent the cooked cake getting stuck to the inside of the tin. Bundt tins, for example, require a lot of greasing.

If you are greasing with an oil rather than butter, always use a light sunflower oil rather than olive oil, which will be too heavy and thick.

LINING › To line our trays and tins, we use non-stick baking parchment. In some cases (in the very delicate Cats' Tongues, page 27) we recommend using a non-stick silicone baking mat instead of parchment, if you have one.

CHOOSING › For more on the tins we use, along with what can be used as an alternative, see page 71. Other options and tips are given throughout the book.

MEASURING › To find the accurate width and length of a tin, always measure from inside edge to inside edge, so the measurement does not include the thickness of the tin. Fluted tins are measured from the inside edge of one outer curve to the inside edge of the curve directly across from it. To measure a round cake tin, measure across the top diameter of the tin, from edge to edge. If the sides are sloping, then also measure the base of the tin. To measure the tin's depth, place a ruler on the kitchen counter and measure straight up from the bottom of the pan. If the pan edge is slanted, do not slant the ruler, measure straight upwards.

This all sounds very prescriptive and strict, we know: we take all these details very seriously. At the same time, though, don't worry if your tin or tray has dimensions which are slightly different to ours. As well as making recommendations for alternative shapes and sizes for tins, where we can, visual guides are given so you'll know when your cake is ready. This should give you the confidence to use a slightly different sized or shaped tin, if you need to, and then make adjustments to the baking time accordingly.

Water ganache

Water ganache sounds like a contradiction in terms – the mixing of chocolate and water doesn't feel as though it should work – but in fact it emulsifies into the smoothest of all ganaches. Using water instead of cream means that nothing distracts from the pure taste of the chocolate. It's also much more stable and easy to work with than cream-based ganaches, which (though they taste great) tend to lose their shine after an hour or two and turn a bit dull and grainy. Water ganache keeps in the fridge for days and can be reheated either in a bain-marie or in a small saucepan over a low heat; you will need to stir constantly and maybe add a touch more water. For instructions on how to make the perfect water ganache, see the Flourless Chocolate 'Teacakes' on page 108.

This is not a comprehensive list of ingredients used throughout the book. It's a list of the ingredients we think are in need of a bit of explanation: what they are, why we like them and, in some cases, what to use as an alternative.

Almond paste

Not to be confused with marzipan. While marzipan can contain as little as 10% almonds, almond paste is made up of 50% almonds. The paste contains much less sugar, as a result, and has a coarser texture. Marzipan is useful for rolling out to drape over cakes (thanks to the liquid glucose), but we use almond paste in our baking for a purer taste of almonds. It's available in most large supermarkets and online. Alternatively, check out the almond percentage in marzipan: the higher the better. Buy the Odense brand of marzipan if you can.

Amaretti biscuits

Shop-bought Amaretti biscuits are either soft and pale (often individually wrapped, in a tin you'll want to keep) or brown and crunchy. We use them to provide a distinctive crunch – not too sweet, with a bitterness from the apricot kernels in the biscuits – in the base of our Rhubarb Galette (see page 230). We also make our own: the Amaretti on page 38. There's more going on in these, flavour and texture-wise, than in the simple shop-bought version, so these should not be used for the base of the galette.

Aniseed

With a flavour somewhere between fennel and liquorice, aniseed is a sweet and complex spice. It is most commonly associated with ouzo, raki or the French pastis, but it also works very well when ground and added to all sorts of cookies and cakes. We use it in our Parsnip and Pecan Cake (see page 128) and Almond Nougat (see page 328). Alternatively, use an equal quantity of finely ground fennel seeds instead.

Apricots

Although we tend to make use of fresh, seasonal fruit, apricots have a relatively short season, so we often use tinned instead. Their quality is good – and far better than unripe or out-of-season fresh apricots – so don't feel as though you're skimping on quality if you are starting with tinned. If you are baking with fresh apricots and they're not as large and juicy as you'd want them to be (when roasting them for the Apricot Cheesecake on page 219, for example), you might need to sprinkle them with a little more water than recommended, to create some added moisture.

Bananas

When choosing bananas for baking, you want them to be ripe but not too ripe. Unripe, they'll have an astringency which will carry right through your cake or cookie; too ripe – if they've been taken to the point of blackening – and the pH of the bananas changes from acidic to alkaline, which makes it difficult for the raising agent to do its work. The resulting cake, though rich in flavour, will be rather heavy and dense. The perfect banana for baking is speckled or mottled: this indicates that it is sweet and full of flavour.

Cardamom (ground)

Ground cardamom is not always easy to get hold of (compared to the whole green pods, which are widely available), but there are a couple of ways to grind your own. If you want to make 1½ teaspoons ground cardamom for the Coffee Pound Cake on page 181, you'll need to start with about 40 pods; the Almond Butter Cake on page 176 needs ¾ teaspoon, so you'll need to start with about 20 pods. You can either crush the whole pods with the flat side of a large knife to release the seeds, then grind the seeds in a spice grinder or pestle and mortar: this will give you the most distinctive and intense cardamom taste. Alternatively, grind the whole cardamom pod in a spice grinder and then pass the mix through a fine sieve. The second option is quicker and easier than the first, but the taste of the spice will not be nearly as intense, so you might want to add a tiny bit more than the recipe suggests.

Chocolate

All dark chocolate used in the book should be cooking chocolate with 70% cocoa solids, unless otherwise stated. In terms of a specific brand, the range of chocolate on offer is absolutely huge. So long as you stick with the recommended cocoa percentage for a recipe, and always buy cooking chocolate, you can go with your preferred brand.

CHOCOLATE CALLETS › In the shops and bakery we use chocolate callets (chips) in our cooking: they come in a range of cocoa percentages and have the great advantage (over starting with a whole block of chocolate and chopping it by hand) of melting through evenly. Callets are widely available – they're sometimes sold as 'chef's chocolate drops' – but for the most part we've specified hand-chopping a block of chocolate, as bars of cooking chocolate are still the most readily available. The exception to the rule is with the Chocolate Chip Cookies (see page 26), where you really need to start with chocolate chips or callets: using chocolate with inconsistent sizing will create an uneven bake and change the consistency of the cookie.

GIANDUJA › In recipes which call for Gianduja, a particularly wonderful chocolate with about 30% hazelnut paste, we have provided an alternative for the home cook who can get hold of Nutella – or another chocolate hazelnut spread – more readily. Do keep an eye out for Gianduja, though: it's really very special.

For more notes on the handling of chocolate – melting and tempering it, for example – see pages 344–5.

Cocoa powder (Dutch-processed)

All the cocoa powder used in our recipes is Dutch-processed (as opposed to natural). The difference between Dutch-processed (also known as 'alkalized', 'European style' or 'Dutched' powder) and natural cocoa powder is that the former is treated with an alkaline. This reduces the acidity of the cocoa, creating a smoother, milder flavour than in the more acidic natural version. Since Dutch-processed cocoa isn't acidic, it doesn't react with alkaline leaveners (like bicarbonate of soda) to produce carbon dioxide. This is why recipes that contain Dutch-processed cocoa powder are usually leavened by baking powder, which has a neutral pH. The colour of the Dutch-processed cocoa is also darker than the natural.

Coconut flakes

In the shops we like to use Baker's Angel coconut flakes, which are sweet, wet and delicious. They are not easy to get hold of in the UK, though, so we have used regular coconut flakes instead. These are sold as either 'unsweetened', 'raw' or 'plain' coconut flakes. Desiccated coconut – the finely shredded version of the unsweetened flakes – can also be used as an alternative.

Coffee

We've tried to keep things simple by mainly using instant coffee granules in our recipes – we tend to use Nescafé. In some cases, though, ground coffee is called for, either for its intensity in the Frozen Espresso Parfait (see page 298), or for the wonderfully speckled look it brings to cakes like our Coffee Financiers (see page 105).

Cream cheese

The texture of cream cheese can vary from brand to brand (and even from country to country, within the same brand), with one batch being much runnier than the next. In the UK, for example, Philadelphia cream cheese is softer and more watery than the same brand version in the USA, where it's sold in blocks and is very firm. The runnier the cheese, the less time it will take to become smooth when whisked, and the quicker the mix will come together for a dough, for example. Watch out for it while making the icing for the Beetroot Cake (see page 130) – if you whisk it too much it will become too runny. The addition of cream cheese to the pastry in our Rhubarb Galette (see page 230) is what makes it so tender and flaky. For more on cream cheese pastry, see page 227.

Date syrup

Date syrup is the same thing as date molasses (but not the same as blackstrap molasses). Using date syrup in a cake is a great way of injecting huge amounts of rich sweetness and moisture into the mix. Golden syrup can be used as an alternative, if necessary.

Eggs

SIZE › Unless otherwise stated, eggs used in all recipes are large. Where the net weight of eggs is important, it will be given in the recipe as a guide, as large eggs can vary in size. We have sometimes called for small or medium eggs (in the Grappa Fruit Cake, page 141, for example) because the net weight of two is perfect.

TEMPERATURE › Unless otherwise stated, we start our baking with eggs at room temperature. This matters more for some recipes than others. For more on the temperature of eggs when baking, see page 346.

WHITES › Several of our recipes call for egg whites only. As a general rule, 1 large egg will provide around 40g egg white; eggs do vary in size, however, so always weigh out the egg whites where specified: it's the weight in grams which is important. If you are not starting with a surplus of saved egg whites, you can buy tetra pak containers of egg whites from most large supermarkets. We find them really useful, as for all our good intentions to use the yolks or whites left over, we know there is only so much mayonnaise or custard you need in your life.

Flour

RICE FLOUR › We use grainy rice flour in baking (in the Orange Shortbread, page 47, for example),

not to be confused with the finely milled Asian variety, which you'd use to make dumpling wrappers. Bob's Red Mill is our chosen brand.

ITALIAN '00' FLOUR › The flour used in our shortbread is the '00' wheat flour (rather than the '00' semolina flour you'd use for pasta).

TAPIOCA FLOUR › We use tapioca flour, available from Asian grocers, to toss with the fruit in our Rhubarb Crumble Cake (see page 148). It has the capacity to thicken without leaving a floury taste. The tapioca flour also looks better – it's not opaque in the way that cornflour is – but they function in the same way. However, cornflour can be used as an alternative, if necessary.

BUCKWHEAT FLOUR › This flour brings its distinctive nutty and slightly sour taste to a bake: the taste is very particular and not one that can be substituted. We add a little to our Persian Love Cakes (see page 74).

SELF-RAISING FLOUR › Not as readily available in some countries as in others. If you need to make your own, sift together plain flour with baking powder. As a guide, use 2 teaspoons of baking powder to every 150g plain flour.

Gelatine

We prefer to use gelatine leaves (rather than powder) as they are odourless, flavourless and dissolve quickly without residue. They come in three different strengths: bronze, silver and platinum. As a guide, four leaves of platinum gelatine is the equivalent of 1 tablespoon of powdered gelatine.

(Stem) ginger

If you can't get stem ginger, use the same amount of finely chopped crystallized ginger, steeped in about 250ml boiling water for 15 minutes, then drained. The ginger flavour won't be as intense, however, so you might want to compensate by adding a teaspoon of freshly grated ginger at the same time.

Glacé fruit

Also called candied or crystallized fruit, don't be tempted to skimp on quality when buying glacé fruit. The top-quality varieties are usually French, but you can also get a really good selection online, which is where we tend to go. You can always vary the glacé fruit you use, according to your own preference (unless a recipe states otherwise). If you can't find mixed peel, then candied citron or orange peel (or a combination of both) is a good alternative.

Lemon

LEMON OIL › A drop or two of lemon oil (or pure lemon extract, as it's also known) is a great way of injecting an intense citrus hit into a simple biscuit or tart. It may seem extravagant to buy a small bottle when only a drop or two is asked for in a recipe, but it keeps well (stored in the fridge) and really does make a difference to the Cats' Tongues (see page 27). A drop or two is also great added to whipped cream, which is then served with fresh or roasted fruit. We use Boyajian pure lemon oil which is top-of-the-range, but there are several other options to choose from: Steenbergs and Nielsen-Massey both do good-quality lemon extracts. Either way, do not confuse this with lemon-infused olive oil, which is commonly sold for use in savoury cooking.

ZEST › Using finely grated lemon zest is another way to bring the citrus hit that we love. When grating your zest (using either a microplane or the smaller holes of an all-purpose grater), take care to avoid the white pith: this has a strong bitterness that will carry through everything it's added to. As a rough guide, 1 regular lemon will give you 1 teaspoon of finely grated lemon zest.

Liquid glucose

Also known as glucose syrup, liquid glucose is a thick, clear syrup usually made from maize but can also come from wheat, barley or potatoes. It's a useful way of controlling the formation of sugar crystals in the making of confectionery such as the Raspberry Lollipops (see page 318) or Almond Nougat (see page 328). Glucose syrup or corn syrup can be used as alternatives to liquid glucose.

Mahleb

Mahleb is a spice made from the ground seed kernel of the St Lucie cherry. It's not widely used outside of Greece, Turkey and the Middle East, so don't worry if you can't get hold of any: a few drops of almond extract work well instead.

Marzipan

See Almond Paste for the important difference between the two. If you do have to use marzipan (instead of almond paste), you can add a drop or two of almond essence to the mix to ramp up the flavour. Marzipan is much sweeter than almond paste, so you might want to reduce the amount of sugar a recipe calls for accordingly.

Mixed spice

Also known as quatre épices, mixed spice is a sweet blend of cinnamon, nutmeg, mace, allspice, cloves and coriander. It's similar to the American pumpkin pie spice, but not to be confused with allspice, the dark berry from the pimento tree.

Nuts

Always taste your nuts before baking with them: the quality can vary hugely, from creamy and nutty on one hand, to dry and rancid on the other.

ALMONDS (SLIVERED) › The 'little sticks' of slivered almonds that we fold through our Coconut Brittle (see page 336) provide a wonderful crunch, but don't worry if you can't get hold of them. Just roast some whole blanched almonds for 10 minutes in an oven set to 180°C/160°C Fan/Gas Mark 4, then roughly chop them – these will be fine as an alternative.

HAZELNUTS › Hazelnuts are very idiosyncratic in baking: they cause a cake to dry out really quickly. As a result, hazelnut cakes are always best eaten on the day of baking.

PEANUTS (RAW) › Raw peanuts – unroasted, skinless and unsalted – are not always easy to find. Roasted (but still skinless and unsalted) are often easier to get hold of, so use these instead, if necessary.

PISTACHIOS › We like to garnish our cakes with slivered bright green Iranian pistachios: it's what we use in the shops, as their length and colour look great. If you are using these, be sure not to toast them, as they'll lose their colour. If using regular pistachios, however, these will need a bit of toasting to really draw out their taste.

WALNUTS (QUALITY OF) › Keep a close eye on walnuts, in particular, and always taste them before adding them to your cake: they won't improve with baking, so if they taste rancid at the outset, they are not worth using.

Oats

When making the 'Anzac' Biscuits (see page 52), don't start with the small quick-cook oats common to some breakfast cereals: they'll turn to mush as soon as they come into contact with liquid. You want rolled oats (rather than steel-cut), so start with either the 'jumbo' version (which will just need a little pulse in the food processor to break them up) or 'regular' rolled oats, which can simply be added as they are – or use a combination of the two.

Orange

BLOSSOM WATER › This is a key ingredient in various Arab and Mediterranean cuisines, used in particular to flavour cakes like baklava, as well as other sweets. Sugar syrup made with orange blossom water can be used to soak into cakes, flavour fruit salads and fold into creams as a dessert. We also use it in a savoury context, where its aroma gives a wonderful exotic hue. Some varieties are more concentrated than others, so have a little try before adding it: you may need to adjust the quantities accordingly.

OIL › With highly scented ingredients like orange oil (or lemon oil, almond extract, rose water, etc), always get the best quality you can: there's such a difference from brand to brand that it can really affect the end result. The better the quality, the more expensive it will often be, but you only really need a drop or two in a cake, so a little bottle will go a very long way. If you can't get hold of a really good-quality oil, some finely grated zest is often a better alternative than reaching for a cheaper brand.

Pandan leaf

Often referred to as the 'vanilla of the East', pandan leaves are used all over South East Asia to flavour (and colour) many dishes, but predominantly cakes and sweets. The leaves look like long blades of grass and are extremely fibrous (and thus inedible), so are used instead to infuse foods. To bring out the flavour of pandan, the blades are bruised with the back of a knife, then tied into a knot and dropped into the food to be infused. They are also often blended with water or coconut milk, then strained through a fine-meshed sieve, to extract the colour and flavour for cakes and puddings. If you cannot find pandan leaves (usually sold in the fruit and veg or freezer sections of Asian grocers), use a quarter of a vanilla pod instead, split in half lengthways to release the seeds.

Passionfruit pulp

We get our strained passionfruit pulp from a French company called Les vergers Boiron. It's super flavourful and tangy and comes frozen, so we can just cut off what we need and keep the remainder in the freezer for future use. Seek it out, if you can – it's readily available online. Ordering products online always feels like a bit of a hassle (until you get into the habit of it), but you can reassure yourself that the alternative is extracting the juice from about a dozen fresh passionfruit by hand!

Rice paper (edible)

Edible rice paper is a useful way to line something sticky like the Almond Nougat (see page 328), to make it easy to handle and store. And as it's completely edible, there's no need to peel it off before eating. You can buy it in sheets, like A4 paper, from speciality cake shops or online. As an alternative, you could use wafer paper made from potato starch, which serves the same purpose, or just line the tin with baking parchment dusted with icing sugar; the latter won't be edible, obviously, so you'll have to peel it off before eating.

Rose water

The difference between pure rose water and rose essence is huge. The ingredients in rose water are literally rose oil and water. Rose essence, on the other hand, contains ethanol as well as rose oil. Undiluted, rose essence is therefore far stronger than rose water and serves a completely different purpose; it's generally added by the drop rather than by the teaspoon or tablespoon. Adding 2 tablespoons of rose water to a cake such as our Pistachio Semolina Cake (see page 165) may seem brazen, but it's what makes the cake both distinct and delicious. The same is true in our Flourless Chocolate Cake (see page 170). Adding 2 tablespoons of rose essence to the same cakes, on the other hand, would make them basically inedible. Confusingly, rose essence is sometimes called rose water, so just have a look at the ingredients to double check. We use the Lebanese Cortas brand, which we recommend: it's not necessarily the absolute best, but it's one of the good-quality brands most readily available.

Salt

We use two types of salt in the book: table salt and flaky sea salt. Table salt is what we use most for baking, as it disperses more evenly through a batter or dough. Flaky sea salt is often used as a garnish, there for its gentler flavour and more prominent texture. In certain recipes – our Chocolate S'mores (see page 47) and our Garibaldis (see page 57) – we use both types of salt.

Star anise (ground)

Ground star anise is not always as easy to find as whole star anise. To grind your own, use a spice grinder or pestle and mortar to blitz whole star anise, then pass through a fine sieve.

Sugar

We use various types of sugar throughout the book: icing sugar, caster sugar, demerara sugar, light brown soft sugar, dark brown soft sugar, light brown muscovado sugar and dark brown muscovado sugar. There's no getting around the fact that baking requires a fair bit of sugar!

ICING SUGAR › 'Pure' icing sugar is not that easy to find in the UK, so we have used regular icing sugar in our recipes (which has about 3% maize starch in it, making it still suitable for those with gluten intolerances). In some recipes – the icing for the Pineapple Chiffon Cake (see page 179), for example – we have mentioned pure icing sugar as option one, if you can get hold of it, as it doesn't have the slightly floury taste from the cornflour as the regular one. Don't worry if you can't find the pure version – regular icing sugar will be fine.

Treacle and molasses

For some recipes – the Soft Gingerbread Tiles (see page 42), for example – you can use either black treacle or blackstrap molasses and you won't be able to tell the difference. While the two names are often used interchangeably, there is a difference, in that molasses are a pure by-product of refining sugar cane into sugar crystals, while treacle is a blend of these molasses with the refinery syrup. Treacle (which is often paler, sweeter and more mellow than molasses) ranges in colour from light gold to almost black, depending on the ratio of the blend.

Vanilla

EXTRACT › As with all extracts and oils, use the best quality you can find: it makes a huge difference. We used the Nielsen-Massey brand for the recipes in this book.

PODS › Rather than discarding vanilla pods once their seeds have been scraped and they've done their work in a recipe, always rinse and dry them, then stick them in a container of caster sugar. It makes a lovely alternative to regular sugar in your cappuccino, and can be added to all sorts of puddings or smoothies.

Yoghurt (Greek)

The rise of fat-free or 2% fat Greek yoghurt has been so great that it can sometimes be hard to find the full-fat version: shelf space is precious in shops, we know, but it seems such a shame! You can use reduced-fat yoghurt if you like – even in recipes like the Yoghurt Panna Cotta (see page 282), which needs to set – but you won't get the wonderful richness that a dessert such as this really deserves.

A

ricotta crêpes with figs, honey
and pistachio 268-9
Roma's doughnuts with saffron custard
cream 113-15
rose petals, candied 165-6
rose water 355-6
flourless chocolate layer cake with coffee,
walnuts and rose water 170-2
pistachio and rose water semolina
cake 165-6
raspberry and rose powder puffs 82-4
rose water cream 170-2
rosemary
chocolate tart with hazelnut, rosemary
and orange 241-2
crystallized rosemary sprigs 241-2
roulades
pistachio roulade with raspberries
and white chocolate 159-60
'training' roulades 348
rugelach, not-quite-Bonnie's 65-6
rum
festive fruit cake 167-8
rum and raisin cake with rum caramel
icing 124
rum butter glaze 42-3
rum caramel icing 100, 124
Speculaas biscuits 37

S

saffron
saffron and almond ice cream
sandwich 301-3
saffron and pistachio brittle 315
saffron custard cream 113-15
saffron, orange and honey madeleines 76-8
sage, crystallized 245-6
salted caramel, sticky fig pudding with 287
sandies, peanut 21
sauce, chocolate 308
schiacciata with grapes and fennel
seeds 250
semifreddo 293-4
semolina
lemon and semolina syrup cakes 111
pistachio and rose water semolina
cake 165-6
sesame seeds
sesame brittle 232-4, 334
soft date and oat bars 45
shortbread
Middle Eastern millionaire's shortbread 341
orange and star anise shortbread 46-7
shortcrust pastry, sweet 226, 232-6, 241-2,
255-6
s'mores, chocolate and peanut butter 48-51
snowballs, pecan 63
sorbet
Campari and grapefruit sorbet 304
prickly pear sorbet 306
sour cherries: almond, pistachio and sour
cherry wafers 23
soured cream
beetroot, ginger and soured cream
cake 130-1
chocolate banana ripple cheesecake 216-17
white chocolate cheesecake with cranberry
compote 203-5
Speculaas biscuits 37

spice 354
Gevulde Speculaas 33-4
Speculaas biscuits 37
spiced praline meringues 323
Tessa's spice cake 186
sponge, genoise 96-9, 346
star anise 356
blackberry and star anise friands 103-4
orange and star anise shortbread 46-7
pineapple and star anise chiffon
cake 179-80
pineapple tartlets with pandan
and star anise 255-6
sticky fig pudding with salted caramel
and coconut topping 287
strawberries
celebration cake 193-4
rhubarb and strawberry crumble cake 148
roasted strawberries 221-2
roasted strawberry and lime
cheesecake 221-2
strawberry and vanilla mini-cakes 95
strawberry icing 95
Victoria sponge with strawberries and white
chocolate cream 96-9
woodland meringues 319-20
yoghurt panna cotta with basil and crushed
strawberries 282
sugar 356
caramelizing sugar 349
cardamom sugar 113-15
sifting caster sugar 348-9
sugar syrup 326-7
sultanas
apple and olive oil cake with maple
icing 132-3
grappa fruit cake 141-3
sweet shortcrust pastry 226, 232-6, 241-2,
255-6
Swiss meringues 347
syrup
honey syrup 268-9
lemon and semolina syrup cakes 111
rose water syrup 165-6
sugar syrup 326-7

T

tahini
halva 341
little baked chocolate tarts
with tahini 232-4
tahini and halva brownies 87
tahini caramel 341
take-home chocolate cake 152-5
tarragon, rice pudding with roasted rhubarb
and 272
tarts 224-57
chai brûlée tarts 239-40
chocolate tart with hazelnut, rosemary
and orange 241-2
fig and pistachio frangipane tartlets 247-9
little baked chocolate tarts with tahini
and sesame brittle 232-4
Mont Blanc tarts 235-7
pineapple tartlets with pandan
and star anise 255-6
walnut and black treacle tarts
with crystallized sage 245-6

teacakes
baby black and orange cakes 94
flourless chocolate 'teacakes' 108-10
lemon, blueberry and almond 'teacakes' 88
temperature
ingredients 350
oven 347-8
Tessa's spice cake 186
thyme: apricot and thyme galettes 253-4
tin can cakes 136-40
banana, date and walnut tin can cake 140
butternut, honey and almond tin can
cake 136-7
pineapple, pecan and currant tin can
cake 139
tins 71, 123, 198, 227, 350
toffee Cape gooseberries 274-5
treacle 356
gingerbread with brandy apples and crème
fraîche 266-7
walnut and black treacle tarts
with crystallized sage 245-6
tropical fruit cake 161-3
truffles, pecan and Prosecco 324
tuiles, brown butter almond 30
Turkish delight: chocolate, rose and walnut
ice cream 308

V

vanilla 356
strawberry and vanilla mini-cakes 95
vanilla whipped cream 82-5, 247-9
Victoria sponge with strawberries and white
chocolate cream 96-9
vineyard cake 134

W

wafers, almond, pistachio and sour cherry 23
walnuts 355
banana, date and walnut tin can cake 140
beetroot, ginger and soured cream
cake 130-1
caramelized walnuts 170-2
chocolate banana ripple cheesecake 216-17
chocolate, rose and walnut ice cream 308
coffee and walnut financiers 105-7
fig, orange and mascarpone
cheesecake 212-13
flourless chocolate layer cake with coffee,
walnuts and rose water 170-2
not-quite-Bonnie's rugelach 65-6
prune cake with Armagnac and walnuts 126
walnut and black treacle tarts 245-6
water ganache 55-6, 108-10, 190-1,
209-10, 350
woodland meringues 319-20

Y

yo-yos: custard yo-yos with roasted rhubarb
icing 19-20
yoghurt 356
lemon, yoghurt and juniper berry
ice cream 307
Persian love cakes 74
yoghurt cream 274-5
yoghurt panna cotta with basil and crushed
strawberries 282

ACKNOWLEDGEMENTS

Our book has been three years in the making and involved lots of very talented people, to whom we are extremely grateful.

Two years out of the three we've been having weekly tasting sessions in which we would taste up to a dozen sweets in one afternoon. In charge of those marathons was one Sarah Joseph, a great cook, colleague and friend, who has dedicatedly tested all the recipes in our test kitchen, many of them several times. Sarah kept her jolly spirit in the face of many a cake adversity. For that, and for all her insights, clever contributions and very hard work, we are utterly grateful.

Tara Wigley had the impossible task of putting all this complexity in order and turning it into an actual book. Baking is already highly technical and the fact that both authors are famously fastidious didn't make it any simpler. As she always does, Tara meticulously collected recipes and information, constantly offered thoughtful suggestions and, generally, kept the ball rolling even when it was veering seriously off course. Her observations, her ability to hold the project together and her brilliant way with words were all priceless assets.

We are also totally grateful to Esme Howarth and Claudine Boulstridge, both of whom were deeply involved in the recipe testing in the UK. On the other side of the pond, Kim Laidlaw happily confirmed our inkling that we've got something good going, also by American standards.

For their part in making this book as striking as it is delicious and as radiant as an Ottolenghi meringue, we would like to thank Caz Hildebrand and Camille Blais (incredible Team Here), and Taylor Peden and Jane Munkvold (awesome Team P+M). A big thank you is also due to Lucy Attwater and to Lindy Wiffen of Ceramica Blue.

For supporting us, trusting us and allowing us to play with our food, we are utterly grateful to our agents, publishers, editors and publicists: Felicity Rubinstein and Kim Witherspoon; Rebecca Smart, Jake Lingwood, Aaron Wehner and Hannah Rahill; Lizzy Gray, Lisa Dyer, Louise McKeever, Helen Everson and Kaitlin Ketchum; Mark Hutchinson, Sarah Bennie, Diana Riley, Gemma Bell and Sandi Mendelson.

We would also like to acknowledge a few colleagues and collaborators to whom we are always grateful: Jonathan Lovekin, Sanjana Lovekin, Bob Granleese, Melissa Denes, Sarah Lavelle and Fiona MacIntyre.

Throughout the book we refer to our colleagues and friends at Ottolenghi. Without them, this work would never have come to pass.

Firstly, we should mention Noam Bar, Cornelia Staeubli and Sami Tamimi. All three of them, in their own particular ways, have contributed to shaping this book and the environment in which it has been created. Noam, Cornelia and Sami are family to us, a constant source of stimulation, support and critical thinking.

Equally important are the heads of the pastry section who worked with us over the years. Paulina Bembel, who is currently in charge, has made the Ottolenghi pastry counter her own. Her smart ideas, her practicality, her striking displays and the way she runs her team are exemplary. Her deputy, Verena Lochmuller, is equally brilliant and a privilege to have around us. Other wonderful 'heads' that have been with us over the years and to whom we are utterly grateful are Savarna Paterson, Sarit Packer, Carol Brough, Jim Webb, and Khalid Assyb.

At the helm of our bakery is Aaron Kossoff who, alongside Irek Krok, runs the little engine that supplies our shops and restaurants with breads, morning pastries, bagged cookies and biscuits, jams, chutneys and much much more. Aaron and Irek's clever innovations, their willing approach and their professionalism have successfully seen us through some very busy Christmases. We'd also like to thank Faiscal Barakat, Charissa Fraser and Mariusz Uszakiewicz, all of whom have have held this ever-challenging position in the past.

Other pastry chefs and bakers, present and past, that we would like to mention here with much gratitude are Jens Klotz, Daniel Frazer, Daniel Karlsson, Przemek Lopuszynski, Brooke Gladden, Julia Frischknecht, Solvita Valaine, Céline Lecoeur, Franceska Venzon, Dan Murray, Rob Wainwright, Vita Shkilyova, Kristina Kazlauskaite, Emily Parker, Simonetta Minarelli, Giulia Bassan, Mirka Strzep, Nelson Fartouce, Daniela Silva, Carley Scheidegger, Jacopo Romagnoli, Michael Strong, Cristina Mehedinteanu, John Meechan, Lingchee Ang, Mariusz Krok, Colleen Murphy, Adam Murawski, Andrea Del Valle Garcia, Artur Matewski, Agnieszka Wozniak, Ernestas Valantinas, Carlos Prachedi Pesca, Robert Jastrzebski, Peter Polgar, Damian Zmijewski, Elimar Viale, Jared Carter, Ali Jannas, Sergio Cava, Robert Czarniak, Arkadiusz Jaroszynski, Magdalena Juhasz and Zbigniew Zubel.

More than anyone else, really, we are grateful to all the sweet-toothed customers of Ottolenghi and NOPI who have been nibbling on our brittles, chewing our biscuits, inhaling our meringues and scoffing our cakes for many many years. Please keep on coming and let us carry on baking to our heart's delight.

—

Finally, we would like to acknowledge a small group of close friends and family and thank them here for being part of everything we do.

HELEN › First and foremost, David Kausman, my rock and confidant, a true *mensch*, and father of my beautiful children; my parents, for their examples of generosity, courage and perseverance; my siblings, Jimmy, Lucy, Lily and Margaret, for their unfailing love and support, and my precious nieces and nephews; Brendan Slater and Eng Ching Goh for their enduring loyalty to our family; Mark, Roma and the entire Kausman/Aflalo/Tauber families – the most incredible in-laws one could wish for; the Lee family who still loom so large and lovingly in my life – your little Ah Nung turned out all right in the end!

I am blessed and grateful to have the wonderful friendship of so many people, in London and Melbourne. There are too many to mention individually, but special thank you to John Redlich, Sherry Strong, Kathy Reed, Felicity Craig, Caroline Lor and Richard Ryan, Chryssa Anagnostou and Jim Tsaltis, Melly Beilby, Nicole Rudolf, Goli Nili and Ali Hazrati, Alice and James Spence, Betsy and David Gottlieb, Shehnaz Suterwalla and Azeem Azhar, and the fabulous mums at Norland Place School.

YOTAM › Karl Allen, Max and little Flynn; Michael and Ruth Ottolenghi; Tirza, Danny, Shira, Yoav and Adam Florentin; Pete and Greta Allen, Shachar Argov, Garry Chang, Alex Meitlis, Ivo Bisignano, Lulu Banquete, Tamara Meitlis, Keren Margalit, Yoram Ever-Hadani, Itzik Lederfeind, Ilana Lederfeind and Amos, Ariela and David Oppenheim.

10 9 8 7 6 5 4 3 2 1

Ebury Press, an imprint of Ebury Publishing,
20 Vauxhall Bridge Road,
London, SW1V 2SA

Ebury Press is part of the Penguin Random House
group of companies whose addresses can be found
at **global.penguinrandomhouse.com**

Text © Yotam Ottolenghi and Helen Goh 2017
Photography © PEDEN + MUNK 2017

Yotam Ottolenghi and Helen Goh have asserted their right
to be identified as the authors of this Work in accordance
with the Copyright, Designs and Patents Act 1988

First published by Ebury Press in 2017
www.eburypublishing.co.uk

Design: Here Design

ISBN: 9781785031144

Colour origination by Altaimage, London
Printed and bound in Italy by Graphicom S.r.l

Penguin Random House is committed to a sustainable
future for our business, our readers and our planet.
This book is made from Forest Stewardship Council®
certified paper.

SWEET

YOTAM OTTOLENGHI
HELEN GOH

The perfect interactive companion to the book

Featured recipes

Cinnamon pavlova, praline cream and fresh figs

This is a stunning dessert for a special occasion. It also has a nice element of surprise, as the meringue base is not quite what you might expect: gooey – almost toffee-like – rather than dry and crispy...

See Recipe

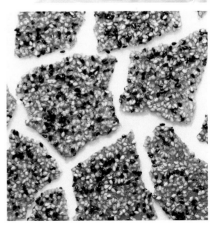

—

All of the recipes at your fingertips, wherever you are

BROWSE Access all the recipes online from anywhere.

SEARCH Find your perfect recipe by ingredient or browse through the chapters.

FAVOURITES Create your own list of go-to recipes and have them at your fingertips, whether shopping on the way home or looking for recipe ideas during a weekend away.

TO UNLOCK YOUR ACCESS VISIT BOOKS.OTTOLENGHI.CO.UK AND ENTER YOUR UNIQUE CODE: AXRT-TV32-CYRZ-VT61

—